A Guru's Journey

MUSIC IN AMERICAN LIFE

A list of books in the series appears at the end of this book.

A Guru's Journey

Pandit Chitresh Das and Indian Classical Dance in Diaspora

SARAH MORELLI

UNIVERSITY OF ILLINOIS PRESS
Urbana, Chicago, and Springfield

Publication of this book is supported by grants from the University of Denver's Lamont School of Music and the AHSS Book Publication Support Fund and from the AMS 75 PAYS Endowment of the American Musicological Society, funded in part by the National Endowment for the Humanities and the Andrew W. Mellon Foundation.

1 2 3 4 5 C P 5 4 3 2 1
♾ This book is printed on acid-free paper.

Library of Congress Control Number: 2019952252

ISBN 978-0-252-04286-7 (hardcover) | ISBN 978-0-252-08468-3 (paperback) | ISBN 978-0-252-05172-2 (e-book)

In Memory of Pandit Chitresh Das, 1944–2015
master performer, educator, pioneer.

This book is dedicated to the kathak artists he trained and to future generations contributing to this lineage.

"Culture does not only affect the mind. It changes the body."
—Catherine Geurts (2002)

"Our frequent admonition—stop thinking and dance—isn't to say that the motion is unthinkable. It's to say that the body is capable of understanding more things at once than can be articulated in language. One has no choice but to *think with the body*."
—Barbara Browning (1995)

"Dance finely tunes sensibilities, helping to shape the practices, behaviors, beliefs, and ideas of people's lives. At the same time, a multiplicity of ethnographic realities shapes the unique and historical occasion of any dance. All this raises questions about the transmission and transformation of dance from one cultural setting to another, as well as from one historical period to another. . . . What do these changes indicate about the mutability of the body? How malleable are our perceptual processes, and what effect might exposure to different dance experiences have on our social perspectives?"
—Cynthia Jean Cohen Bull (1997)

"To be received like this in a foreign land, my god, it is overwhelming. I have never felt so much warmth and openness, so much love for our music. It inspires me so. But I wonder how much they can understand? And where all this will lead to?"
—Ravi Shankar (in Worth 1991)

Contents

Illustrations

Figures

Music Examples

Map

Tables

Video Examples

All videos are accessible on the companion website, www.press.uillinois.edu/books/morelli/journey. References in the text are accompanied by the symbol ▶.

Note on Transliteration and Pronunciation

Most non-English terminology found in this work is from Hindi or Urdu. I generally follow orthography for Devanagari script used in McGregor (1993) with a few exceptions, noted below. I do not utilize diacritics in the transliteration of proper names such as Das (Dās), or Krishna (Kṛṣṇa). Similarly, I have elected to transliterate the names of specific *rāg*s without diacritics, using their most common English spellings. For plurals, I generally employ the English *-s* or *-es*, as it is the method used most often by my research associates: *chakkar*s and *qamīz*es instead of their Hindi pluralizations *chakkar* and *qamīzeṅ*.

Many Indian languages include both short and long versions of specific vowels. In Hindi, the vowels *a*, *i*, and *u* are distinct from longer versions, transliterated as *ā*, *ī*, and *ū* and pronounced thus:

a	as in g*u*tter or r*u*t	ā	as in f*a*r or f*a*ther
i	as in b*i*n or s*i*mple	ī	as in m*ea*n or cr*ea*ture
u	as in s*oo*t	ū	as in typh*oo*n

The vowels *e* and *o* each have only one form:

e	as in b*e*t
o	as in b*oa*t

Diphthongs have rough equivalents:

ai	as in b*i*te
au	as in c*ow*

In Hindi, as with many South Asian languages, a short *a* is implied with every consonant unless marked by another vowel. Therefore, words transliterated with an end consonant (such as *tāl*) may also be written with a short *a* (*tāla*); however, the final *a* is more commonly dropped in colloquial speech. I use both spelling possibilities, depending on common pronunciation. The final *a* is often pronounced when singing and therefore is included in the song texts transliterated in this work.

Hindi has a nasal sound roughly equivalent to the *n* in the English sa*n*g, transliterated here as *ṅ* or *ṁ*, and has two slightly differing *sh* sounds, transliterated as *ś* and *ṣ*. There are also retroflex consonants, which are differentiated with a dot below the transliterated consonant such as *ṭ*, *ḍ*, and *ṇ*.

Unlike English, many consonants have both non-aspirated and aspirated versions. Each of the aspirated consonants, including *kh, gh, jh, ṭh, ḍh, th, dh, ph* and *bh*, requires a small exhalation after the pronunciation of the consonant that does not otherwise affect its pronunciation. For example:

th is pronounced po*th*ole, not *th*ing or *th*is
ph is pronounced shep*h*erd and not *ph*one

The *ch* sound also has non-aspirated and aspirated versions that are often transliterated as *c* and *ch*. In most cases, I have transliterated this pair as *ch* and *chh*, which I feel more accurately reflects the sounds produced. Furthermore, the kathak school discussed in this book, Chhandam, uses this method of transliteration. I have also transliterated the Hindi vowel ऋ as *ṛi* rather than *ṛ* for ease of pronunciation, so for example *nṛitya* instead of *nṛtya*. The

Table 0.1. Vowels and consonants in Devanagari script with corresponding Roman transliterations used in this book

Vowels						
अ a	आ ā	इ i	ई ī	उ u	ऊ ū	ऋ ṛi
ए e	ऐ ai	ओ o	औ au	अं aṃ	अः aḥ	
Consonants						
क ka (क़ qa)	ख kha (ख़ kha)	ग ga (ग़ ga)	घ gha	ङ ṅa		
च cha	छ chha	ज ja (ज़ za)	झ jha	ञ ña		
ट ṭa	ठ ṭha	ड ḍa (ड़ ṛa)	ढ ḍha (ढ़ ṛha)	ण ṇa		
त ta	थ tha	द da	ध dha	न na		
प pa	फ pha (फ़ fa)	ब ba	भ bha	म ma		
य ya	र ra	ल la	व va			
श śa	ष ṣa	स sa				
ह ha						

superscript signs *anusvāra* ं and *chandrabindu* ँ nasalize the previous vowel; both are transliterated in this work as *ṅ*.

A few words contain consonants used in Urdu or in loanwords from Arabic, Persian, Portuguese, and English: क़ (ق) is transliterated as q, ख़ (خ) as k̲h̲, ग़ (غ) as g, ज़ (ز, ظ, or ض) as z, झ़ (ژ) as zh, and फ़ (ف) as f. The Urdu ط is transliterated here as ṯ; *hamzah* (ء), found only in the medial position in this work, indicates a diphthong and is represented by ', such as in *ṯavā'if*.

Note on Names and Honorifics

Many of the dancers and musicians discussed in this book are among the most respected artists in their fields, with honorific titles such as Ustad, Shrimati, and Pandit. Thus, I generally employ culturally appropriate titles of respect, particularly the first time a name appears. Chitresh Das will most often be referred to as Pandit (meaning one of great learning) Das. The suffix *-jī* may also be appended to the first or last name as a form of respect, so Chitresh Das is also referred to as "Chitresh-jī." For male Muslim names, the suffix *-sahib* (*sāhab*, pronounced "sāhb") may be added to the last name; in particular, Ali Akbar Khan will sometimes be referred to as "Khansahib." Additionally, the term Ustad (*ustād*) is an honorific title used for respected male Muslim musicians such as Ustad Ali Akbar Khan and his father, Ustad Allauddin Khan. The names of senior female kathak gurus and performers in this text are noted with the respectful Shrimati (*śrīmatī*) or with -jī. At times, these titles are replaced by the term Guru.

While for Pandit Das I write out the full honorific title, for other artists, I also use the following abbreviations:

Pt.	Pandit
Ust.	Ustad
Smt.	Shrimati

For the sake of clarity, in all captions, an artist's given name is used without honorary title.

Familial terms also are commonly used in South Asian cultures to create extended networks of fictive kinship and to designate a person's age and status relative to one's own. In Tamil, for example, older women are referred to as *mā* (mother), or *akkā* (older sister), depending on the extent of age difference. In Bengali and other North Indian languages, similarly, women are often referred to as *dīdī*, or older sister, and men may be referred to as *dādā,* or older brother. The shortened forms *-dī* and *-dā* can be appended to first names to denote respect and/or a warm bond. In the artistic world, these terms can be used between students or by students for their teachers.

Note on Musical Notation

Most music examples in this book use a modified version of Hindustani notation. Ruckert 1991 contains a more complete description of this system.

Writing Melody

Hindustani melody utilizes a solfège system called *sargam*. It employs a "movable do," meaning that the tonic note, Sa, can be set at any pitch and will not change for the course of that particular performance. The system used in this book transliterates the notes of *sargam* into the Roman alphabet. Each note has a full name, which can be shortened to one syllable. In music notation, only the first consonant of each note's name is utilized, but it is pronounced using the first syllable when singing. A lower-case consonant indicates the flatter variant of a particular interval, and an upper-case consonant indicates the sharper variant (table 0.2).

Table 0.2. *Sargam* pitch names and intervals

Pronounced	Written	Interval from the tonic	Full name
Sa	S	tonic	*ṣaḍja*
re	r	minor second	*komal ṛiṣabha*
Re	R	major second	*śuddh ṛiṣabha*
ga	g	minor third	*komal gāndhāra*
Ga	G	major third	*śuddh gāndhāra*
ma	m	perfect fourth	*śuddh madhyama*
Ma	M	augmented fourth	*tīvra madhyama*
Pa	P	perfect fifth	*pañchama*
dha	d	minor sixth	*komal dhaivata*
Dha	D	major sixth	*śuddh dhaivata*
ni	n	minor seventh	*komal nishāda*
Ni	N	major seventh	*śuddh nishāda*

Any notes produced in the octave below the main performance octave are indicated with a dot below the written note, and any notes the octave above are given a dot above the written note. Notes appearing in superscript with a slur marking (curved line) above indicate a slide from that note to the note on the main line (or vice versa). Other slur markings above groups of notes indicate those notes are to be sung to one syllable of the accompanying text. Similar slurs placed below the notation (called scoops in this artistic community) indicate rhythm, as described below.

Writing Rhythm

Most Hindustani music is performed within a cyclical rhythmic framework known as *tāl* (or *tāla*). Each *tāl* contains a given number of *mātrās* (counts or beats) with varying degrees of emphasis and importance. The rhythmic framework of the two *tāls* notated in this book, *tīntāl* and *rupak tāl*, are included below (see music examples 0.1 and 0.2), with full dashes each indicating one count of silence. In these examples and in music example 6.2, each *mātrā* is further highlighted by the addition of its number in parentheses.

Within each *tāl*, beats can be grouped into subdivisions known as *vibhāgs* that are either designated as *tālī* (lit. clap), basically meaning they include bass tones, or as *khālī* (lit. empty), in which bass tones are, generally speaking, not to be performed. The beginning of each *vibhāg* is preceded by a vertical line. A symbol is placed above the first beat of each *vibhāg* designating that *vibhāg*'s value as *tālī* or *khālī*, and if *tālī*, identifying its placement within the complete rhythmic cycle.

Tīntāl consists of sixteen *mātrās* subdivided into four *vibhāgs* of four counts each (see music example 0.1). The first *vibhāg* is marked by a plus sign (+) to indicate that its first beat is *sam*, the count of primary importance (see the glossary). Its second *vibhāg* is the second *tālī* subgrouping, marked with a number two. The third *vibhāg* is a *khālī* subgrouping, designated by a zero. The fourth and final *vibhāg* is the third *tālī* subgrouping, indicated with a three.

Vibhāgs	+				2				0				3			
Mātrās	(1)	(2)	(3)	(4)	(5)	(6)	(7)	(8)	(9)	(10)	(11)	(12)	(13)	(14)	(15)	(16)
Notation	—	—	—	—	—	—	—	—	—	—	—	—	—	—	—	—

MUSIC EX. 0.1. *Tīntāl* framework

Vibhāgs	0			2		3	
Mātrās	(1)	(2)	(3)	(4)	(5)	(6)	(7)
Notation	—	—	—	—	—	—	—

MUSIC EX. 0.2. *Rupak tāl* framework

Rupak tāl is a cycle of seven *mātrās* with one *khālī* subgrouping of three counts and two *tālī* subgroupings of two counts each (see music example 0.2). *Rupak tāl* is uncommon in that each *sam* (beat 1) is also the beginning of the cycle's *khālī* subdivision, marked with a zero.

To designate smaller subdivisions occurring within one beat, "scoops" under groupings of single consonants (*sargam* or abbreviated *bols*), syllables (*bols*), and/or dashes (silence) indicate that each discrete unit within the particular scoop receives equal rhythmic value (see Hindustani notation example, music example 0.3).

Reading Rhythm in This Book

Rhythmic phrases embedded within the main text of this book are generally written without rhythmic value; in some cases, commas may divide a longer phrase into subgroupings. Where written "with rhythm" (often in the notes), discrete drum or dance syllables (*bols*) are joined to indicate that they fall evenly within one rhythmic grouping, with each grouping separated by a space. As in Hindustani notation discussed above, a dash indicates a rest of equal value to the other syllables within that particular grouping. Whenever possible when writing with rhythm (either in text or in Hindustani notation), each beat of the notated example has the same number of subdivisions. To compare, note the same phrase below as (1) written in text without rhythm, (2) in text with rhythm, and (3) in Hindustani notation within the framework of *tīntāl*:

1. In text without rhythm:
   "tā theī tat tat theī, ā theī tat tat theī, theī tā theī tā theī, theī theī tat tat"
2. In text with rhythm:
   "tā– theī– tattat theī– ā– theī– tattat theī– theī– tātheī –tā theī– theī– theī– tat– tat–"

3. In Hindustani rhythmic notation:

+ 2
|Tā – theī – tat tat theī – |Ā – theī – tat tat theī – |

o 3
|theī – tā theī – tā theī – |theī – theī – tat – tat – |

MUSIC EX. 0.3. Hindustani rhythmic notation

In this book, where Hindustani notation contains particularly dense passages, kathak *bols* are abbreviated to the first letter of each syllable. In music examples 4.2 and 6.1, "TtttĀttt" replaces the more complete *bols* "tā theī theī tat, ā theī theī tat" of *tatkār*. In music examples 7.1, 7.2, and 7.3, "tddd" replaces the *naṭavarī bols* "tiga dhā diga diga." Some music examples utilize longer vertical lines to visually connect several horizontal lines of notation meant to occur simultaneously (found particularly in chapter 6). Finally, chapter 3 contains music examples using a modified version of western staff notation; a key and discussion of that notation can be found in the text of that chapter.

Acknowledgments

I begin with deep respect and boundless gratitude to Pandit Chitresh Das for engaging me, in his uniquely perceptive and energetic way, to develop my abilities in dance, music, and scholarship. While writing a book must always be a daunting task, I have felt this to be especially the case when the work is so centered on one person. His trust in sharing his life and teachings with me as a student and a scholar was a tremendous gift. I wish, similarly, to express everlasting appreciation to Ustad Ali Akbar Khan for sharing his teaching, mastery, and wisdom. Heartfelt thanks also to George Ruckert and Gretchen Hayden for the solid training and support they provided, for their countless kindnesses and generosities, and for giving form and direction to my love of North Indian performing arts.

In the academic world, I am particularly grateful to Kay Kaufman Shelemay for her ongoing support, insights, guidance, and friendship. Sincere thanks to Beth Bullard, Truman Bullard, and Carol Babiracki for their formative and lasting influences on my intellectual and artistic path. Thanks also to scholars Gordon Thompson, Liz Tolbert, Tomie Hahn, Deborah Wong, Marina Roseman, George Ruckert, Deborah Foster, Martha Selby, Richard Wolf, Ingrid Monson, and Joan Erdman. I hold special gratitude for my friends and colleagues Patricia Tang, Jeremy Wallach, and Zoe Sherinian, each of whom invaluably supported me in completing this book; also for Elyse Carter Vosen, David Kaminsky, Esther Clinton, Brenda Romero, Jeffrey Cupchik, Mekhala Natavar, Nilanjana Bhattacharjya, Victoria Levine, Judah Cohen, Shanti Pillai, Grete Viddal, Adam McGee, Sharon Kivenko, Darya Pinton, Kiri Miller, Corinna Campbell, Katherine In-Young Lee, Petra Gelbart, Marc Gidal, Natalie Kirschstein, and Sheryl Kaskowitz.

For her excellent editorial assistance and insightful contributions to this manuscript, sincere thanks to dancer, choreographer, and editor Parijat Desai. Patricia Tang and Stephen Scaringe also provided important input on several versions of this manuscript. Several other colleagues have read and commented on all or portions of this manuscript, including Tomie Hahn, George Ruckert, Eliana Schonberg, Kay Kaufman Shelemay, Zoe Sherinian, Jeremy Wallach, Richard Wolf, Elyse Carter Vosen, Antonia Banducci, Seibi Lee, Rina Mehta, and Juli Parrish.

Thanks also to many of my colleagues, past and present, at the University of Denver, in particular Jack Sheinbaum, Antonia Banducci, Aaron Paige, Arthur Jones, Roger Holland, David Montaño, Ginni Ishimatsu, Haider Khan, Pavithra Prasad, Lynn Baker, Jeremy Reynolds, Scott Bean, Kristin Taavola, Mitch Ohriner, Chappell Kingsland, Jonathan Leathwood, Heidi Leathwood, Linda Wang, Tom Miller, Ricardo Isnaola, Richard Slavich, Kitty Knight, Woody Colahan, and Lamont School of Music directors F. Joseph Docksey, Nancy Cochran, and Keith Ward.

I am grateful to Director Laurie Matheson and to Dawn Durante, Julie Laut, and Jennifer Comeau of the University of Illinois Press for their help and patience throughout this process. This manuscript received a subvention grant from the AMS 75 PAYS Endowment of the American Musicological Society, funded in part by the National Endowment for the Humanities and the Andrew W. Mellon Foundation. Publication of this book was also supported by the University of Denver's Lamont School of Music and the Arts, Humanities & Social Sciences (AHSS) Book Publication Support Fund. Portions of chapters 1 and 6 contain revised text from "'A Superior Race of Strong Women': North Indian Classical Dance in the San Francisco Bay Area," *The Music of Multicultural America: Performance, Identity, and Community in the United States*, edited by Kip Lornell and Anne K. Rasmussen, Copyright © 2016 by University Press of Mississippi. Other portions of this manuscript have been excerpted and revised from "Intergenerational Adaptation in North Indian Kathak Dance," *Anthropological Notebooks*, vol. 16, no. 3 (2010): 77–91. I thank University Press of Mississippi director Craig W. Gill and *Anthropological Notebooks* editor Gregor Starc for permission to reprint.

Several people have invited me to present this work at various stages. For these opportunities and their feedback, I am grateful to Daniel Neuman and Abhiman Kaushal at UCLA; David Harnish, Jeremy Wallach, Katherine Meizel, and Esther Clinton at Bowling Green State University; Brenda Romero, Jeremy Smith, and Thomas Riis at the University of Colorado at Boulder; Carol Babiracki at Syracuse University; Beth Bullard at George Mason University; Birendra Sinha of the Anila Sinha Foundation; and Anagha Sundararajan, Maheema Haque, and Apsara at the University of Chicago.

This book would not have been possible without the time and input of many artists. Thanks to the following disciples and students of Pandit Das for sharing their thoughts and experiences in interviews with me: Gretchen Hayden, Valerie Gold, Michele King, Marni Wieser Ris, Michele Zonka, Joanna de Souza, Noelle Barton, Amrit Mann, Jaiwanti Das Pamnani (in loving memory), Charlotte Moraga, Pratibha Patel, Seibi Lee, Jenny Baker Zangpo, Farah Yasmeen Shaikh, Joanna Meinl, Rachna Nivas, Rina Mehta, Anjali Nath, Cimeron Ahluwalia, and Farhana Huq. Sincere gratitude to the following artists for taking time out of their busy schedules to be interviewed: Kathakali master Govindan Kutty (rest in peace), sarod players Swapnamoy Banerjee and Chris Ris; vocalist Debasish Sarkar; and tabla players Abhijit Banerjee, Kousic Sen, Satyaprakash Mishra, and Jim Santi Owen. Thanks also to Pandit Das's first wife, Julia Maxwell, to his brother Ritesh Das (who generously told me stories of his parents and their school, Nritya Bharati), and to former Nritya Bharati student, Ipsita Mitra.

Many in India also patiently answered questions both informally and in interviews. My thanks extends to kathak artists Madhuri Devi Singh, Chetna Jalan, Bachan Lal Mishra, Ruby Badopadhyaya, Maya Chatterjee, and one anonymous *dīdī* for sharing their memories of Pandit Ram Narayan Mishra and Pandit Das's youth, and to the former chairman of Kathak Kendra and vice president of the Sangeet Natak Akademi, the late Shyamanand Jalan, for his time and insights. Thanks to sarodist Anindya Bannerjee for his assistance in a variety of contexts, to master instrument maker Hemen Chandra Sen (rest in peace), industrialist and philanthropist B. K. Birla and family, and Ramakrishna Mission Secretary Prasanna Maharaj. Thanks to Manju Mishra for her assistance in Kolkata and to her daughter, dance-sister Kasturi Mishra.

I am tremendously grateful to Richard Harrington and to Sean Campbell for the many hours they spent respectively engraving the Hindustani and western music transcriptions appearing in this book. Thanks to Paul Arroyo at the University of Illinois Press for his assistance with the book's accompanying videos, to Bill Nelson, who created the map accompanying chapter 1, and to Deborah Oliver for her editorial work in the project's final stages. Thanks also to Pallavi Salvi, Shilpi Sharma, Rina Mehta, Poonam Narkar, Ria DasGupta, and Indira Walia for their assistance with Hindi translations and transliterations.

Many dancers and friends provided assistance in filming, including Shipra Shukla, Antara Bhardwaj, Rina Mehta, Trina Chaudhuri, Anjali Nath, and Jason McCauslin. Shipra Shukla and Shefali Jain contributed invaluably to this book in their roles as Chhandam video archivists; Gretchen Hayden, Noelle Barton, Celine Schein Das, Seibi Lee, Rachna Nivas, Rina Mehta, Poonam Narkar, Shefali Jain, Labonee Mohanta, Rucha Chitnis, Christopher Ris, Marni Wieser Ris, and Mary Khan also assisted with gathering video and photo materials accompanying this book. Darlene Dhillon, Brandon Brown, Juhi Dubey, Macklin Kowal, and Joanna Meinl each provided prompt and helpful responses to my requests of the Chhandam Chitresh Das Dance Company office; thanks also to Manik Khan, Joel Schoolnik, Ben Kunin, and Wallace Harvey for their assistance at the Ali Akbar College of Music. And special thanks to Celine Schein Das, Pandit Das's widow and former executive director of the Chhandam Chitresh Das Dance Company (CCDDC).

In addition to those listed above, my full appreciation goes to those others who have buoyed me in various stages of writing through their various gifts and kindnesses, including Stephen Scaringe, David and Hali Morelli, Billi Morelli, Joel Schoolnik and Seibi Lee, Rina Mehta, Rachna Nivas, Shefali Jain, Stephen Wade, Leslie Schneider, Kim and Steve Weiner, Robert Castillo, Jenny Bertrand, Matthew Diekman, Bill Woodall, Jeff Honert, Wendy Turner, Mahea Uchiyama, Tim Witter, Susan Morgan, Timothy Stokes, Bruce Tift, Sasha Rubel, Kunga Dawa, Valentino Romero, Christine Shin, and Derek Chiou. I extend my appreciation to the following musicians who have continued to teach me or inspire more indirectly: Pt. Rajeev Taranath, Steve Oda, Debasish Sarkar, Kalinath Mishra, Shweta Jhaveri, Jayanta Banerjee, Ben Kunin, Abhiman Kaushal, Ty Burhoe, Vaibhav Mankad, and Satyaprakash Mishra. Thanks also to the following supporters of the arts in my Colorado community: James Bailey, Pushpa Mehta, Sharad and Vinod Tewary, Michael McGoldrick, Paul Docktor, Meena and Maulin Desai, George and Beth Ann Taylor, Geeta Sharma and Sukumar Vijayaraghavan, and Ajay Menon, and as well as those with whom I've had the pleasure of performing, particularly Jason Fellin, Swagata Banerjee, Sulakshana Jayaram, Joginder Singh Virdi, Vinata Gangoly, V. K. Arun Kumar, Priya Hariharan, Jeffrey Rogers, Ty Burhoe, Nabin Shrestha, Bijay Shrestha, Megan Yalkut, Aakash Mittal, Tejas Hemsell, Anil Khare, Harsh Agrawal, and Dustin Adams.

Thanks also to the students I've worked with over many quarters in various seminars, classes, and ensemble rehearsals at the University of Denver. In particular, Carrie McCune and Cailey Salagovic, who have continued their kathak training well past graduation, have each been integral in helping build the kathak community in Denver through the Sureela Academy. Thanks also to university and academy students Rebecca Moritzky, Pallavi Salvi, Shilpi Sharma, Thomas Jennings, Julia Emery, and Katrina Yoshida, as well as Rose Martin, Andrew Ferdig, Victoria Mogollón Montagne, Sonora Dolce, Maria Souliotis, Jonathon Parker, Emily Stephenson, Jane Carter, Katie Aiken, Sarah Kleinsteiber Morrison, Kelsey McIsaac, Sean Campbell, Derek Sumpmann, Mary Hannig, Miranda Teske, and Daniel Vargas. My sincere apologies to those I've inadvertently left out.

Finally, I owe an indescribable debt of gratitude my parents, Richard Scott Morelli and Sylvia McAllister Morelli, for their love and support.

A Guru's Journey

1

Encountering the Dance

October 23, 1999, Medford, Massachusetts: The group assembled on the floor of Tufts University's Jackson Gymnasium was a motley one, dressed in an array of dancewear ranging from tight leggings and leotards to śalvār qamīzes*, the loose pants and long tops common in South Asian cultures. Some people stretched in preparation for the dance workshop; others simply sat on the floor, casually talking. A few, dressed in T-shirts and jeans, appeared to have seen the event flyer and decided to attend at the last minute. The flyer read, "Kathak Dance Workshop by Chitresh Das. A rare chance to try a kathak class with a master . . . for free!!" and had been posted around the Tufts campus by students of Gretchen Hayden, then my kathak teacher of just two months. In turn, Chitresh Das (referred to throughout this book as Pandit Das or Chitresh-jī) was Gretchen Hayden's dance guru. She had studied this North Indian classical dance form with Pandit Das in the San Francisco Bay Area for some twenty years before establishing her own kathak school in Boston.*

Several years later, my impressions of this, my first experience of Pandit Das's teaching, were still powerful: *He arrived in a flurry of activity and after a quick assessment of the group, set us in motion. Some of the movements were already familiar to me from my initial classes, but most were new. As in every class I had taken thus far, we first performed* pranām*, a reverential salutation, centering of the self, and sanctification of the space. Our lesson then got under way with* tatkār*, kathak's most basic footwork pattern, comprised of eight slaps of the feet: right left right left, left right left right, or as it is more commonly expressed in spoken syllables called* bols*: "tā theī theī tat, ā theī theī tat."*[1] *After practicing this footwork pattern at different speeds, the same syllables were reconfigured into a* tatkār kī bandiś, *a composition using the* bols *of* tatkār, *beginning with the phrase "tā theī tat tat theī, ā theī tat tat theī."*[2]

"TĀ–THEĪ–TAT TAT THEĪ–Ā–THEĪ–TAT TAT THEĪ–!" Pandit Das urged us to increase our energy level and physical commitment to what were (for me and many others) still awkward movements. I struggled not to stumble while moving sideways, crossing my feet one behind the other, keeping my hips facing the front of the room, turning my head to the side, and cupping my hands slightly to "scoop" the air in time with the recited composition. The room was so crowded that our sideways stepping occasionally produced small collisions between some with less finely attuned spatial sensibilities.

Through dance, we were then introduced to the Hindu tale "Kaliya Daman." Each of us assumed the character of divine young Krishna playing with a ball, teasing his friends, and suddenly throwing the ball into the Yamuna River. Despite his friends' warnings, Krishna dove into the water and, in searching for the ball, found the tail of the serpent-demon Kaliya, who was sleeping deeply. Instead of avoiding the dangerous creature, Krishna yanked on his tail, waking and angering the massive Kaliya. We quickly switched roles to portray Kaliya: as a struggle between the two commenced, we "toe-flatted" our way to the right and left.[3] *To the* bols *"diga diga diga diga" we were Kaliya, our arms arched above our heads to outline the serpent's hood, holding our eyes wide open in the unblinking fashion of a snake. On "taka taka taka taka" we became confident young Krishna, spiritedly pulling the serpent-demon's tail. Back and forth, back and forth, we learned to switch between the two with greater frequency.*[4] *Emerging from the river as Krishna triumphantly riding the hood of the defeated and now devoted Kaliya, I reflected on how physically and emotionally engaged I had become in this epic battle, waged in a Boston-area gymnasium* (▶ see video 1.1).

Pandit Das's skill at drawing on unknown recesses of energy from dancers of any level was something I would later come to expect of all his classes. But in the middle of this, my first class with him, as we were catching our breath and wiping sweat from our faces, Pandit Das began what seemed to be his real lesson: "To be a kathak dancer is not so easy; it takes discipline, *riyāz, sādhanā.*" Playing off the hypothetical question of an uninformed student he continued, "What is *sādhanā*? *Sādhanā* is discipline with *mehnat*—with effort, work!" Here he paraphrased one of his favorite quotes by the legendary kathak dancer Smt. Sitara Devi, known for her spirited, outspoken style.[5] He next applied the concept of discipline to our US context: "Out of that *sādhanā* comes your true freedom. Some people think that freedom is, 'Yeah, man, I'll just do what I want because I'm free.' Sometimes in America you will hear that. That is your average definition of freedom. *Real* freedom comes from refined discipline with responsibility." When he felt his point was made, in characteristic fashion, he said, "OK, I've given you a lot of rest," and launched back into the rhythmic cycle, reciting, playing his tabla, and calling out the next exercise (adapted from field notes, October 23, 1999).

This encounter with Pandit Das opened the door for my study over the next fifteen years, and particularly between June 2000 and August 2003. In conducting ethnographic research in the dance studios of Pandit Das, I found that the contrasting notions of freedom and discipline he described that first day worked as core distinctions informing and directing his pedagogical philosophy and creative directions. The following chapters, focusing on the kathak community that developed around Pandit Das's teaching in the United States, consider how these and other ideas about what is often seen as "Indian" culture and "American" culture influenced this dance subculture. How Pandit Das and his students responded—artistically and otherwise—to questions regarding identity and meaning in their work reflect and embody the complexity of the American cultural landscape.

Pandit Das's career in the United States began in 1970. Over the subsequent forty-five years, his teaching was based mainly in the San Francisco Bay Area but also grew to include other cities in North America and India where his student-disciples founded related schools. This book, however, focuses on the community in the San Francisco Bay Area, the primary site of his own work. In examining how the kathak dance form was utilized and modified by Pandit Das and his students in response to changing cultural contexts, I necessarily introduce readers to various aspects of kathak and of Hindustani music, which are often, though not unproblematically, glossed as North Indian classical dance and music (see, e.g., Schofield 2010).

Kathak is a multifaceted dance form involving dynamism and refinement; precise, staccato footwork and graceful, fluid gesture; dramatic expression and musicality. Together, musicians and dancers create the sonic world of kathak, which in turn is integrated with kathak's movement expression in the term *saṅgīt* (here meaning the combination of melody, rhythm, and movement).[6] The English labels "music" and "dance" are cumbersome when writing about kathak, and become particularly problematic when discussing someone like Pandit Das, who developed what most might consider the "musical" aspects of kathak in unique ways. Because of the art form's complexity and richness, this book is designed to unfold in such a way that each ensuing chapter progressively introduces the reader to various kinesthetic and musical aspects of kathak, from relatively basic to increasingly subtle and complex. At the same time, the book is structured roughly chronologically in examining Pandit Das's life and career, and the development of his dance style, which was influenced by his interactions with different generations of dance students, audiences, and critics.

Saṅgīt: Interweaving Melody, Rhythm, and Movement

One of the classical dances of India, kathak encompasses a wide range of performance styles including storytelling (*nṛitya*), as in the tale of Krishna and Kaliya, and dance without explicit narrative (*nṛitt*), such as the *tatkār kī bandiś* described above.[7] Regardless of whether narrative is present or not, kathak performance shares the same musical framework and terminology as Hindustani music. Performances of Hindustani music and kathak may include a fluid combination of precomposed and improvised material, and both can last anywhere from several minutes to several hours. In what is deemed its most traditional presentation, kathak is performed by a solo dancer accompanied by musicians, although choreographed group presentations are also common. The sequence of a kathak solo "is not codified or prescribed by any manual or treatise" but typically follows a standard progression (Walker 2004, 11). Today the solo often begins with an elaborate *pranām* or *raṅgmañch*, both relatively formalized sections of performance based in Hindu belief that serve to sanctify the space and prepare dancer and audience for the ensuing performance (▶ see video 1.2). This may be followed by an invocation, or *vandanā*, to a particular Hindu deity (▶ see video 1.3). In Muslim contexts, or those that are otherwise less explicitly Hindu, the dancer might instead begin with a *salāmī*, a formalized salutation (Natavar 2000, 494). In either case, the dancer will likely then transition into a longer *nṛitt* (nonnarrative) section generally commencing with *āmad* and *ṭhāṭ*, in which the performer highlights grace and subtlety of movement, interspersed with displays of athletic and rhythmic prowess. With some exceptions, the order of items follows a format of gradually increasing tempi as is found in Hindustani music performances.[8]

Because kathak and Hindustani music share the same musical structure, many dancers train in one or more aspects of Hindustani music. The number of musicians and specific instruments may vary for any particular kathak performance, but accompanying ensembles almost always include a tabla player, though other drums are sometimes used, and one or more stringed instrumentalists playing sarangi, sitar, sarod, violin, or other (figure 1.1). Often, a vocalist and harmonium player, and occasionally a bansuri player, perform with the ensemble. Finally, fellow dancers frequently support the soloist by playing *manjīra* (cymbals used to keep time) and *tānpūrā* (the stringed instrument providing a drone), by reciting the syllables of dance compositions, and sometimes by playing *svaramaṇḍāl* (a zither).

FIG. 1.1. Chitresh Das in performance with musicians (*left to right*) Sabir Khan (tabla), Debasish Sarkar (vocal, harmonium), Jayanta Banerjee (sitar), Seema Mehta (*manjīra*). At the Karamatullah Khan Festival, National Centre for the Performing Arts, Mumbai, April 13, 2014. Photo courtesy of Showhouse Event Management.

One of kathak's most notable characteristics is the fast, percussive footwork dancers perform by slapping or striking their bare feet on the floor using various techniques. Dancers also wrap strings of bells called *ghuṅgharū* around their ankles (figure 1.2). Usually numbering between one hundred and two hundred individual bells per leg, the weight of the *ghuṅgharū*s slightly shifts the center of gravity, grounding dancers in their movement; and the sounds of the bells emphasize the rhythms of footwork. Footwork patterns dancers produce can be imitated by tabla players; further, these rhythms can be communicated orally when performers recite *bol*s, onomatopoeic syllables that imitate the tones and timbres of particular drum strokes or are specific to kathak footwork patterns. In *bol-paran* sections of a kathak solo, the dancer generally determines which specific compositions will be performed, drawn from a broader repertoire including compact, pithy *ṭukṛā*s or *toḍā*s, longer *paran*s, and *ginti*s, compositions based on numbers (▶ see video 1.4). The soloist may recite then immediately dance each composition; and the musicians' challenge—particularly the tabla player's—is to grasp the composition and the dancer's intentions as quickly as possible in order to play in synchrony with their footwork and other movements.

FIG. 1.2. Promotional image for *Masters of Tradition* performances with Swapan Chaudhuri. At the Marin Center Showcase Theater, San Rafael, CA, April 21, 2001, and, at Cubberly Theater, Palo Alto, CA, April 28, 2001. Photo by Marty Sohl.

North Indian classical dancers and musicians structure their performances through the framework of *tāl*, rhythmic cycles each with a given number and pattern of beats. They communicate *tāl* in a variety of ways. When reciting compositions, performers often show the *tāl* visually with their hands, using specific claps, waves, and finger taps. While a kathak soloist is dancing, the accompanying tabla player might signal the *tāl* audibly by playing *ṭhekā*, the signature pattern of drum strokes for a given *tāl*. More often, instead of playing *ṭhekā*, the tabla player will match whatever footwork patterns or other movements the kathak soloist is performing, highlighting and reinforcing accents. As Pradhan writes, "The *tabla* player is . . . expected to produce *bols* that simulate the footwork, while also keeping in focus the overall aesthetic appeal created by gesture and movement" (2008, 112). If the dancer is enacting a story, the tabla player may accentuate its various elements, for example with light drum strokes to amplify the plucking of flowers, or with louder booming tones to accompany the dancer's portrayal of a rainstorm. In sections when the tabla is following the dancer closely, melodically focused musicians usually mark the passage of the underlying rhythmic cycle by playing a repeated melody called a *laharā* or *nagmā* (as in video example 1.4) or (particularly in dance sections involving narrative) by repeating one or more lines of a song (▶ see video 1.5, cue point 7:31).

The role of "keeping *tāl*" is of vital importance because of the emphasis on *sam*, the first beat of the *tāl*, in kathak and Hindustani aesthetics. Compositions and sections of improvisation commonly end on *sam* and its occurrence is noted in various ways. Musicians and dancers may approach and "land on" *sam* with a *tihāī*, a cadential figure in which the same phrase is repeated three times. They also might give slight accentuation to *sam* in the middle of a longer, multi-cycle composition. Melodically oriented musicians such as vocalists or sarod players often emphasize the note that falls on *sam*, and according to Hindustani melodic (*rāg*) theory, only some notes are appropriate for this distinction. Performing artists also note the arrival of *sam* gesturally: vocalists perhaps by lifting a hand with an upward palm or a gripping motion, or by tapping the thigh; and instrumentalists (whose hands are otherwise occupied) with eye contact or a nod of the head (Clayton 2007, 80; Rahaim 2012, 79). Kathak dancers often finish rapid footwork or a series of swift turns on *sam*, marking the moment with contrasting stillness accentuated by a crisp pose, a turn of the head, a sharp look, and a raised eyebrow (▶ see video 1.6).

While kathak generates movement in many areas of the body, present-day dancers often keep their torsos—and particularly their hips—relatively still. This provides physical stability for footwork and movements of the upper body and also serves sociological functions relating to concepts of respectability (discussed in chapter 2). The dynamics of the upper and lower parts of the body are usually quite distinct but complementary. In contrast to sharp, percussive kathak footwork, movements of the upper body are often graceful and fluid. Dancers combine facial expression, other upper-body movements, footwork, and turns to portray different characters in enacting a story. In storytelling (*nṛitya*), dancers portray all of a tale's characters, depicting a range of emotions and character-types. Characters might be male, female, human, god, or demon, and are drawn most often from Hindu mythology (▶ see video 1.7, cue point 3:16).

Social Changes to Kathak

The term *kathak* has uncertain but widely accepted origins in the Sanskrit root, *kath*, related to the Hindi word *kathā*, or "story." Through this etymological connection, "ancient storytellers" are associated in the postcolonial period with kathak's practice of depicting tales, commonly drawn from Hindu sources including India's principal epics, the Rāmāyaṇa and Mahābhārata. "References to the 'ancient Kathakas' who travelled the countryside in Vedic times reciting sacred stories and epics are standard fare in almost all the books on *kathak* dating after 1965 (see for example Bhavani 1965, Singha and Massey 1967, Devi 1972 and Kothari 1989)," though as Margaret Walker notes, "earlier writers do not make such claims" (2014, 37). In studying the British Colonial Census Reports, Walker posits that "a lower caste group of performing artists assumed the new, and arguably Sanskritized, name of 'Kathak' (i.e., story-teller) sometime in the late-1700s and began an ascent from being enumerated as Shudra or serving caste in the 1832 census (Princep 1832) to being 'regarded' as Brahmin or priestly caste by 1900 (Crooke 1896)" (2006, 56). As she observes, "questions regarding caste, status, and identity hover, largely unexamined, around the edges of the *kathak* world" (56), though her work has done much to elucidate these questions.

Like Hindustani music, which developed in the same geographic locales and sociocultural environment, kathak was developed and refined due to royal patronage, particularly from Rajput kings throughout Rajasthan and in the Mughal courts of sixteenth- through nineteenth-century India (see, e.g., Natavar 1997, 65). From Walker's study of manuscripts written following the establishment of the British Raj in 1858, it appears the dancing presented in Mughal courts by male performers, called Bhāṇḍs or Kathaks, differed significantly from that performed by women, for whom the term *kathak* was not yet applied (2010, 283). Much historiography has privileged male contributions to the amalgamated dance form we now call kathak; however, it is clear that by the eighteenth century women were "prominent holders" of this knowledge and practice (Walker 2010, 280; see also Chakravorty 2008; Walker 2014). At that time, female practitioners were primarily courtesans, called *bāījī*s or *ṯavā'if*s, and the most highly trained among them were versed in the combined arts of song, dance, and poetry. While more experienced *bāījī*s often taught the younger women of their community, male gurus were *bāījī*s' publicly recognized teachers. Artistic knowledge was thus passed on through different lines of transmission: from male gurus to their (primarily male) family members, from those male gurus to their (primarily female *bāījī*) students, and from one *bāījī* to other (female) *bāījī*s.

Rulers and other wealthy landowners patronized the arts until major societal shifts in the twentieth century drastically changed the lives of Hindustani performers. A movement to dispossess *bāījī*s and other female performers of their social position took hold during the years of the British Raj, led first by the British and later by Indian elites. With independence in 1947, the feudal system of patronage ended. As Natavar writes, "The patrons of Kathak dance were no longer the Hindu and Muslim rulers. . . . Urban elite upper and middle class connoisseurs, the Tourism Departments of various states, the television and film industries, and the Indian government became the new benefactors of Kathak" (1997, 26). The new Indian government, artists, and interested patrons also opened music and dance institutions across India, making study accessible to a larger cross section of the populace. Yet, the same nationalist zeal that led reformers to elevate and disseminate knowledge of Indian artistic traditions in defiance of decades of colonial oppression simultaneously disenfranchised many of the (often Muslim) hereditary performers who had maintained the arts for generations (Katz 2012). Regardless of individual identity and status, however, with the earlier system of patronage dismantled, dancers and musicians were compelled to compete for opportunities to perform in concerts attended by a broader spectrum of concertgoers and therefore, to appeal to the tastes of audiences not necessarily deeply knowledgeable about the arts (e.g., Ruckert 2004, 14–16).

With sociopolitical and economic changes taking place throughout the twentieth century, kathak was altered in both subtle and pronounced ways. Change came in part through the broader participation of nonhereditary (often middle- or upper-class) dancers, many who received training in independence-era arts institutions such as Nritya Bharati, founded in Calcutta by Pandit Das's parents, and later, in diasporic locations like Pandit Das's Chhandam School of Kathak in northern California. Today, as kathak is practiced internationally and performed in large venues with high-quality sound amplification and sophisticated lighting design, the dance's connection to "ancient storytellers" may indeed seem tenuous. Like other South Asian dance forms including bharatanatyam and odissi, present-day kathak is influenced by twenty-first-century aesthetic preferences and desires, transnational sociocultural dynamics, and the competition for economic gain and artistic status (O'Shea 2007; Sikand 2016). Some artists have utilized kathak in more radical or self-consciously new ways (e.g., S. Chatterjee and Lee 2017; Garlough 2013; Lee 2017; Prickett 2012); however, as with many performance practices, change has also taken place within lineages and in contexts considered quite traditional.[9]

While much has been written on stylistic development in Hindustani music, such changes have been more complicated to assess in kathak. Reasons echo those for most dance forms, including the later development of video technology in comparison to audio technology and inherent challenges in describing and transcribing movement. Readers interested in a broader history of kathak will find particularly detailed studies by Margaret Walker (2004, 2006, 2010, 2014), whose work critically examines the development of the dance form and social history of its performers, and Pallabi Chakravorty (1998, 2000, 2000–2001, 2004, 2006, 2008), whose monograph, *Bells of Change*, analyzes dynamics of gender, modernity, and globalization in the development of kathak in the nineteenth and twentieth centuries. Contributing to this literature by focusing on more recent and particularly diasporic history, this book examines stylistic changes led by Pandit Das over the course of his performing and teaching career, and sociocultural factors that spurred such changes. This work also adds to a long and perhaps growing vein of ethnomusicological research on the individual's role in musical culture (see Rice 1987; Ruskin and Rice 2012) and a subgenre of ethnographies focusing on the lives and distinctive contributions of individual master-artists (e.g., Danielson 1997; Guilbault and Cape 2014; Muller and Benjamin 2011; Veal 2000; Williams and Laoire 2011).

Pandit Das and others sometimes referred to the style he developed as the "California *gharānā*" of kathak (e.g., Chakravorty 2006, 127; Swapan 2015). Deriving from *ghar*, or "house," *gharānās* are both social and artistic categories, connecting specific lineages of performers with particular styles of performance. Daniel Neuman's research indicates that the *gharānā* concept developed in the nineteenth century and came into use first by solo musicians in the twentieth century ([1980] 1990). Although a relatively new phenomenon, because *gharānās* were created by emphasizing preexisting linkages of ancestry and discipleship, they quickly "assumed an appearance of being ages old" (146).

Daniel Neuman asserts a connection between the formation of *gharānās* and the advent of the telegraph and train travel in India, which allowed patrons to book artists from afar and for artists to travel relatively long distances in a short period of time (1978, 206–7). While this technology enabled many to perform concerts for wider audiences, artists correspondingly experienced greater anonymity as they worked to secure performances from a larger number of patrons in a more geographically dispersed marketplace. *Gharānā* identity thus helped communicate the details of an artist's style and pedigree to audiences who might not know them personally. Neuman suggests the formation of *gharānās* by solo (Kalāvant) musicians also served an exclusionary function, to differentiate themselves from rural (Mirāsī) accompanist musicians of lower social strata, who likely were moving to major urban centers in greater numbers in the early twentieth century (201).[10] Whether they developed to attract patrons or exclude other artists, *gharānās* served to communicate identity and a particular set of musical values based in lineage and artistic style.

While the concept was first used by hereditary lineages of solo Muslim vocalists, in the early twentieth century other artists began using the term *gharānā*, beginning with solo instrumentalists, followed by accompanists (including tabla players), and kathak dancers (Daniel Neuman 1978; Walker 2014). As with musicians, Walker suggests that for kathak dancers, "the decision to form . . . *gharānās* was made as dancers from various areas came into increasing contact with each other in the early twentieth century" and experienced "competition for patronage and need for stability in the new marketplace" (2014, 108). In kathak, two *gharānās* are the most common. These, the Jaipur and Lucknow *gharānās*, are respectively named after major cities in Rajasthan and Uttar Pradesh where they developed. Lesser-known *gharānās* include those from Benares and Raigarh.[11] Two communities of dancers are both identified as Benares *gharānā*; one, considered "a bifurcation of the Jaipur gharana," was founded by Janaki Prasad of Rajasthan, who moved to Benares in the 1800s, and includes kathak artist Smt. Sunayana Hazarilal (Natavar 1997, 75). Exponents of the other Benares *gharānā* include disciples and relatives of Smt. Sitara Devi, some of whom still reside in Varanasi (Benares) and likely have familial ties to members of the Lucknow *gharānā* (Walker 2014, 20, citing Narayan 1998, 176). In the decades preceding Indian independence, the princely state of Raigarh (in present-day Chhattisgarh) became an important center for kathak due to the patronage of Raja Chakradhar Singh, who ruled as feudatory chief (Kothari 1989, 67). While Raigarh's style is considered an amalgamation of the other three schools and thus its status as a *gharānā* is disputed, Walker suggests that Raigarh's role as a center for artists from different regions to come together may have been a central motivation in creating distinct kathak *gharānās*, as dancers "realized that separate identities and styles would be advantageous and also offer a certain sense of security" (2014, 107).

Music or dance "style" may be difficult to pinpoint; and indeed, whether a particular approach is characteristic of a particular *gharānā*, or whether an individual artist's interpretations fall within the understood parameters of their *gharānā*, are common topics of debate. As with music, the articulation of regional styles of kathak as discrete *gharānās* was "as much political as artistic" (Walker 2014, 108). Nevertheless, stylistic distinctions are drawn between kathak *gharānās*, particularly Lucknow and Jaipur, by focusing on the use of specific types of compositions, differing techniques, and approaches to the dance. Pallabi Chakravorty provides a succinct description of their characteristics by noting that "the two major *gharanas*, Lucknow and Jaipur, are marked by sensuous and delicate movements of the limbs and complex and vigorous footwork respectively" (2006, 133 fn. 8). Mekhala Natavar similarly writes that "the Jaipur school is known for its emphasis on technical virtuosity and enactment of religious and heroic tales, while the Lucknow school is considered more lyrical, with a focus on interpretive themes of love" (1997, 64; see also Walker 2014, 20–21).

Pandit Das, whose own guru was trained in both Jaipur- and Lucknow-*gharānā* kathak, characterized their distinctiveness by highlighting the environments in which each style developed, as well as by distinguishing specific kinds of footwork and turns used for each. He described Jaipur-*gharānā* kathak, as a "vigorous, 'warrior-like' style," arising from the arid semideserts of Rajasthan, western India, and characterized by *tārikiṭa* footwork (C. Das et. al. 2001, 85).[12] In contrast, the Lucknow *gharānā*, which he noted flourished in the lavish courts of eighteenth-century Lucknow, was characterized by a "graceful, decadent style," utilizing *tatkār* and *nā dhin dhin nā* footwork (85) (▶ see video 1.8).[13] In his teaching, Pandit Das clearly distinguished Jaipur-style and Lucknow-style turns as well, primarily through differing hand and arm movements. For Jaipur-style turns, his dancers hold their arms in a strong, outstretched position at or slightly below shoulder height, with the hands quickly moving in toward the chest and back out again for each turn (▶ see video 1.9, cue point 0:53). By contrast, in Lucknow-style turns, dancers' hands begin and end in a more easeful position in front of the chest; as the arms move away from the body to initiate a turn, they may drop well below the shoulders with a *parī* or "fairy" style of fluid wrist and hand movements (▶ see video 1.10, cue point 1:19).

While Pandit Das clearly articulated stylistic differences between Jaipur and Lucknow *gharānās* (as in video 1.8), these are by no means universally-recognized distinctions.[14] As Daniel Neuman exhorts, "one has constantly to keep in mind that gharanas are essentially abstract categories" ([1980] 1990, 146). The challenges in distinguishing *gharānās*, again, derive from multiple and differing social and artistic viewpoints, and from the general difficulties in characterizing "style," as well as from continued contact between artists. The "exchange of material and students between Lucknow and Jaipur *gharānās* seems to have been a constant process throughout the twentieth century," as Walker notes (2014, 108). And these distinctions, if they ever were clear-cut, continue to be blurred. Today it is common for kathak dancers to study with multiple teachers over the course of their training, and although generally discouraged, for some to train in several styles of dance, reflecting the increasingly broad, often transnational scope of both the artists and the forms they practice.

Particularly in diasporic sites of artistic transmission, we may distinguish participants as heritage learners, those whose familial roots connect them to the place identified with an artistic practice, or as affinity learners, those who do not share a common ethnic or national affiliation with the art form they practice, and whose involvement develops primarily through a sense of individual connection or affinity (Shelemay 2011; Slobin 1993).[15] In the case of affinity learners, academic inquiry has arisen slowly, although, as Cowdery writes, "serious students have been crossing cultural boundaries for decades" (1995, 50). And while we find a growing literature on Indian dance forms practiced and performed by heritage learners in diasporic contexts, scholarly research has "tend[ed] to focus on the diaspora in isolation from the 'host' society," which Thobani observes "obscur[es] the actuality that diasporic practices are part of and related to the wider multicultural context—and politics—in which they are located" (2017, 8).

In examining the community of kathak dancers in the United States that coalesced around Pandit Das's teaching, I consider all members—heritage and affinity practitioners from a variety of backgrounds—as belonging to a specific artistic diaspora, while acknowledging and examining individuals' various subjective positionalities. With a diverse group of students such as this, how does a teacher transmit cultural and dance knowledge? In an artistic diaspora, how does a culture bearer maintain, modify, and frame repertoire, cultural norms associated with being a dancer, and philosophies surrounding the dance? And how do dancers negotiate the challenges of cultural expression in such manifestly intercultural contexts? Questions posed within this community—one of the longest-running sites of kathak transmission in the United States—serve to illuminate aspects of contemporary expressive practice in multicultural America as well as their embedded values.

Pandit Das's Career

Pandit Das's US career was marked throughout by a passion for bringing diverse groups of students into the world of kathak dance. While he described a strong desire to move to the United States as a young man, like most other immigrants, his decision involved both strong push and pull factors. The States offered new possibilities as well as an escape from frustrations in India, where he felt he lacked opportunities: "I was not getting anywhere because I was very young, and I did not have that recognition. My parents had a very big dance school and they were situated in Calcutta, but things were happening in Delhi. Anything that came through Delhi was marked, acknowledged, and approved with the government of India seal" (C. Das interview, June 17, 2004). As Pandit Das alludes, Delhi was the site for India's National Institute of Kathak, Kathak Kendra. Established in 1964, the institute was led first by celebrated guru of the Lucknow *gharānā*, Pt. Shambhu Maharaj, and then, from 1970 to 1988, by his nephew, Pt. Birju Majaraj, whose style of kathak became the national standard. "As a result," Chakravorty writes, "performing artists had to politically align themselves with the central government" (2008, 67). Pandit Das, based first in Calcutta and then in the United States, distanced and unaffiliated with Delhi's powerful kathak scene, had felt disenfranchised from those artistic opportunities. However, that very distance from hegemonic forces shaping kathak in India conversely gave him the space—socially, politically, and geographically—to develop himself as an artist, and to crystallize a signature style of kathak profoundly influenced by his experiences in India and the United States, ultimately embodying his own vision for the art form.

In 1970, Pandit Das arrived in the United States on a one-year Whitney fellowship at the University of Maryland to teach kathak and study modern dance (figure 1.3). The following year, he moved to the San Francisco Bay Area to teach at the Ali Akbar College of Music (AACM), in Marin County just north of San Francisco. By 1979 he had left the AACM faculty to form his own dance school called Chhandam, and in 1980 he incorporated the Chitresh Das Dance Company (CDDC); later the two projects coalesced as one organization, the Chhandam Chitresh Das Dance Company (CCDDC).[16]

FIG. 1.3. Chitresh Das putting on his *ghuṅgharū* before a kathak lecture-demonstration at the University of Maryland, 1970.

In his ensuing decades in the United States, he trained generations of kathak dancers of varying backgrounds, some of whom attained professional-level facility to perform nationally and internationally, both independently and with Pandit Das.

Until the late 1980s, Pandit Das's teaching was based largely in Marin County, where his dance students were primarily young, white women whom he affectionately labeled "the blondes and brunettes." With the 1988 opening of a branch of his school in Fremont, a city in the southeast region of the Bay Area where growing high-tech employment attracted and recruited an increasing population of South Asian professionals, Pandit Das took up the opportunity to teach more first- and second-generation South Asian American students. Beginning in the late 1990s, Pandit Das's Chhandam School of Kathak dramatically expanded in the southern and eastern regions of the Bay Area, with branches opening in Berkeley, Mountainview, San Bruno, and San Jose (table 1.1 and map 1.1). By the time I began fieldwork in 2000, the large majority of Chhandam students were of South Asian origin, and Pandit Das's dance company, no longer solely "blondes and brunettes," was stridently self-declared his "rainbow coalition," after the Reverend Jesse Jackson's nonprofit organization of the same name.

Table 1.1. Overview of Pandit Chitresh Das's US teaching career and kathak schools affiliated with Das, 1970–2015

1970	Pandit Das arrived in the United States on a fellowship to teach kathak at the University of Maryland
1971	Began teaching kathak at the Ali Akbar College in Marin County, CA
ca. 1978	Taught classes in Berkeley (at world music performance venue Ashkenaz) intermittently until 1996
1978	Taught classes regularly in Los Angeles as a guest artist with Aman International Folk Ensemble (until 1986)
1979	Established the Chhandam School of Kathak Dance with classes in Marin County (San Rafael/San Anselmo; closed in 2003) and San Francisco
1980	Incorporated the Chitresh Das Dance Company (CDDC)
early 1980s	Taught a weekly class in Stockton, CA
ca. 1988	Taught a kathak course at San Francisco State University (until 2005)
1988	Began teaching classes in Fremont/Union City, CA (which later became a branch of Chhandam)
1988	Joanna de Souza established M-DO (now M-DO/Kathak Toronto) in Toronto, Canada
1992	Gretchen Hayden established Chhandika, the Chhandam Institute of Kathak Dance in Boston, MA
1998	Established a branch of Chhandam in Berkeley, CA
1999	Established a branch of Chhandam in Mountain View, CA
2000	Established a branch of Chhandam in San Bruno, CA (closed in 2005)
2002	Established the Chitresh Das Youth Company (later the Chhandam Youth Dance Company)
2002	Established Chhandam Nritya Bharati kathak school in Kolkata, India
2003	Closed Marin branch of Chhandam
2003	Established a branch of Chhandam in San Jose, CA
2007	Pratibha Patel established a branch of Chhandam in Sacramento, CA (closed in 2014)
2008	Rina Mehta established a branch of Chhandam in Los Angeles (later the autonomous nonprofit Leela Institute for the Arts)
2010	Seema Mehta established a branch of Chhandam Nritya Bharati in Mumbai, India

In the late 1980s and early 1990s, Pandit Das's teaching extended beyond the Bay Area when two of his longtime students, Gretchen Hayden and Joanna de Souza (then Das) began their own schools.[17] In Boston, Gretchen Hayden founded Chhandika: Chhandam Institute of Kathak Dance when her husband, ethnomusicologist George Ruckert, joined the music faculty at MIT. Joanna de Souza moved to Toronto with her then-husband, Pandit Das's brother, Ritesh Das, and founded the kathak institution M-DO. In 2001, driven by a desire to influence the direction of kathak in India, Pandit Das opened a new school in Kolkata, Chhandam Nritya Bharati, named for his parents' institution, Nritya Bharati.[18] In subsequent years, other students established branch institutions: Seema Mehta established a branch of Chhandam Nritya Bharati in Mumbai and Pratibha Patel and Rina Mehta established California branches of Chhandam outside the Bay Area.[19] By 2004, the

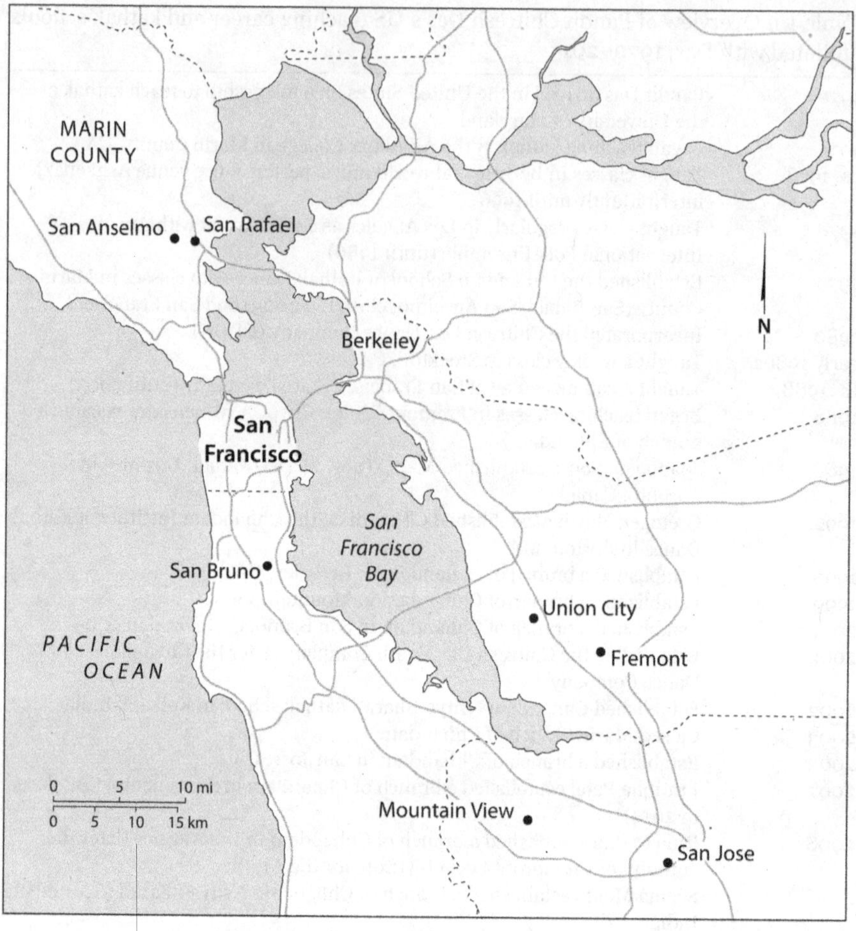

MAP 1.1. Locations of the Chhandam School of Kathak in the San Francisco Bay Area.

Chhandam School confidently proclaimed itself the largest classical Indian dance school in North America.

Articulating Immigration

Pandit Das was an innovator, "a pioneer emigrant who settled in the Bay area 30 years ago and blazed a trail, firmly establishing Kathak among American dancers and the Indian diaspora" (Kothari 2004). In addition to documenting the development of Pandit Das's style of kathak performance, this book examines how living, teaching, and performing in the United States influenced Pandit Das's pedagogy and the culture of his dance school and company. My interest in these questions is in part a reflection of Pandit Das's own understanding of his positioning in and between India and America, which evolved over the course of his lifetime. For many years when he lived and taught primarily in the United States, this relationship was expressed with the simple phrase, "from Calcutta to California," which became the title of a twenty-four-page promotional booklet created in 1986 by his then-wife, Julia Das (now Maxwell; J. Das 1986a). The same phrase featured prominently in the advertisements and concert program for Pandit Das's 1990 choreographic work, *Impressions of California Goldrush*, in which the gold rush symbolized his own westward journey (▶ see video 1.11).[20] Themes of relocation and adaptation explored in this production are central both to Pandit Das's life experiences and kathak's history, as captured in the following *San Francisco Chronicle* review:

> Chitresh, who arrived in the United States 20 years ago with $8 in his pocket, feels that "Gold Rush" is an extension of the kathak tradition of dance drama and virtuoso technique. Just as in its ancient form, when kathak moved away from being a devotional expression to the Hindu gods, evolving into lavish entertainment in the courts of Hindu maharajahs and Muslim nawabs, it is entirely appropriate to expand its borders with further immigration. . . . "I am that part of India that is always traveling," Chitresh remarked. . . . "My role

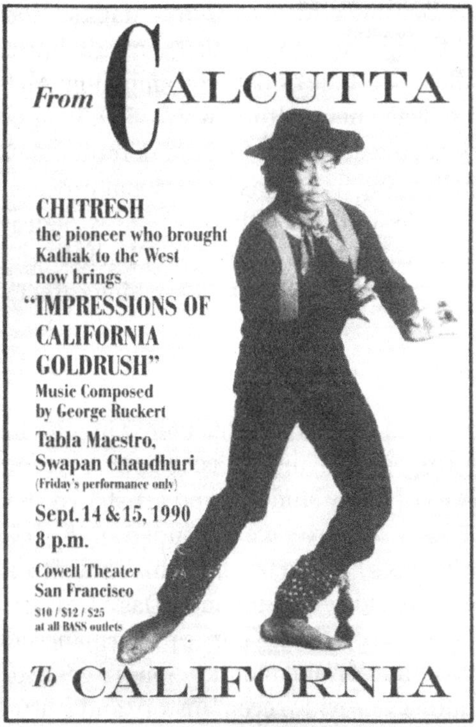

FIG. 1.4. Advertisement for *Impressions of California Goldrush* from *In Dance*, September 1990. Photo by Marty Sohl.

was not just to be a famous Indian dancer. I could have stayed in Calcutta for that. I am a pioneer, the Johnny Appleseed of kathak dance." (Tucker 1990)

While Pandit Das highlighted his move from Calcutta to California as central to his life path, his evolution as an artist and teacher was not unidirectional. His work resulted from ongoing interactions with a variety of students in the United States and in India, and more nominally with other artists, critics, audiences, and promoters; many times over, this evolution involved community building, artistic experimentation, disagreements, rifts, and sometimes even dissolution, followed by more community building and more experimentation. In order to help capture this complexity, this book regularly shifts focus among the perspectives of Pandit Das, his dance students, and the author (as both dancer and ethnomusicologist).

Particularly in his early days in the United States, Pandit Das's interactions with students frequently produced culture shock on both sides. Pandit Das struggled to replicate for his adult US students the rigorous training he received as a child in India. For his students, this confrontation with strict Indian-style discipleship conflicted sharply with romanticized notions about Indian spirituality, freedom, and liberation propagated in America's counterculture. As the dance culture of Pandit Das's school developed over almost forty-five years of teaching in the United States, ideas of India and Indian-ness transmitted by Pandit Das and critical to his teachings similarly evolved. Further, these concepts differed from those initially brought into the classroom by his students, regardless of ethnic or national affiliation. All his dancers, to varying degrees, had to learn new cultural ways of being in taking on the particular type of student role necessary for kathak training with Pandit Das. Responses to the challenging and transformational process of discipleship varied significantly, and as such, this ethnographic work draws on interviews and experiences with students from a range of backgrounds, who were active during different periods of Pandit Das's teaching career.[21]

Themes of the Book

Through his combination of deep-seated love for kathak, intense inquiry into the form, and unmistakable showmanship, Pandit Das became a groundbreaking artist who shaped the lives of many students and artists. To share this story and examine its implications, I interweave various strands of narrative throughout this work: Pandit Das's life and teaching, his students' experiences, and analysis of the dance form itself.[22] In Pandit Das's transition from India to the States, arguably every aspect of his dance performance and teaching underwent processes of examination and modification. To contextualize these processes, in most chapters I provide recent history and cultural analysis in dialogue with music/dance analysis. For example, in chapter 6, I describe how Pandit Das evolved a system of integrating dance with basic Hindustani rhythmic and melodic structures, while also examining how his students understood and articulated the relationship of racial and ethnic identity to dancing kathak in the United States. One central issue Pandit Das and his students explored was whether or not in dance—where the body itself is the medium of expression—one can "transcend" ethnic, racial, and national differences. These interrogations resulted in Pandit Das privileging the technical and rhythmic prowess of kathak over its lyrical and narrative elements, which I reveal through description of several of his key practices and stylistic approaches.

Chapter 2 illuminates the history Pandit Das told about himself and the dance form, focusing on the sociohistorical context in which he was raised and trained in kathak. This chapter provides background on Pandit Das's parents, guru, and fellow students. In addition, beginning in chapter 2, I examine ideals of guruship held by Pandit Das, and ways he adapted the model provided by his own guru over time, and in response to changing contexts for kathak transmission.

Chapter 3 situates the performance choices Pandit Das made within the history of Indian culture bearers in the United States. Like many who preceded him, he experimented with various strategies to make his tradition comprehensible to US audiences. After some years of overwhelming his audiences by performing lengthy concerts with more complex and dense material than they could understand, Pandit Das learned to abridge the more technical aspects of his kathak performances and expand the narrative aspects—helping audiences better appreciate the art. He also highlighted pieces that sonically portrayed the material world, including his solo piece *The Train*, which was long the subject of controversy in part due to its radical emphasis on the sounds of footwork. Chapter 3 examines this, his best-known solo work, and other key technical and choreographic innovations that heightened the variety and virtuosity of his performances in response to US audience and critic expectations, while still working to remain within the shifting parameters of tradition.

Pandit Das taught that kathak demands four complementary sets of skills: *taiyārī*, physical agility and "readiness" for dance; *layakārī*, rhythmic virtuosity; *khūbsūratī*, beauty in movement; and *nazākat*, subtleness in gesture and facial expression. Pandit Das's strategies to teach his earliest US students in the 1970s and '80s involved intensive training focusing on *taiyārī*. Chapter 4 introduces some basic technical aspects of kathak while discussing both the physical and emotional challenges Pandit Das's students experienced in navigating the *guru-śiṣya paramparā*, or "teacher-disciple tradition" of pedagogy.

Chapter 5 examines what are generally considered to be feminine and masculine stylistic developments in Pandit Das's manner of teaching and performing kathak. During the late 1980s and '90s, when Pandit Das began teaching more South Asian American students, the style of kathak he taught changed noticeably, emphasizing the arguably more feminine elements of *khūbsūratī* and *nazākat*. After analyzing specific ways the style he taught softened during this period, the second section of the chapter discusses the more masculine aspects of Pandit Das's own dance, particularly his practice of dancing with dumbbells. Together, these sections consider how ideas of masculinity and femininity emerged in Pandit Das's kathak style and how the half-male, half-female Hindu deity *ardhanārīśvara* influenced Pandit Das's dance philosophy.

Chapter 6 considers various metaphors Pandit Das and his dancers employed to represent the diversity of the Chitresh Das Dance Company, and ways they discussed ethnic and racial difference in the early 2000s, the period of my primary fieldwork. In this community, technical virtuosity was long considered the great equalizer, an emphasis that culminated in Pandit Das's creation and development of a practice he called kathak yoga. In addition to analyzing kathak yoga's physical mechanics and performance examples, this chapter addresses its philosophical foundations, exploring how it might appeal to Americans of diverse backgrounds.

Kathak yoga also serves to heighten a dancer's *layakāri*, or rhythmic facility, an essential skill for performing a "traditional kathak solo." As addressed in chapter 7, a full-length kathak solo is considered the primary rite of passage for a senior dance student transitioning into a performance career. For Pandit Das's students, this performance was particularly formidable because he expected them to include the element of *upaj*, or spontaneous, non-choreographed dancing. Chapter 7 also explores different types of improvisation found in kathak and methods by which Pandit Das's students practiced the skills needed to improvise. Finally, this chapter considers the means by which Pandit Das inserted *upaj* and other forms of *layakāri* into the large-scale and largely choreographed format of "new productions" expected by promoters, funders, and audiences.

The final chapter discusses pedagogical, philosophical, and performance contributions Pandit Das made late in life. In 2001, he began teaching in Kolkata, marking his return to India as a teacher after thirty years in the United States. In subsequent years, he performed in cities across India as a soloist and collaborator (most notably with tap dancer Jason Samuels Smith), and deliberately taught students from different strata of society, including children from a red-light district in Kolkata that used to be home to *bāījīs*, former purveyors of this artistic tradition. Pandit Das's creative work flourished from 2005 to 2015, a period of both greater influence in India and more mainstream recognition in the United States.

This ethnographic study of a kathak master and community concludes that the well-worn dichotomy of "tradition" and "innovation" is not navigated alone but instead is negotiated by individuals and groups within a complex network of relationships involving in this case, audiences, supporters, critics, and most importantly, student-artists who in relationship with their mentor prompted and supported artistic change. Through these intense interactions, Pandit Das's pedagogy, artistic philosophy, and creative genius coalesced into what some call the California *gharānā* of kathak. Chapter 8 closes by examining some of the central questions for members of this kathak community, who, following Pandit Das's death in 2015, continued working to uphold and advance his artistic legacy.

In the Field

In the remaining portion of this introductory chapter, I address the important topic of the ethnographer's position in this study. It is by now a widely recognized aspect of ethnography that the fieldworker's presence influences the very field they are studying (e.g., Barz and Cooley [1997] 2008; Karp and Kendall 1982).[23] In the words of Jane Cowan, "the fieldworker's personality, temperament, and a whole gamut of intangible, contingent factors inevitably affect the fieldwork process and the social relations it entails" (1990, 55–56). A reflexive turn may be particularly valuable here because of the close nature of the transmission process in North Indian classical dance and music.

My relationship with this dance community was, like most in the field, complex. While in my second year of graduate study at Harvard University, I began kathak classes with Gretchen Hayden at the suggestion of her husband George Ruckert, an ethnomusicologist with whom I was taking Hindustani vocal lessons. As senior disciples of Pandit Chitresh Das and Ustad Ali Akbar Khan, respectively, they had an enduring dedication to the arts and their insight and generosity as teachers easily drew me into the study. As my interest deepened, I began to consider going to California to study with their gurus, wrestling with the possibility of foregoing earlier plans to conduct fieldwork primarily in India. Over the course of three trips, I had previously spent over a year in India, but as I learned more about the relatively longstanding music and dance communities in the San Francisco Bay Area, I became fascinated with investigating how practitioners of the Hindustani arts adapted to such a different sociocultural environment.

When I arrived in California, I realized just how valuable my previous study had been. Everyone seemed to have words of kindness and respect for George-dā and Gretchen-dī (meaning elder brother and sister), as some called them; and in introductions to other community members I came to rely on the good feelings engendered by mentioning their names. During my studies with

Pandit Das and Ustad Ali Akbar Khan (respectfully referred to as Khansahib), I often drew on my experiences with them, and sought to emulate in my own interactions their gracious way of being. I came to think of them as my Schieffelins, after the mentors who prepared Steven Feld for his fieldwork (1982). However, unlike Feld's introduction to the Kaluli of Papua New Guinea, it was not necessary to invent familial ties with my new community (11). By virtue of studying with George-dā and Gretchen-dī, I had already become part of overlapping communities of fictive (and partially real) kinship.

In Cambridge, Massachusetts, my dual studies of music and dance were a natural, unproblematic combination; training in one proved to inform my understanding of the other. However, before I left for California, Gretchen-dī suggested that at some point I would have to choose between the two. When I arrived in San Francisco, it became apparent that serious study with two master artists was an uncommon and perhaps impossible enterprise. I was astonished at the level of dedication with which many had undertaken their study of kathak or Hindustani music—and the sacrifices some made to do so. I took on a similar intensity in my own studies, and for most of my three years of fieldwork I participated in dance and music classes five to six days each week. The weekends often were taken up with concerts for my attendance or participation as a dancer, vocalist, or sarod player. I was also called on to accompany dance performances by singing or playing sarod, reciting dance compositions, playing harmonium, *manjīra*, *tānpūrā*, or *svaramaṇḍāl*, or usually some combination of these.

In addition to logistical complications and limitations of physical and mental energy, serious study in more than one area of these classical arts is made problematic by the concept of guru. George Ruckert describes a guru as a teacher of the kind "one sees daily for years and years . . . with whom one lives nearly as a family member" (1994, 2). This quasi-familial tie expresses itself in the terms with which students refer to their teachers: Khansahib's students referred to him as Bābā (father); Pandit Das's students often called him Dādā or Dādā-jī (elder brother) and, increasingly toward the end of his life, Guru-jī. Extending the familial network, a fellow student is a guru-*bhāī* or guru-*bahan* (guru-brother or guru-sister). If older, he or she could be referred to as *dādā* or *dīdī* (elder brother or sister), terms that can be appended to the first name (such as George-dā and Gretchen-dī) to convey respect. Students of Pandit Das also used the Anglicized term *dance-sister*.

"No one can have two gurus," Pandit Das once said, expanding on the familial theme. "Having two gurus is like having two husbands or two boyfriends; your heart cannot be in two places at once." At the time, Pandit Das was referring to dancers studying with more than one kathak teacher; however, I experienced a similar pull between my kathak and Hindustani music studies. Khansahib openly discouraged my situation, likening it to "trying to cross the river with your feet in two different boats."[24] Nevertheless, the experience afforded me a unique perspective on the inner workings of the Hindustani system of *saṅgīt*—instruments, voice, and dance—and on the two interrelated, yet distinct communities at the schools led by Ali Akbar Khansahib and Pandit Chitresh Das.

Joan Erdman argues: "In most Indian performance arts, both fine and folk forms, music and dance and drama are intertwined and inseparable parts of a presentation whole. To insist on studying them separately is to deny the indigenous aesthetic and constructs, thereby destroying the very process one is trying to understand" (1991, 113). The integration of music and dance has historical underpinnings as well, found most explicitly in the performances of *bāījīs* or *ṯavā'ifs*, singer-dancers who had a valued position in Indian society until the late nineteenth century (Qureshi 2006). Music and dance practices were pulled apart in a movement supposedly to restore Indian arts to a position of moral decency and bourgeois respectability (Oldenburg 1990). Today, although some artists study more than one instrument or performing art in the early stages of training, at some point they find it necessary to focus on one. My experiences confirmed for me the wisdom of this approach. Whenever one of the two schools (the Chhandam School of Kathak and Ali Akbar College of Music) was on break, my studies became immensely more pleasurable. This was not due simply to the pressures of time and logistics; regardless of which school was on hiatus, I found myself delving into my study of the other with greater depth, facilitated by the lack of inner friction created by regularly shifting between the two.

Prior to arriving in California, I had expected to focus my research on the Ali Akbar College of Music, an assumption informed partly by the paucity of dance research in ethnomusicology at that time, and relative lack of attention given to dance scholarship in academia (Desmond 1993/1994; Farnell 1999; Reed 1998). I initially approached kathak classes as a time away from my fieldworker persona, but this stance became difficult to maintain. Pandit Das's teaching methods explicitly drew on the personal and political by relating our kathak study to issues of race, ethnicity, gender, age, and even marital status, challenging his students individually and collectively. Inside his classroom, I found a fascinating world where issues of contemporary America seemed to be almost bouncing off the walls along with the sounds of dancers' bells and bare feet slapping the floors. Here was an ongoing conversation about the dance, its place in contemporary America, and these dancers' positioning in the larger world of kathak.

I eventually decided to switch my approach toward these two areas of study, cultivating an ethnographer's perspective on the kathak scene, while focusing on music making and less formal observation within the Hindustani music community. Having spent a significant amount of time previously developing relationships with Pandit Das and members of his school and dance company, I experienced a relatively smooth transition when adding other elements to my own participation congruent with traditional fieldwork methodology, such as interviewing and videotaping classes.

As the only dancer at that time also studying voice and the sarod with Ali Akbar Khansahib, I was drafted as a musical accompanist for dance concerts and classes almost immediately upon my arrival in the Bay Area. Within months, I regularly played sarod for Thursday company classes, closed-door training sessions for members of the Chitresh Das Dance Company led by Pandit Das. Under these circumstances, my positioning was distinct, physically and socially. I sat facing the dancers on a raised platform at the front of the room, and Pandit Das would usually stand in front of the dais, simultaneously playing tabla and dancing while leading the company members through various repertoire. In that context, Pandit Das sometimes turned to me in his role as teacher, challenging me to play with more clarity or speed; at other times, he would simply play with me, smiling and having fun. The bulk of Pandit Das's attention, however, would be squarely on the dance company members, giving me room to observe.

Sitting with my sarod, I could see somewhat more objectively the intense physical and emotional dramas unfolding in front of me each week. I had a front-row seat to the process of crafting a dancer. As one dancer commented, this dynamic interaction "is at the heart of what Pandit Das does, and what [his students] are all participating in." While fascinating, this process could be difficult and sometimes even painful for the students. Another dancer suggested that Pandit Das had a unique ability and willingness to "let others sit in their own unease." Pandit Das himself likened this process to holding a mirror in front of someone, and the combination of physical and emotional adversity in his classes often brought unexpected results.

As other ethnomusicologists have noted, teachers sometimes become more critical as a student's skill level increases (e.g., Tang 2007, 16–17). Similarly, early in my studies I danced in what Pandit Das nicknamed the happy-hour class. More experienced dancers often advised us to enjoy this time, because Pandit Das would not always be so easygoing in his teaching style. As my own dance classes became more challenging, I took in intense training situations with an entirely different point of view than when playing sarod. The crucial difference seemed to lie in the intense physicality of the dance training. Reaching the point of physical exhaustion, as we commonly did, seemed to make me much more emotionally vulnerable to verbal criticism. The sheer anticipation of that criticism brought with it a heightened awareness sometimes even manifesting as intense anxiety. We were being kept on our toes, as it were, despite the dance form's inherent groundedness. As suggested by some of the senior dance students, this was in fact a crucial aspect of our training, preparing us to be ready for anything.

When I decided to focus my academic work on kathak, I began interviewing Pandit Das and his students and occasionally videotaping classes. My first videos are from late 2001, and Pandit Das was slow to accept the presence of my camera. After I videotaped interviews, classes, rehearsals, and other events for several years, two other dance students, Shipra Shukla and Antara Bhardwaj, were recruited to shoot. After watching a kathak performance in 2006, noted author and psychologist Daniel Goleman encouraged Pandit Das's students to "overdocument" their teacher's work. It was then that Pandit Das became more amenable to the presence of video cameras, which became even more commonly part of his life from 2007 to 2013, when he and tap dancer Jason Samuels Smith were filmed as the main subjects of the documentary *Upaj: Improvise* (Uchiyama 2013).[25]

During the years of my primary fieldwork, however, Pandit Das maintained an ambivalent stance toward video as a means of communicating the dance, and I felt an important level of trust had been reached when I was allowed to bring my video camera into the classroom.[26] Particularly early on, he would tell me to "Turn that thing off!" when he had something to say that he considered inappropriate to record. What followed often involved chastising a particular student or railing against some aspect of the highly charged politics of North Indian classical performance. His candid remarks in those moments were often more direct and revealing than when Pandit Das was more mindful of maintaining diplomacy. Since I was often dancing or playing sarod in the classes that I taped, I began to give him the remote control so he could turn off the camera himself, usually with a dancer's flourish. Giving Pandit Das control over the recording also gave him the agency to determine what was appropriate to record, which was a successful means of ameliorating the potentially disruptive presence of a video camera.

During my final summer living in California (2003), I accompanied Pandit Das to Kolkata where, following his lead, the camera seldom left my side. I interviewed many of his guru-brothers and -sisters, other dancers, musicians, and dance critics. My video camera recorded almost everything Pandit Das was involved with: from concerts to classes, conversations with students, journalists, and colleagues in music and dance; and it captured many unexpected moments of inspiration. This six-week period was my closest experience until then of being a *śiṣya* (pronounced "shishya"), or disciple. Over the course of his life, Pandit Das had relatively few official disciples, women who trained with him for more than ten years and took part in a *gaṇḍā bandan*, or string-tying ceremony.[27] Since none of the current *śiṣyas* were there that summer, my dance-sister Rina Mehta and I took care of all those things a

FIG. 1.5. *Left to right*: Chitresh Das with Charlotte Moraga, Seema Mehta, and the author, all soaked with sweat following practice in Mumbai, July 2007.

disciple would: offering tea to visitors, managing telephone communications, and even massaging sore muscles.[28]

My fieldwork also continued after physically leaving the field. Pandit Das made short yearly trips to Boston to work with Gretchen Hayden's kathak students; while I lived in Cambridge from 2003 to 2006, his visits allowed me to work with him in a less hectic environment than his schedule typically permitted. Pandit Das's trip in 2004 culminated in our joint presentation to the Harvard Music Department on aspects of his style of kathak. I accompanied Pandit Das to India again in the summer of 2007 (figure 1.5) and made several yearly trips to California to lend my assistance during particularly busy concert seasons, to participate in and sometimes teach music classes during kathak retreats, to revisit the CCDDC archives, or to conduct follow-up interviews. Fieldwork in the United States made it convenient to continue discussions and formal interviews with dancers over the telephone and via Skype. These conversations largely proved to be even more fruitful than interviews conducted while I was in California. Though I was a known and trusted member of the dance community, my absence in the daily social network seemed to allow my dance-sisters to open up more freely and share insights about their dancing lives.

On my return to Cambridge in 2003, I renewed my studies with Gretchen Hayden, and for a time taught dance classes at her Chhandika school, a situation that brought about its own challenges. While Gretchen-dī received her formative training in an early period of Pandit Das's teaching in the United States, over the years Pandit Das continued to modify his vision and version of kathak. Thus, when I came back to Boston, we found that the way I moved was very different from that of her other students. The problem for us both lay in determining which aspects of my dancing were the result of transformations in Pandit Das's teaching, and which were instead my own stylistic idiosyncrasies. As Tomie Hahn described of her own fieldwork process, "the very 'data' I sought were . . . entrenched in my very body—ready to be mined" (2007, xiv). This embodied data and my work with Gretchen-dī were key in understanding the extent to which Pandit Das's style evolved over the course of his career.

In subsequent years, I came to understand the challenges Gretchen-dī experienced in teaching me from a different perspective. In 2006, I began teaching kathak at the University of Denver, where I faced similar questions of how to maintain the style in which I was trained—which lived, developed, and matured in my own body and artistry—while, as Pandit Das put it, "the guru is still evolving." The challenge included developing my own teaching and maintaining my own dance practice, while remaining open and flexible enough to "move with the guru" as his dance style and repertoire evolved. These challenges helped me recognize that differences in my dance-sisters' styles might develop because of individual strengths and proclivities, but also might stem from having trained during different periods of Pandit Das's life, further reinforcing my understanding of the dance form as a living, breathing tradition.

Pandit Das's own evolution as a pedagogue, performer, and guru came to an end when he passed away January 4, 2015. Over forty-five years of teaching in the United States and later India, Pandit Das developed a distinctive and recognizable style of kathak. Today, with kathak schools run by senior students and disciples of Pandit Das in various cities in the United States, Canada, and India, central questions include whether and how his disciples might work to maintain consistency across these schools. It remains to be seen how much the style of kathak danced and taught by his disciples in different locations might differ from one another forty-five years after his passing; yet the inevitable variations certainly will contribute to the rich, multifaceted style of kathak that was developed by Pandit Das and his students on Californian soil.

2

Dancing History

October 13, 2001: The audience in San Francisco's Cowell Theater hushed as the lights dimmed for Pandit Das's latest premiere, titled Sadhana. *Darkness revealed the soft glow of a* dīyā, *a ceremonial lamp surrounded by flowers and placed in the front right corner of the stage. As a projection screen center stage lit up with an image of the sun rising over Indian marshland, the hum of a* tānpūrā *swelled to fill the room, accentuated by the descending pitches of a* svaramaṇḍāl *and birdsong. The gritty strains of sarangi next entered the soundscape, not with the tonic stability of* Sa, *but instead a whole step below on* komal ni, *a minor seventh scale degree. Evoking pathos and nostalgia with slow, oscillating* āndolan, *the sarangi player lingered over the note's microtonal shadings, touching on its chromatic lower neighbor,* śuddh Dha, *before descending another whole tone to* Pa *to close the phrase.*[1]

Natural sounds superimposed over the music accompanied on-screen images that shifted from mountaintops to ocean waves, to finally rest on the performance title.[2] *Next, the hall resounded with Quranic recitation, conch shells, and church bells as the silhouettes of secular and sacred spaces—a city park, mosque, temple, and cathedral—faded one into the next. These images dimmed slightly to reveal Pandit Das behind the screen. As he performed* pranām, *an invocation to the dance, it seemed the audience was being given a glimpse of an exceedingly private ritual. Ringing church bells gave way to a train whistle, and the images again shifted: to Kolkata's Howrah Bridge, and then to a crowded Indian train station. Like* darśan *(viewing the deity) in a crowded temple, the audience's view of the dancer was also fleeting, quickly obscured by the ever-brighter image of a train rushing past. Pandit Das disappeared, seemingly swallowed by India itself, depicted here as ancient and eternal, yet modern and ever in motion* (▶ see video 2.1).

I begin this chapter describing *Sadhana* in order to initiate a nuanced reading of Pandit Das's understanding and presentation of himself as a kathak dancer. An atypical production, *Sadhana* portrayed personal and cultural experiences that informed and infused his kinesthetic experience of dance. This chapter works to do the same by introducing readers to key stories from Pandit Das's life and examining how those experiences informed his social and artistic choices.

In kathak, as in other storytelling traditions, narrative is created and recreated in moments of performance. Though most stories presented in kathak have been enacted countless times, for performer and audience they may contain nuances and lessons relevant to immediate life concerns. Similarly, Pandit Das recounted most of the biographical episodes he presented in *Sadhana* many times over the years; and for his longtime students, they were part of a larger collection of well-known tales. Over the course of my training with him, as I would listen to Pandit Das launch into a familiar story, I sometimes likened myself to an audience member watching a performance from one of India's epics, for whom the point is not to experience a new story but rather to savor the progression of a familiar tale, appreciate its distinct development and interpretation in a particular iteration, note how it may differ from other tellings, and apply its lessons to present circumstances—as Purnima Shah describes it, to "engage . . . in a new aesthetic experience each time" (1998, 14).

Most of the dancing performed in *Sadhana* could be considered "traditional"; however, the performance conceptually diverged from the norm in its intent to portray (for a San Francisco audience) the cultures, philosophies, and experiences that informed Pandit Das's dance and infused his daily practice, or *sādhanā*.[3] While this work was autobiographical, its purpose was not to re-create scenes from the past but instead to portray how the past lives on in the present dancing body—to illuminate the self that arises out of, and indeed is created in, the very act of dance. Dance works as a catalyst for calling up memories, sensations, and stories that often then find their expression as well as their meaning in the dance. Thus, if the self is "constructed in and through performance," then so too the self as dancer may be best understood and communicated through the dancing self (Sax 2002, 6).

The contradictions and complexities found in Pandit Das's life history are analogous to the history of kathak itself, which "is neither simple nor straightforward. It is not the story of one family or one tradition . . . [but] is a cultural collage, as multi-faceted and fascinating as the collage of cultures that produced it" (Walker 2004, 21). Kathak's "multiple genealogies," as Chakravorty suggests, "articulate a complex intersection of regional histories," including influences from folk traditions, Bhakti and Sufi religious movements, and the patronage of royal courts, in which differing male and female styles of dance were cultivated (2008, 26; see also Walker 2010).[4] In the section of *Sadhana* described above, Pandit Das acknowledged the multifaceted nature of the dance and his own life by including sonic and visual symbols representing Islam, Hinduism, and Christianity. The significance of these religious referents was made clear later in the performance, when he described the manner of his upbringing as photos from his youth faded in and out of the background: "My mother is a Bengali Protestant, but she was very open to all the religions. We had a mosque in front of our house and every morning I woke up at four o'clock in the morning with *ajān* [*azān*: the morning Muslim call to prayer]. And then my dance would begin" (▶ see video 2.2, cue point 1:41).

The cultural synthesis of elements in kathak considered Hindu and Muslim continues to be both a strength of the art form and a matter of some controversy.[5] Most kathak practitioners will claim, as they have been taught, that its storytelling aspects were developed centuries ago as itinerant troupes of dancers and musicians traveled from village to village telling stories from the Hindu epics, and that kathak acquired greater technical virtuosity during the Mughal period (1526–1857), when wealthy Muslim as well as Hindu rulers and landowners patronized musicians and dancers (see Bhate-Jathar 1990; Massey 1999; C. Das et al. 2001; Chakravorty 2008).[6] However, both North Indian music and dance saw an explicit Hinduization coinciding with the independence movement in the early twentieth century. As Regula Qureshi argues, "it became the agenda for middle-class Hindu music lovers for a generation: to take music out of the hands of the Muslim hereditary professionals and win it for the Hindu elite through discipleship and devotion" (1991, 161). In kathak, newer nonhereditary Hindu practitioners developed dance repertoire that drew inspiration from Hindu antiquity such as *śloka*s, from Sanskrit religious texts, and *vandanā*s, each depicting the attributes of a particular Hindu deity (Walker 2010, 294).[7]

Kathak's varied cultural influences and the religious diversity of its patrons and practitioners have led some to eschew the practice. Even in South Asian American diasporic communities in the 2000s, some parents discouraged their children from studying kathak for religious reasons: Hindus because the dance was "too Muslim," and Muslims because it was "too Hindu" (Shaikh interview, December 12, 2002). As a young man growing up next to a mosque, with a Rajasthani Hindu guru, a Bengali Hindu father, a Bengali Protestant Christian mother, and graduating from the Roman Catholic Don Bosco School in Calcutta, Pandit Das was introduced early on to a range of cultural practices and confronted with multiple and competing priorities.[8] These experiences perhaps prepared him to think more carefully about how he represented the dance's cultural complexity as a cultural emissary in the United States. For example, in response to sectarian sentiments and because of his family's heterogeneous religious affiliations, Pandit Das often placed only a *dīyā* (lamp) on stage as in *Sadhana*, rather than using other Hindu iconography common in some kathak performances. He felt the flame, while still a symbol with Hindu religious overtones, represented one of the basic elements of nature and carried more universal meaning than would the image of a specific deity.[9]

Pandit Das was born in 1944 and grew up in Calcutta (now Kolkata) at the end of the British Raj and beginning of independent India. His formative years and training reflected this juncture of old and new political and social structures. His father, Prohlad Das, was a dance scholar and choreographer who used traditional dance forms to express modern issues, particularly in his anticolonialist dance-drama *Abhyudaya* (Awakening), staged several years before India's independence in 1947. Though he wasn't particularly close to his father, Pandit Das often proudly described how his father was "responsible for presenting the first revolutionary dance-drama in Calcutta," once adding that "all the great Congress leaders of that time, great leaders watched" and highlighting the danger of doing so, for others "were put to jail for doing that—that was before Independence" (C. Das 1984).[10] Additionally, Prohlad Das "taught at the Birla Academy and lectured at Rabindra Bharati (Tagore University). He had developed a system of dance notation and was widely acknowledged for having contributed to the national standardization of dance education" (Maxwell 2012, 31). He published *Kathak Dance (Bol)* (1961) on kathak dance theory and for his many contributions was awarded the honorary title of Nritya Acharya by the state of Bengal.

In 1942, Pandit Das's parents founded Nritya Bharati, one of India's early institutions for dance, which sponsored teachers of several classical and folk styles (figure 2.1). His mother, Smt. Nilima Das, was a talented Manipuri dancer and the backbone of the school, caring for the students, cooking for them if their classes ran late, even for a time driving students to and from classes in the school's own bus. Nilima Das was the primary influence in Pandit Das's life; in an interview conducted late in his life he described his mother (and by extension all mothers) as such: "Mother is the ultimate protection; mother is the first guru. . . . Mother is also unconditional love. So, where can you go beyond that?" (Mishra 2014).

In their support of traditional arts, Nilima and Prohlad Das's work was an outgrowth of a largely nineteenth-century movement in Bengal known as the Bengal Renaissance (*nabajāgoraṇ*), which was "based on the intersection of the Oriental scholarship of rediscovery of ancient Hindu achievements and modern Western thoughts inculcated through English education" (Chakravorty 2008, 43). In the independence era, Nritya Bharati and other dance academies played an important role in the changes taking place in India's dance traditions. While men from hereditary families continued to exert a strong influence on the dance

FIG. 2.1. Nritya Bharati school and the home of Prohlad (*pictured*) and Nilima Das. Calcutta, ca. 1959.

form, for young women in particular, these new dance academies provided acceptable (read: respectable) contexts for study, and facilitated kathak's shift from a practice of hereditary professionals to mostly nonhereditary dancers from the middle and upper classes, who were not necessarily expected or encouraged to take up kathak as a professional career.

Although Prohlad and Nilima Das's institution and others helped make Indian dances accessible to nonhereditary students through lessons that functioned more like western-style classes, Nilima Das saw to it that their son's training would be in the traditional teacher-disciple method, or *guru-śiṣya paramparā*.

> My mother's dream was for me to study with her friend Jai Kumari-jī, one of the greatest of the Jaipur *gharānā* dancers. . . . She came one day, the great Jai Kumari-jī, and had lunch with my mother. My mother called me to dance. Jai Kumari was very sweet to me; she was like an auntie.
>
> She said, "Hey *beṭā*, son, come here. Do *tatkār* footwork." . . . She said, "Oh, his *tatkār* is good." They talked and [Jai Kumari-jī] left.
>
> My mother said, "Hey do you want to study with her?" I kept quiet. I don't know why; I was very naughty. . . . I didn't answer so she gave me a little [tap], "Eh, why don't you answer me?"
>
> I said, "I don't want to study with a woman." She got so angry at me, she *jhāṁp*ed [smacked] me. (C. Das interview, July 25, 2003)

As suggested by Pandit Das's recollections, even as a boy he likely picked up on societal prejudices regarding female dancers that "arise from the context of asymmetrical power relations of gender and class in Kathak" (Chakravorty 2008, 2). After her initial response, Pandit Das's mother suggested a male teacher. "She told my father, 'Look at this arrogant boy. He doesn't want to study with a woman; what does he think he is? Then my mother asked my father, 'Who is this man you go and visit in the *bāījī* quarters?' That is how it started" (C. Das interview, July 25, 2003). With the support of his parents, young Chitresh was formally "tied" to the kathak guru Pandit Ram Narayan Mishra in a *gaṇḍā bandan* ceremony in 1955 at age ten. He trained with Pandit Mishra until leaving for the United States in 1970 and continued to learn from him during two visits to India before Pandit Mishra's untimely death in 1973.

Pandit Ram Narayan Mishra died by falling down the unfinished elevator shaft of his apartment building. It was suspected that he had been pushed to his death by a neighbor who owed him a large sum of money (Maxwell 2012, 2; Uchiyama 2013). Forty years later, Pandit Das recalled to me his experience of his guru-jī's death:

> I had just seen him about three days earlier. I came after the New Year's and asked, "Where is Guru-jī?" . . . To see his dead body lying on a vegetable vendor's cart, his hair hanging out from under the shawl they covered him with. . . . Bachai [guru-brother Bachan Lal Mishra], another person and I took his body from the hospital to the morgue. At the morgue [they] would not allow my guru-jī's body to be admitted until they had a judge's signature because the death was suspect. When they left Guru-jī's body on the street in the heat, with flies and feces—from dogs, from humans—that is when I started crying. I did not feel anything before, but then I couldn't hold it back any longer. From then on, I accepted the fact that he was gone. (C. Das, pers. comm., December 17, 2013)

At that point in sharing memories with me, Pandit Das shifted to considering how the experience impacted his understanding of his own life's purpose. "I thought, what am I teaching? How am I living? Julia [his then wife] had told me, 'Your mother's unquestionable faith in your guru-jī made you what you are today.' And the words of my mother rang in my ears. She said your guru-jī taught you dance and that is your profession, your way of life" (C. Das, pers. comm., December 17, 2013).

Sadhana Vignette 2: In the Times of Pandit Das's Guru

With the whistle of a train still echoing in the audience's ears, the next sounds to emerge from the dark hall were the crisp jingling of ghuṅgharū.

A spotlight revealed Pandit Das's feet engaged in tatkār *footwork: right, left, right, left, left, right, left, right. The sound of a sarangi returned to accompany new images fading one into the next on the proscenium screen: Chitresh as a toddler in his mother's arms, close-ups of his father—first gazing into the distance, and then as a younger man in an extravagant dance costume—and Chitresh as a young boy leaning against a wall, looking defiantly out the corners of his eyes, straight into the camera. Continuing footwork implied that as Pandit Das grew, a constant in his life was dance—particularly the act of practice, called* riyāz *or* sādhanā. *His fundamental relationship with dance became even more apparent when a spotlight focused in on Pandit Das's feet doing the simple practice of* tatkār. *As his feet continued their practice, on the opposite side of the stage a picture of Pandit Ram Narayan Mishra appeared and Pandit Das's prerecorded voice described his first encounter with his guru. "My guru-jī came and had a lovely lunch; after the lunch I was ushered in. I was very little . . . he was sitting so his eyes and my eyes were almost [at] the same level, and he said, 'Son—*beṭā, nāch sikhnā hai?*' 'Do you want to study dance?' And I just—I was mesmerized with his eyes, and I just bent my head [in acquiescence]. I didn't even say yes or no"* (▶ see video 2.2).

FIG. 2.2. Chitresh Das receiving blessings from his guru, Ram Narayan Mishra. Calcutta, ca. 1962.

FIG. 2.3. *Left to right*: Chitresh Das with his guru, Ram Narayan Mishra, and his father, Prohlad Das. Taken at the Nritya Bharati house, Calcutta, ca. 1972.

Despite his untimely death, Pandit Ram Narayan Mishra was a crucial figure in kathak's transmission, and his role as a guru to students from disparate social backgrounds reflected the shifting status of Indian dances before and during his lifetime. Pandit Mishra was born on August 10, 1911, in the Rajasthani village of Dungarpur. He studied kathak with his father, Pandit Gobardhan Prasad, until his father passed away when Mishra was ten years old. By 1934 he had moved to Calcutta, where he studied with Gurus Acchan Maharaj and Shambhu Maharaj of the Lucknow *gharānā*. There, he took up residence on the outskirts of Bowbazar, famous for its *bāījī*s, or courtesans.

By the 1930s and '40s, several Indian dance forms had been the subject of considerable controversy and change. In the North Indian courts of the Mughal Empire, courtesans known as *bāījī*s or *ṯavā'if*s practiced the arts of song, dance, and poetry, as well as seduction.[11] A heterogeneous group of female performers, "the most refined among them were urbane, literate, and highly trained" (Walker 2010, 281). In South India, formally trained dancers were called *devadāsī*s, literally "servants of god," who were each dedicated to a particular temple at a young age. There, they performed music and dance for much of their lives; though they were considered "married" to the temple deity, they were free to take lovers and bear children (see Ramberg 2014; Soneji 2012; A. Srinivasan 1985; Sundar 1995).

As the British increasingly exercised power across the diverse subcontinent, beginning with the founding of the East India Company in the 1600s and from 1858 through the direct political control of the British Raj, the climate for such professional female performing artists shifted dramatically. During British rule, most regions were directly annexed through battle or, as in the case of the kingdom of Awadh, through a bloodless coup. The last Nawab of Awadh, Wajid Ali Shah, was deposed to Calcutta in 1856; a great patron of the arts, he brought with him "ustads and entertainers" including at least three hundred courtesans, "providing Calcutta with an important cultural and artistic resource" (Barlow and Subramanian 2007, 1786; Sarker n.d.). Despite the influx of courtesans to the imminent capitol of the British Raj, or perhaps partly because of it, intolerance for "nautch girls" (an anglicized version the Hindi *nāch*, or "dance") increased. The British Contagious Disease Acts, implemented in India in 1864, effectively equated courtesans with prostitutes and "signal[ed] the gradual debasement of an esteemed cultural institution into common prostitution" (Oldenburg 1990, 260). These acts required courtesans to register and undergo the same medical examinations forced on prostitutes serving British soldiers in cantonment cities.

Although some courtesans actively supported rebellion against British rule, Indian nationalists in the late twentieth century adopted a negative view of this class of formerly culturally sanctioned, unmarried female artists.[12] Like the colonial government, they "linked dancing girls to prostitution and urged a 'boycott of nautch dancing at formal occasions' (Meduri 1996, 56)" (P. Srinivasan 2012, 70). This movement led finally to the passage of several laws in British India and then in independent India, whose net effect was to bar the profession and disenfranchise courtesans and their children (Soneji 2012, 110).[13] Chakravorty writes: "The effect of the [anti-nautch] campaign was devastating for the nautch and devadasi institutions. They not only lost their traditional patrons but they were ostracized by society which provided them with no alternative means of livelihood. Not surprisingly, a large number of the dancing girls were driven into prostitution" (2000, 64).[14]

After independence, culturally conservative and often British-educated members of the Indian elite maintained an anti-courtesan stance while, simultaneously, the arts were undergoing a "revival," in which forms of music and dance traditionally practiced by courtesans and other hereditary artists were appropriated and modified by members of the middle and upper classes in the name of nationalist pride.[15] As Matthew Allen writes in discussing South Indian dance, this pan-Indian revival was not only "a re-vivification or bringing back to life, it was equally a re-population (one social community appropriating a practice from another), a re-construction (altering and replacing elements of repertoire and choreography), a re-naming (from *nautch* and other terms to *bharata natyam*), a re-situation (from temple, court, and salon to the public stage), and a re-storation (as used in Schechner 1985, 69, a splicing together of selected 'strips' of performative behavior in a manner that simultaneously creates a new practice and invents an historical one)" (1997, 63–64). Similarly, changes in the social background of its practitioners and performance repertoire took place in kathak, which shifted from being an enjoyment of wealthy royals and feudal landlords, to an outlawed practice, and soon thereafter to a crucial tool in building cultural capital for the independent Indian nation.

Pandit Mishra purportedly made his living in Calcutta solely from teaching courtesans until he was "discovered" by Pandit Das's father, Prohlad Das, who helped him procure prestigious teaching positions at the Birla Academy, Sangeet Shyamala, and the Das's own dance school, Nritya Bharati. At these new institutions, he taught sons and especially daughters of middle- and upper-class families.[16] Pandit Mishra later was awarded the prestigious title Nritya Acharya by Dr. Rajendra Prasad, first president of independent India (C. Das 1985). Pandit Mishra continued to train women in the *koṭhās* (courtesan quarters), and his growing renown certainly had positive ramifications for them, as the social position of a courtesan was largely dependent on the status of her male guru (Daniel Neuman [1980] 1990, 101). In the twentieth century, however, his increased status did not open doors to possible name and fame as it might have in the past. As Walker writes, courtesans "became no more than an embarrassing footnote in the history of Indian music and dance" (2010, 291). Thus, although Pandit Mishra's courtesan students like Smt. Madhuri Devi Singh had received training by a guru of renown, the audience for their talents and artistry all but disappeared.

Sadhana Vignette 3: Pandit Das and His Guru-Sisters

The second half of Sadhana *opened with Pandit Das kneeling and performing* bhāv batāna*—a practice of singing accompanied by facial and upper-body gesture that is reminiscent of courtesan performances—as a photo of his guru-sister, Madhuri Devi Singh, appeared behind him (▶ see video 2.3).*[17] *As he concluded the song, Pandit Das reminisced: "When I was a young boy, . . . I used to go to my guru-jī's house in a tram. And from my guru-jī's house, I used to go to the courtesans, the* bāījīs, *the* ṯavā'ifs*—my guru-sisters. And my guru-jī used to go and teach . . . my guru-sisters, Madhuri, Kalavati, Shah Jahan . . . and what a powerful memory: the last of the courtesans." In the subsequent video, black and white images showed a Calcutta streetcar like one he might have ridden as a boy. Smt. Madhuri Devi Singh's singing voice mingled with street sounds as the video camera focused on the moving wheels of a wooden rickshaw, the fingers of her harmonium accompanist, and then her face as she sang and enacted the lyrics in* bhāv batāna.

Although the section of *Sadhana* described here was presented in a particularly nostalgic way, Pandit Das did not dismiss his living guru-sisters as a remnant of the past, but rather, he worked to advocate continued respect for and acknowledgment of them, their artistic accomplishments, and their role in the kathak tradition. During a tour of India in 1996, for example, he supported a courtesan association by performing at a house concert they sponsored in one of the *bāījī* residences of Bow Bazaar. Pandit Das involved courtesans and former courtesans, including his closest guru-sister, Smt. Madhuri Devi Singh, in events he sponsored, such as the 2002 inaugural gala for his Kolkata school, "Chhandam Nritya Bharati" (named in honor of his parents' school), anniversary celebrations in subsequent years, and annual school shows.[18] In 2006, Pandit Das brought Madhuri-dī (as we call her) to the United States to perform at *Kathak at the Crossroads*, an international festival and symposium involving kathak dancers, scholars, and journalists. She was given a standing ovation—particularly meaningful because of the lack of recognition she received in India. Surprised by the warm reception in San Francisco, she responded, "So much love, so much respect as if they [contemporary conservators of the kathak tradition] have forgotten who I am" (S. Roy 2006) (▶ see video 2.4 and figure 2.4).

FIG. 2.4. Madhuri Devi Singh in performance at *Kathak at the Crossroads* at the Yerba Buena Center for the Arts, San Francisco, September 29, 2006. Pictured behind (*left to right*): Swapnamoy Banerjee, Kasturi Mishra, Chitresh Das, Ramesh Mishra.

I had speculated that Pandit Das's overt support of courtesan women developed while living outside of India, distanced from the ambivalence or outright aversion surrounding the profession. However, in a 1970 article about Pandit Das, published just before he left India for the first time, he was quoted as supporting courtesan women with just as much zeal as I had observed in later years: "Sometimes with [my guru] I would visit the baijee quarters. You know professional women dancers. People call them nautch girls, immoral. Why? I don't think so. Even today you will find the finest dancers, the finest artistes there" (Suraiya 1970, 18–19).

With the moral climate in India largely opposed to courtesans and courtesan culture during Pandit Das's youth, it is somewhat surprising that his parents allowed him to accompany his guru when he taught *bāījīs* in Bow Bazaar. Perhaps he was permitted to do so because his father had already spent significant time with Pandit Mishra in Bow Bazaar or because, as Pandit Das often emphasized, his mother had absolute trust in her son's guru. Being a mixed-caste, multireligious, and thus unorthodox family to begin with, perhaps his parents realized that giving their son the chance to experience the rich, then-endangered courtesan tradition was more valuable than any possible resulting social stigma. Pandit Das's descriptions of his mother reveal her to be an iconoclast more than willing to challenge various customs and social norms. For example, Pandit Das often described instances in which his mother, a Christian, would take him outside their house to a private area of their property and compel him to eat beef, once saying, "Let's see which one of your Hindu gods will strike you down!"

When he was older, Nilima Das encouraged her son to express as wide a range of sentiments in his dance as possible, in any social context—as he recalled her exhorting, "dance from the gutters to the heavens." And Pandit Das followed suit, embracing social connections across the spectrum of Indian society. For example, in August 2006, I accompanied him to Sonagachi, the largest red-light district in Kolkata, and on the same day we visited B. K. and Dr. Sarala Birla, among India's major industrialists and philanthropists, at their elegant estate. Moreover, Pandit Das followed his mother's example of challenging social convention by admonishing negative societal attitudes toward courtesans and even prostitutes, reminding cultural insiders—and his students—that Bengali marriages are not considered complete until dirt from the quarters of prostitutes (*beṣyā*) is brought to sanctify the union. He would ask, "How can they pooh-pooh the *bāījīs* on one hand and sanctify their marriage with the prostitutes? It's a double standard and hypocrisy" (C. Das interview, August 17, 2005). Blessing a marriage with this dirt signified both humility and symbolic community consensus; as Pandit Das noted, "even a woman who is disregarded as nobody in society—even a little dirt from her house is necessary" (pers. comm., December 17, 2013).

Despite his mother's open-mindedness, it is less likely that Pandit Das would have been permitted to visit the courtesan district in his youth were he female, for generally, the new waves of nonhereditary female dance students were kept at a remove from the culture and even movement styles of the courtesans. His guru-sister Smt. Chetna Jalan recalled: "He [Pandit Ram Narayan Mishra] of course deliberately took that part away from me, because I was young and it—it would have been fire [scandalous] at that time, that *koṭhā-ka* dance [dance of the courtesans' salon]. It would have been fire" (Jalan interview, July 31, 2003).

Pandit Mishra thus acted as a mediator, purposely altering the dance to suit differing sensibilities and societal expectations. Most practitioners of kathak and other performing arts faced similar decisions during the independence era. South Indian dancer and reformer Rukmini Devi consciously downplayed *śriṅgāra rasa,* or the depiction of erotic love (Allen 1997; Meduri 1988). In kathak, the seductive swaying of the hips, an important element of courtesan dances like that presented by Smt. Madhuri Devi Singh (▶ see video 2.4), was discouraged in the dance's transmission to nonhereditary, middle- and upper-class students. Chakravorty reports that her guru, Smt. Bandana Sen, "repeatedly made sure while teaching that we did not swing our hips akin to the 'khemta' style prevalent among the baijis" (2000, 54n10). Walker similarly notes that "one is constantly reminded in dance classes not to move the hips" (2004, 5). On occasions, Pandit Das choreographed pieces for his dance company members that utilized hip swinging when explicitly evoking the courtesan world, such as in "Nautchwali" (▶ see video 2.5). However, he generally discouraged side-to-side movements of the hips, less because of its association with *bāījīs* and more because hip movement detracted from the speed of his students' footwork.

Pandit Das presents an interesting mixture of competing, contradictory, or controversial attitudes and stances. While remaining a self-confessed "macho" dancer, he consistently advocated for maligned female artists like his guru-sister Smt. Madhuri Devi Singh. And while the asymmetrical power relationship between himself and his female disciples was decidedly problematic (and one which students sometimes considered unhealthy), he also advocated for women's power, pushing these students to develop their own self-confidence and strength.

Pandit Das credited his guru's training for his own physical and emotional strength. Pandit Mishra reportedly modified his training style according to the social status and gender of each student, as indicated above, but also to suit their inclinations: "He . . . taught according to the personality, strength, and capacity of each individual. This was one of his great achievements, and it was very interesting to see the various disciples dancing the same compositions with totally different emphasis—either soft, or fast, or with extra turns or strong footwork. Due to my fiery nature as a child, for me it meant endless hours of practicing footwork, turns, and recitation, often to the point of exhaustion" (C. Das 1986b, 29).[19]

Though the qualities of movement Pandit Mishra taught might have varied, strict discipline was an important aspect of his training method for each of his students. As many scholars and artists have noted, in North India the discipline imparted by a guru is both intense and a source of pride (see, e.g., Daniel Neuman [1980] 1990; Nuttall 1998; Ruckert 1994). Smt. Chetna Jalan animatedly recalls Pandit Mishra's training style, describing it as "very torturous training for me . . . because of his strong regime, and no intervals in between" (Jalan interview, July 31, 2003). She continued, noting that "there [was] no sitting down, no chatting, nothing . . . *riyāz* [a term meaning practice involving effort] *mane riyāz*"—practice means practice. But she also suggested that his intense training gave her a "good spine," saying "I singularly thank him for giving me this kind of training." Similarly, Pandit Das provides the following description of his training routine with Pandit Mishra:

> It would still be dark when I woke up and wrapped almost five kilos of bells around my ankles. I did my *pranam*, touched my guruji's feet and began my practice. I would dance from four until seven A.M. Guruji would have me start with a slow *tatkar* . . . creating a continuous series of clearly defined slaps on the floor. Soon the pace would increase, and increase again, and continue for over an hour until I felt nearly consumed by the sounds of the bells. As the sky grew pale light, I would begin to dance compositions of various types, with fast turns and crisp stances. I would have to recite compositions without sounding out of breath. If I showed any signs of breathlessness I would be severely reprimanded. I danced on a polished concrete floor in a space approximately five feet square. Losing balance or accidentally touching anything was absolutely forbidden. In this way I learned to be constantly aware, developing the span, focus, and intensity of my attention. (C. Das 1986b, 28)

As is typical of the *guru-śiṣya* pedagogical style, Pandit Das's training also extended outside of the formal classroom context: "I had to be able to respond instantly to any demand. I remember times in the *baiji* quarters in front of gatherings of other gurus and *ustads*, my guruji would tell me to dance. There was no previous warning, no opportunity to warm up. It was a test of spontaneity, and a time for him to measure the speed of my thoughts against the speed of my movements. If I could not remember or present a composition with ease and accuracy, I would receive a stern verbal rebuke" (C. Das 1986b, 28).

Pandit Das continued in his own teaching certain aspects of training described by Pandit Mishra's students, particularly the imperatives not to sit down, talk, or drink water during class, and the possibility of being asked to perform at a moment's notice. This intensive training was very difficult to implement in the West. More difficult, however, was negotiating the role of guru amid US expectations and discomfort surrounding the term (see chapter 4).

Becoming a Disciple, Becoming a Guru

The role of the guru is one of the most common topics Pandit Das and other artists discuss with one another. Over the years of being privy to such conversations, I heard several phrases repeated—"a guru gives blood," "a guru leads one from darkness to light," "a guru shows the way"—such as in this conversation with Smt. Chetna Jalan: "What is a guru? The guru is one who not only gives blood, but there is an accountability, and there is a bonding. . . . It is a bonding that is very personal, like religion, politics, or anything else. . . . 'Guru' means accountability, a tremendous amount of accountability" (C. Das to Jalan, from fieldwork video, July 31, 2003).

While the guru-*śiṣya* relationship develops over the course of several years, it is formalized in a ritual string-tying, or *gaṇḍā bandan*, ceremony. Pandit Das recalls the string-tying ceremony in which he formally became a disciple of Pandit Ram Narayan Mishra:

> Saraswati Puja, the day of worshipping the goddess of learning, was approaching; it was Vasant Panchami, the days of spring festivities, and the children were wearing yellow *saris*, *kurtas* and *dhotis*. My mother and father planned for the special ceremony where my guruji would initiate me as his disciple. The day arrived. Priests chanted from the Vedic scriptures; sparkling brass and copper trays were laden with tropical winter fruit; and the smells of marigolds, sandalwood incense, and the *ghee* and *myrrh* upon the fire permeated the rooms. On a silver platter my parents offered my guruji a new *kurta*, a *dhoti*, a gold chain, diamond earrings and money. They also offered him a special tray with vermillion paste, dry rice, sweets and a small red thread. He accepted the gifts and then the special tray. My guruji sat in the sacred place in front of the image of the goddess Saraswati, and began the initiation ceremony. Chanting *mantras*, he tied the red thread around my wrist, put vermillion paste mixed with rice on my forehead, and fed me a sweet from the tray. He placed his hand on my head and blessed me. Then he took the bells, touched them to his forehead and gave them to me, telling me to do the same. He told me to stand. I felt shy as he wrapped the rows and rows of bells around my ankles. My playmates stood on the side giggling, but somehow I didn't mind. As the bells became heavier and heavier on my legs, I sensed that something

> very special and important was happening for me. My guruji started instructing me and my guru "brother" played *tabla*. At the end of my first lesson, the many older women and men blessed me. (C. Das 1986b, 27)

Because of the many differences distinguishing Pandit Das's period of study from his students' experiences, their stages of study are marked in different ways. In his school, the first ritual students experience is a *ghuṅgharū* ceremony, in which they receive their first sets of dance bells (usually between six months to a year into the study). The final stage is the *gaṇḍā bandan* ceremony, which Pandit Das, like others, sometimes called the beginning of true study. Pandit Das's *gaṇḍā bandan* ceremony was held with his guru when he was ten years old. Although many studied at Pandit Das's school in the United States, he formally tied strings in *gaṇḍā bandan* ceremonies with only a small number of students—fewer than ten over the course of his lifetime—and only after they had invested at least ten years of study.

This long period of apprenticeship, and the logistics involved in arranging for a *gaṇḍā bandan* ceremony in India added to the ritual's significance. Pandit Das stated, "I don't do it just anywhere; I go to the banks of the Ganga River opposite the Kali temple beside the Shiva temple, behind me

FIG. 2.5. *Gaṇḍā bandan* ceremony: Chitresh Das and Charlotte Moraga. Pictured behind (*left to right*): Manju Mishra and Jaiwanti Das Pamnani. Kolkata, 2002.

a Shakti temple—two feminine energies" (C. Das interview, July 12, 2002) (figure 2.5).[20] Pandit Das held his first *gaṇḍā bandan* ceremony in 1998 with Gretchen Hayden and Joanna (Das) de Souza, kathak artists who trained with him in the 1970s and '80s and went on to lead their own kathak schools in Boston and Toronto, respectively. Hayden recalls the decision to tie strings:

> Why after all this time? People were saying, "They've been here twenty-six years! If they're not your disciples by now." . . . I think for one that the time was coming in himself, because his mother always said, "You're not ready to be a guru yet."
>
> And he kept saying, "I'm not a guru yet."
>
> And I kept thinking, "Well when does one *become* a guru?"
>
> I still wonder about that phrase in itself. I think he was feeling ready to. He was having younger students coming up who he would go through this process with, and I think he would never do it with his younger students without first tying with us." (Hayden interview, January 18, 2003)

The process of becoming a guru was a lengthy one for Pandit Das. For many years, he resisted this designation, first because the early generations of his students were close to his own age, and later out of respect for the responsibilities guruship entailed. A deeper appreciation of the role crystallized after he had moved away from India. "I only began to respect and understand my guru-jī when I came to America and was cut off from India. I was far away and faced challenges and difficulties, then I began to think, 'What would my guru do? What did my parents do? What would the people of my country do?'" (C. Das interview, July 12, 2002).

As a young man, Pandit Das was looking for an opportunity to move to the United States when he performed for US dancers and choreographers, including Pauline Koner and Murray Louis, who were then touring India. The first time he was invited to perform for Murray Louis, however, his preparations ended in a near tragedy:

> A few days prior to the scheduled performance, my tabla player called to say he would not accompany me—as a result of a dancer-musician exchange we had had on stage the previous night, in the Kathak tradition of improvisation, which he felt had insulted him. Standing in front of a huge window made of numerous small glass frames in my parent's [*sic*] house, my anger and frustration rose at the thought of a missed opportunity, and I shot my fist through one of the frames. I collapsed onto thousands of pieces of shattered glass, and was rushed to the hospital where they removed a two-inch piece of jagged glass and operated on my wrist. The tendon of my right hand was severed, and it was not yet known just how much use of my hand I would regain. (C. Das 1986b, 30–31)

Pandit Das described this event not only to dramatize his desire to come to the States, but also to emphasize the intimate role of his guru, both as disciplinarian and father figure: "My guruji came, and when he saw me he melted into tears, which he wiped with the corner of his dhoti. I never believed that the man who taught me with such an iron fist could weep. We wept together" (31).

Pandit Das did regain most of the use of his hand, and though he missed out on performing for Murray Louis at that time, he later performed for Louis and several other foreign visitors. In fact, his chance came just a few weeks later in Patna, where he performed while still wearing an arm sling (Maxwell 2012, 55). Pandit Das's life path shifted dramatically soon thereafter, when he received a fellowship to study in the United States. He later noted that performances like the one he gave in Patna "helped me develop a format that would make my dance accessible to foreigners, yet maintain the tradition and technical integrity" (C. Das 1986b, 31). For him as an Indian artist based in the United States, the challenge of balancing artistic integrity and accessibility would become a fundamental factor shaping his performance, choreography, and teaching. Because of his deep and conscious engagement as a teacher and artist, Pandit Das's path serves as a potent vehicle to examine how the pedagogy and performance of "tradition" can be both consciously modified and staunchly maintained in response to new contexts.

3

On the American Stage

Cross-cultural performance is a critical site of negotiation between performers and spectators, with performers—when they have sufficient agency—often working to find a middle ground in which the art is "true" to connoisseurs, yet comprehensible to inexperienced audience members (e.g., Tang 2005). Pandit Das developed several strategies to engage audiences while he lived and worked in the United States. In two of the best-known pieces from his repertoire, *Twelve Minutes* and *The Train*, he respectively condensed and expanded on elements of the kathak tradition in specific ways examined below. As with many diasporic artists, Pandit Das's adaptations of Indian performance practices reveal deliberate efforts to attract, educate, and retain new audiences—a time-intensive process not available to some of the performing artists who preceded him (Erdman 1987, 76–77; P. Srinivasan 2012). This chapter situates Pandit Das within the history of South Asian culture bearers who performed and taught in the United States and whose experiences helped influence American attitudes and set the stage for how Pandit Das's work was received.

Pandit Das described arriving in the States in 1970 with his bell bag in one hand, tabla bag in the other, and, "like all *desīs*," eight dollars in his pocket—then the maximum US currency the Indian government would sell Indian nationals leaving India (C. Das in Mishra 2014). In January 1971, while on winter break from his studies at the University of Maryland, he married Julia Maxwell, whom he had met in Calcutta in 1966 when she began studying dance with his father. Julia and her daughter, Jennifer, joined Pandit Das for his final semester in Maryland, and in the fall of 1971 they moved to the San Francisco Bay Area, where he gained employment at Ali Akbar

Khansahib's recently established Ali Akbar College of Music. With a teaching position at the esteemed musician's institution secured, Pandit Das's career was launched.

America, he later reminisced, was a chance to start anew, "to become rich and famous overnight," and to follow the path of successful Indian artists who preceded him (C. Das 2001). In 1988, in several handwritten, memoir-style pages, he described his impetus to travel westward: "The late 1960s was a time when, like many restless students throughout the world, I too looked for a change. The rebel in me wanted to break away to unknown adventures. As a child of free India, I knew little of the hardships my father's generation had faced. I was eager to travel and my urge was to go West. I had heard of the successes of the great musicians Pandit Ravi Shankar and Ustad Ali Akbar Khan abroad" (C. Das ca. 1988). Fifteen years later, Pandit Das seemed to pick up the very same conversational thread: "And before [them] came Swami Vivekananda; spiritually the foundation was already laid by him and Swami Yogananda, great Indian spiritualists. Then came Pandit Ravi Shankar-jī and Ustad Ali Akbar Khansahib. Both laid the foundation that we are now following" (interview, April 22, 2002).

India Comes West

As Pandit Das notes, his path to finding success in the West had already been navigated by a number of noted teachers of South Asian spiritual and artistic practices who profoundly influenced US attitudes toward India. Among the first cultural emissaries to the United States were attendees of the Chicago Parliament of Religions in 1893. This watershed event brought several religious figures from South Asia, including Hindu delegate Swami Vivekananda. Vivekananda's charismatic presence at the parliament attracted several American followers and led to the establishment of religious centers around the United States. San Francisco was a particularly receptive site for Vivekananda and his teachings. During his first visit to the Bay Area in 1900, he founded the Vedanta Society of Northern California and sparked a "fevered pace of activity" among his followers (French 1974, 74). In 1906, the Vedanta Society completed construction of the first Hindu temple in the United States, still at the corner of Webster and Filbert Streets in San Francisco.

Despite the warm welcome for some culture-bearers, fears of a "Hindu invasion" or "Turban tide" grew, beginning in the US Pacific Northwest, where South Asians (particularly Punjabi Sikh men) who had worked on the Canadian Pacific railroads in western Canada moved south into Washington, Oregon, and California (Campi 2005). Hostility in the United States toward

South and Southeast Asian immigrants culminated in congressional passage of the Immigration Act of 1917, also known as the Asiatic Barred Zone Act. Whereas the 1882 Chinese Exclusion Act had barred immigration by laborers from China, the 1917 legislation banned immigration from a larger swath of Asia and the Pacific Islands, including India. Most South Asians already living in the United States were denied citizenship with the 1923 Supreme Court ruling *United States v. Bhagat Singh Thind*, which concluded that, although Indians might be "Caucasian," they were not "free white persons" (Rangaswamy 2000, 44; see also Hess 1969, 65).[1]

During the more than forty years these Immigration Acts were in place, some artists and spiritual teachers from India managed to travel to the United States, including Swami Paramhansa Yogananda. Best known for his *Autobiography of a Yogi* (first published in 1946), Yogananda first came to the United States to attend a Unitarian-sponsored conference in Boston (Mann, Numrich, and Williams 2001, 76). He traveled across America on spiritual campaigns, teaching and advocating Kriya Yoga from 1920 until his death in 1952. His teachings continue through the Self-Realization Fellowship, an international organization operating almost two hundred centers throughout the United States (Self-Realization Fellowship 2017).

The roots of such spiritual organizations in the United States can be traced back as early as the eighteenth century. Concepts from India's religious traditions, particularly Vedanta philosophy, reached the States through translations of sacred texts such as the Bhagavad Gita, which influenced the work of American transcendentalist writers including Ralph Waldo Emerson and Henry David Thoreau (Versluis 1993).[2] Nineteenth-century Americans were also exposed to Vedanta philosophy through spiritual movements, including the New Thought Movement; its offshoot, the Society of Silent Help, which eventually became known as the Unity Church; and the Theosophical Society (P. Goldberg 2010).

While this history of US interest in Asian religious philosophies partly accounts for the successes of Indian spiritual teachers such as Swamis Vivekananda and Yogananda, the first South Asian dancers to perform in the United States did not receive a similarly positive reception. Dance scholar Priya Srinivasan's 2012 monograph, *Sweating Saris*, excavates the history and reception of early Indian dancers in the United States, who had been "written out of both U.S. and Indian dance histories" (70). According to her research, the first known troupe to arrive in the United States, in November 1880, included male musicians, jugglers, snake charmers, and a theater manager, as well as five female "nautch" dancers, whose names were recorded as Saheb, Oomdah, Bhoori, Ala Bundi, and Vagoir (48). The group performed in the theatrical production, *Zanina*; according to the concert program, they were "expressly imported to the country" to appear in an "East

Indian Divertisement" after the second act (Locke 1920, in P. Srinivasan 2012, 54–55). The US media heralded these performers' arrival from Bombay and Calcutta, but their positive reception soon soured.[3] Reviews indicate that audiences had wanted the dancers to dress and perform with more overt eroticism and did not recognize or value some of the other aesthetic and technical elements of their performances (57–58).

Within a few weeks of their initial performance in January 1881, Indian performers were removed from *Zanina*, marking a "swift end" to their high-profile performances, which, Priya Srinivasan notes, "had larger ramifications for the future of Indian dance in the United States" (P. Srinivasan 2012, 59). The dancers were replaced in the production by white females who performed in brownface, imitating the nautch dances while showing more skin and otherwise playing to the audience's orientalist imagination (59). As critic Cecil Smith puts it, "it was easier to provide counterfeit Oriental art, and the audience preferred it" (1950, 81). Subsequently, original troupe members and other Indian and Sri Lankan artists found most of their work on relatively lowbrow stages such as dime museums and world fairs, as well as in P. T. Barnum's circus.

Nautch dancers continued to perform in less distinguished venues through 1906, but by 1907 they "had disappeared from the U.S. stage" (P. Srinivasan 2012, 43). Until then, dancers primarily from northern India were performing what Srinivasan hypothesizes was an earlier form of kathak on Coney Island. Millions of visitors came to Coney Island in the summer of 1904 alone, including Ruth St. Denis, credited as one of the founders of American modern dance (74). Srinivasan persuasively argues that St. Denis's impression of the Indian dancers on Coney Island was the first and key inspiration for her development of Orientalist performances including *Incense* (1906), *Nautch* (1908), and *Radha* (1906)—the piece that launched her career.[4] Further, Srinivasan suggests the success of these works and of St. Denis's early tours was largely due to unacknowledged labor of Indian men. These "native informants" participated in extended discussions with St. Denis as she developed her productions, and performed until 1911 as supernumeraries, lending authenticity to her early tours (P. Srinivasan 2012, 91, 87–88; St. Denis 1939, 56). One of these men, Mohammed Ismail, unsuccessfully tried to sue St. Denis, asserting he had taught her and had not been acknowledged or compensated for dance movements she utilized in *Radha* (P. Srinivasan 2012, 99; Kraut 2015, 87–91).

Because few performers came to the United States who could challenge St. Denis's authority or present alternate versions of Indian dance, St. Denis's productions were, by and large, the only works informing Americans' view of Indian dance in the early years of the twentieth century (P. Srinivasan 2012, 97). St. Denis continued to tour and develop these and other dance pieces, drawing inspiration from Egypt and East Asia, as well as South Asia. In 1915, she formally partnered with Ted Shawn, opening the Denishawn School of Dancing and Related Arts in Los Angeles. There, St. Denis's technique and choreographed works were taught to students who would influence the direction of US modern dance, including Doris Humphrey, Charles Weidman, and Martha Graham.[5] For four months in 1926 the Denishawn Dance Company toured India, giving over one hundred performances. Uttara Coorlawala describes their pieces as "unashamedly inauthentic" but argues that their presentation had a widespread impact that may have energized India's own dance revival (1992, 144).

While on tour in India, St. Denis and Ted Shawn met a courtesan named Bachwa Jan, with whom St. Denis was greatly impressed, but they otherwise had difficulty finding the "authentic nautch" they sought (Coorlawala 1992, 127). During the same era, Coorlawala notes that Russian prima ballerina Anna Pavlova met with and "directly inspired" Rukmini Devi Arundale, Leila Sokhey (known as Madame Menaka), and Uday Shankar, "three of the moving forces of the revival of Indian dance" who each gained some notoriety in the West (142). Today, Rukmini Devi's influence particularly endures through legions of dancers studying and performing the style of bharatanatyam she spearheaded; but in their own time, Shankar received the most attention of the three in the West.[6] While he was a student of painting in London, Pavlova asked him to choreograph two pieces, *Hindu Wedding* and *Radha-Krishna*, for a suite titled *Oriental Impressions* (1923) (Erdman 1987, 72). Their association led Shankar to an influential career in dance, beginning with a US tour of *Oriental Impressions* in 1923 and 1924.

After several years of developing his style of performance, Uday Shankar returned to India to found his own dance company in 1929 (Abrahams 2007, 384). Over seven years in the 1930s, Uday Shankar and His Company of Hindu Dancers and Musicians toured much of the world, including a US tour with eighty-five performances—a record number for that season (Erdman 1996, 295; "Largest Tour" 1933). Shankar's performances adapted Indian movements and themes to western theatrical sensibilities, generally following established orientalist conventions of portraying exoticized, romanticized versions of the East. Erdman notes, however, that while Shankar's productions were "like the 'oriental dances' of westerners . . . what distinguishe[d] Shankar from every western interpreter is that he spent his childhood in India, where he learned dance" (1987, 66).

At the same time that Uday Shankar's productions were garnering success internationally, US dancer La Meri (née Russell Meriwether Hughes) was also staging performances of Indian and other dance forms in the United States and abroad. La Meri commonly sought out and studied with local dance masters during her travels and was particularly known for her presentations of dances from Spain and India. In 1937 she trained for three months under Guru Vadivelu Pillai in Madras and in 1940, she and Ruth St. Denis founded the Natya School of Dance in New York.[7] La Meri also played a role in bringing Indian dance practitioners to the United States, including two of Pillai's students, *devadāsīs* Varalakshmi and Bhanumati, who performed in New York in 1942 (P. Srinivasan 2012, 111).

Beginning in the late 1930s, other Indian performers began touring the United States, including Ragini Devi (1937), Ram Gopal (1938), Rukmini Devi (1953), and T. Balasaraswati (1954) (P. Srinivasan 2012, 110–11). These and other artists presented a style of dance less overtly adapted to western sensibilities as previous performances by Uday Shankar and his troupe. They called the dance they performed bharatanatyam.[8] In India, the term *bharatanatyam* served to transform the South Indian *devadāsī* dance form *sadir* into one that would fulfill the needs of respectability, purity, and tradition for a colonized nation struggling for independence (e.g., Allen 1997; Meduri 1988 and 1996). In the United States, as Priya Srinivasan notes, "the emergence of Bharata Natyam as the classical and 'traditional' form now rendered Uday Shankar's dance 'neoclassical' and other Oriental dancers as 'inauthentic'" (2012, 111). Beginning in 1939, dance forms from Asia that were formerly glossed as "Oriental" gained the moniker "ethnic dance."[9]

The United States Opens Its Borders to Asian Immigration

The Immigration and Nationality Act of 1965 repealed the Asiatic Barred Zone Act, which had blocked immigration from Asia to the United States for almost fifty years. Although resulting in a dramatic increase in Asian immigration to the United States, the 1965 act also imposed a preference system by which "immigrants had to meet new requirements in order to migrate: they either had to possess the high skills in demand in the United States or they had to be family members of these highly qualified migrants" (Purkayastha 2005, 1). As a result, 83 percent of Indian immigrants between 1966 and 1977 (approximately eighty-five thousand people) were classified as "professional/technical workers," including approximately forty thousand engineers, twenty-five thousand doctors, and twenty thousand scientists with PhDs (P. Srinivasan 2012, 38; Rangaswamy 2000). Many of the new, mostly male immigrants arranged for their wives and children to join them from India soon thereafter.

While this first generation of post-1965 white-collar professionals and their families began to establish themselves in the United States, interest in Indian culture by other Americans continued to grow. As with Swami Vivekananda six decades earlier, San Francisco was a chosen destination for Hare Krishna (International Society for Krishna Consciousness, or ISKON) movement founder Bhaktivedanta Swami Prabhupada, who relocated to San Francisco's Haight-Ashbury district in 1967 (see Goswami 1981; Hawley 2004). Interest in India soared when, in early 1968, members of the Beatles (including George Harrison, who had already begun studying the sitar with Ravi Shankar) traveled to India with other western celebrities to practice meditation with Maharishi Mahesh Yogi. Philip Goldberg colorfully describes the scene: "The Beatles' journey to the banks of the Ganges blew the gates between East and West wide open. In a flash, more Americans learned about Indian spirituality than in all the previous centuries. Baby boomers read books about Eastern philosophy, took up meditation and Yoga, grooved on the sound of the sitar, chanted Sanskrit in the streets, flocked to gurus, and in some cases trekked to ashrams in India" (2010, 8). In the Bay Area, this confluence of factors provided an atmosphere ripe for the emergence of a local Indian classical music and dance scene.

Until the 1960s, US exposure to Indian music was generally limited first to recordings of Indian classical music, then to recordings by a handful of western pop musicians who incorporated elements of Indian music—particularly the sounds of sitar and tabla—into their songs.[10] This trajectory of Indian classical music in the United States from the elite fine-arts realm to the popular-music scene can largely be credited to George Harrison's widely publicized study with Ravi Shankar, and his subsequent Indian-inspired musical experiments with the Beatles (Wade 1978).[11] Exposure to Indian dance was more limited, though the study of both Indian classical dance and music traditions was to become increasingly possible in the United States.

In 1962, ethnomusicologist Robert Brown invited renowned bharatanatyam dancer Smt. T. Balasaraswati to return to the United States to teach for several months in the Bay Area.[12] Her students included Louise Scripps, who, with her husband, arts patron Samuel Scripps, founded the American Society for Eastern Arts (ASEA) the following year in order to host performing artists from Asia (Cowdery 1995, 51).[13] In the summer of 1965, the group invited Balasaraswati and her ensemble of Karnatak musicians, as well as Ali Akbar Khansahib and tabla player Pt. Shankar Ghosh, to the Bay Area to teach at Oakland's Mills College (Knight 2010, 205–6).

The success of Ali Akbar Khansahib's first classes profoundly influenced the future of Hindustani music in the United States, particularly in the San Francisco Bay Area. ASEA brought Khansahib to teach again in the summer of 1966, during which he taught approximately forty students at a Methodist church in Berkeley. According to George Ruckert, the following year eighty students came to study with Khansahib; this time his classes were held at UC-Berkeley's Chi Phi fraternity house, which ASEA rented for the summer. In 1968, he taught approximately 150 students and established a branch of his then Calcutta-based Ali Akbar College of Music (AACM), which has offered classes in the Bay Area ever since (pers. comm., August 4, 2015). However, the college moved out of Berkeley relatively soon after its inception due to political unrest. At the height of the Vietnam War protests during the summer of 1968, a state of emergency was declared in Berkeley, curfews were imposed, and barricades prevented people from moving from one section of town to another. The college moved to Oakland to avoid the rioting in Berkeley, but that fall, when a tabla student was returning to his apartment in Berkeley after class, he crossed a police barricade and was struck by a policeman's baton, breaking his hand. This incident left Khansahib feeling the area was no longer conducive to studying Hindustani music, and by the summer of 1969, the college moved to quieter Marin County.[14] Over the next several years, other leading Indian artists were invited to teach at the college, including Ust. Zakir Hussain, Pt. Swapan Chaudhuri, Pt. G. S. Sachdev, and Pandit Chitresh Das, all of whom became permanent residents of Marin County (figure 3.1).

Swami Vivekananda, Ali Akbar Khan, and Ravi Shankar, whom Pandit Das often called his "three influences," each had a strong presence in California.[15] Other important artists who traveled to the United States in the early twentieth century include Uday Shankar, Hazrat Inayat Khan, and Rabindranath Tagore. As Gerry Farrell suggests, each of these figures "in his own way

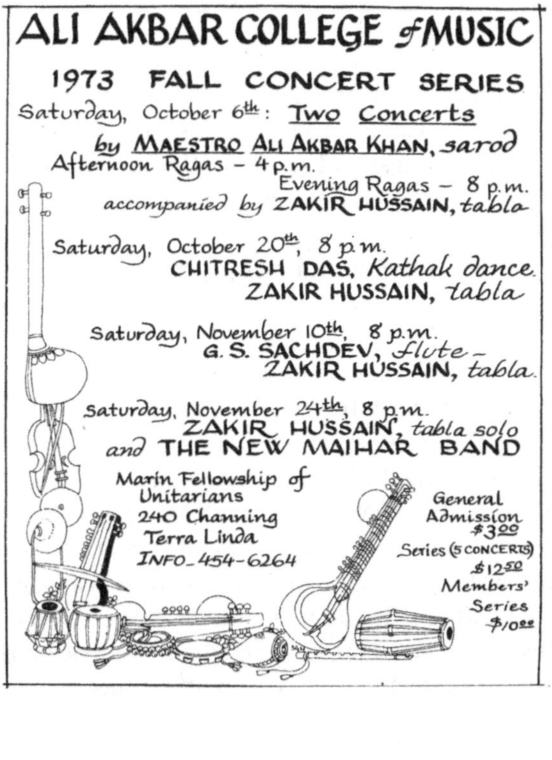

FIG. 3.1. Poster advertising the 1973 Ali Akbar College of Music Fall Concert Series, featuring Ali Akbar Khan, Zakir Hussain, Chitresh Das, G. S. Sachdev, and the New Maihar Band (an ensemble of Khansahib's students).

FIG. 3.2. Chitresh Das performing at Lincoln Center, New York, mid-1980s.

perceived himself as an ambassador from an ancient, complex culture that was largely misunderstood by the West. Each saw it as his role to interpret and explain this culture, to create bridges and synthesis through the media of music and dance—in other words, to educate the West about Indian art and philosophy" (1997, 145).

Although the cultural ethos of the 1960s and '70s generally encouraged Americans to put in more effort to understand the South Asian performances they encountered—particularly as compared to turn-of-the-century audiences—to succeed in the United States, dancers still needed to make strategic adjustments to effectively convey their art. It is clear from Pandit Das's writings about his early years in the United States that he underwent a conscious exercise in trial and error as he learned what would and would not work: "Very few people knew what kathak dance is in [the early] days. It was very difficult to dance and make it accessible to the American audience at the same time. It was an education for me to understand first what an American audience is and then very slowly I had to make adjustments" (C. Das ca. 1988). Pandit Das's learning process involved adapting the content and style of his teaching (discussed in the next chapter) as well as his performances.

Adjusting for Audience Expectations

As a performer, Pandit Das found that success in the United States necessitated both making specific changes to the material he performed, and developing strategies for preemptively shaping audiences' expectations. The changes he made, like those by Uday Shankar and other successful artists discussed above, were "the result of a learning and intuition honed by many cues and experiences in presenting Indian performances in the west" (Erdman 1987, 76–77). For example, an important aspect of kathak performance in India is the direct interaction between dancer and audience, in which dancers speak to the audience, and knowledgeable audience members respond to the performers' moments of excellence verbally, with hand gestures and other body language (see, e.g., Nimjee 2018). Pandit Das noted, however, that talking to US audiences led them to view his performances as lecture-demonstrations, considered less valuable by presenters, critics, and other audience members. In early interviews, he suggested these assumptions prompted him to choose to talk less during performances. However, by the time of my fieldwork in the 2000s, Pandit Das regularly spoke throughout his performances, telling audiences that kathak comes from the word *kathā*, meaning "story," that the *kathaka* (kathak dancer) is a storyteller, and as such, talking to the audience is part of the tradition.[16]

Negative responses Pandit Das received from early US audiences for not maintaining what they perceived as a consistent stage persona also impacted his movement choices. In *bol-paran* sections of solo performances, kathak dancers present a series of compositions, first reciting then dancing each one. Each composition usually will begin on *sam* (beat 1) of the chosen rhythmic cycle and also end on *sam* one or more cycles later. This pattern leaves a gap of time between the *sam* ending one composition and the *sam* beginning the next. During these intervals, dancers in India often dropped their performance persona and walked around the stage waiting for the rhythmic cycle to elapse, or retreated to the back of the stage, "often in a rather perfunctory manner" (Jairazbhoy 1977, 267). Nazir Jairazbhoy notes, "Within the conventions of this tradition, it is understood that the rear of the stage is a kind of private zone, as though it were out of sight of the audience. Here the dancer may slouch, wipe his brow, or converse with the musicians while he prepares for the next series of movements" (267). Pandit Das realized that this "looked very unprofessional to the western world" (interview, November 14, 2005). In order to maintain a more dancerly presence, he developed what his students termed fillers, fluid movements that would lead the dancer from the finishing pose of one composition to the next.

During the 1960s and '70s, Indian and western performers also were influenced by the performance durations expected in one another's culture. For some US musicians, exposure to lengthy Indian music performances led to "*a sudden re-assessment of the idea of musical time*" which resulted in extended melodic experiments lasting well beyond the typical three- to four-minute pop song (Reck 1978, 10, original emphasis). Indian musicians and dancers in the West experienced the opposite effect. As Bonnie Wade reports, Ravi Shankar—a master of gauging western expectations—shortened the length of his concerts to two or two and a half hours from the four to five hours typical in India, and other Hindustani musicians followed suit (1978, 32).

Pandit Das's early solo performances in the United States included extended portions of dense, intricate footwork in which he would produce one composition after another, often with subtle variations that only other professional artists or the most sophisticated connoisseurs could appreciate. As Gretchen Hayden described, "he'd dance on the stage for several hours. . . . he'd just execute *bols* [compositions] one after another. *Bol* after *bol*—recite, dance, recite, dance—and five variations of 'dhā ta ke thungā'" (interview, January 18, 2003). As other students and I speculated, these performances seemed to be in response to elite audiences who hadn't paid him enough attention in India. But for US audience members newly introduced to the Indian classical arts, Pandit Das's extended sets involved much more material than they could absorb, let alone understand.

Many of Pandit Das's early US performances were accompanied by the up-and-coming star of the tabla, Ust. Zakir Hussain, who then also taught at the AACM. Christopher Ris is among the AACM students who remember these concerts vividly: "In the early days he [Pandit Das] would play with Zakir a lot. They would have these knock-down, drag-out concerts that would go on for four hours, just cranking one *bol* after another until the audience was just delirious, like, 'Stop, I just can't take another onslaught!' With these *bols*, they just went at it, one after the other, drenched in sweat" (Ris interview, July 5, 2003) (▶ see video 3.1 and figure 3.3). The competitive nature of the relationship between these two gifted young artists was also likely a contributing factor to the density and technical difficulty of these early concerts.

With time, Hayden observed that Pandit Das "gradually shaped his performances to adjust to what an audience can digest that doesn't know anything about kathak. I think he realized," she said, "people didn't care about five versions of 'dhā ta ke thungā'; they can't tell the difference" (interview, January 18, 2003). Pandit Das confirmed in interviews that he was increasingly aware of his new audiences' capacities, asserting, "if you dance [in] the way and manner I dance in India—straight three hours . . . in America, nobody is going to watch you, except students of Indian music or dance" (C. Das 1984).

FIG. 3.3. Chitresh Das performing with Zakir Hussain (tabla), James Pomerantz (sitar, pictured), and Kathy Jan (*tānpūrā*) at the San Rafael Improvement Club, ca. 1978.

Twelve Minutes and the Kathak Solo

Condensing and modifying Pandit Das's performances was also part of a play for more widespread recognition. Longtime student and former partner Michele Zonka describes the impetus to expand his audience: "The early goal was to go mainstream, to try to land an appearance on TV—on Johnny Carson![17] And so there was an effort to adapt performances to shorter choreographic 'pieces' to make it appealing for a mass American audience while at the same time not compromising the authenticity and traditional values of the art form" (Zonka interview, November 14, 2005). The process of adapting his kathak performances was an ongoing one that developed in fits and starts. As Julia Maxwell reports, Pandit Das's "first big chance in Los Angeles" came about when he was offered a twelve-minute slot at the 1984 Olympic Arts Festival, a performance at the Dorothy Chandler Pavilion in Los Angeles that was organized by the AMAN International Folk Ensemble (2012, 117). Maxwell writes: "Chitresh first turned down the offer, explaining that kathaks sometimes dance for hours at a stretch. Leona [Woods, artistic director of

AMAN] said that he could take it or leave it, and it's a good thing he changed his mind. His new choreography became his second signature piece" titled *Twelve Minutes* (117–18).

Pandit Das's performance of *Twelve Minutes* for the 1984 Olympic Arts Festival provided an important opportunity to showcase this streamlined style of kathak to a broader audience. In this performance, he synthesized the full kathak solo into condensed form. Just as early phonograph recordings of Hindustani music, because they were much shorter than typical performances, provide a valuable crystallization of the music's essential elements (Farrell 1993, 47–48), so too *Twelve Minutes* offers insight into what Pandit Das judged to be the key aspects of a kathak performance—or at least those aspects he felt would be most appreciated by audiences drawn to Los Angeles for the Olympics.[18]

The sequence of a kathak solo, as Margaret Walker writes, "has been developed and accepted through performance practice" and thus "can be designed to express a dancer's personal interests and style" (2004, 11). Many present-day dancers begin a solo performance with one of several forms of Hindu invocation.[19] Using a Sanskrit poem (*śloka*) or song (*vandanā*), the dancer may praise and enact the attributes of a particular Hindu deity. In a similar invocation, *raṅgmañch* (lit. "coloring of the stage"), the dancer performs a *pūjā* or worship, taking on the role of the devotee rather than that of the deity. *Pranām* entails a more generalized sanctification of the dance space, not necessarily referencing a particular deity. In his extended solos, Pandit Das typically presented either *pranām* (▶ see video 1.2) or *raṅgmañch* followed by a *śloka* or *vandanā* (▶ see video 1.3). However, for *Twelve Minutes* he danced only an abbreviated version of *pranām*, already the shortest of the various introductory invocations, preceded by a fast *tihāī*, during which he moved downstage to begin the performance (▶ see video 3.2).

Typically, a kathak performance commences in a slow speed, or *vilambit laya*, increasing to medium (*madhya*) and fast (*drut*) tempi. In *Twelve Minutes*, Pandit Das instead began in *drut laya*, a fast tempo accompanied from the outset by both tabla and the double-headed pakhawaj drum (played by Ritesh Das and Peter Peringer, respectively) and joined by the melodic instrument *jal taraṅg* (played by Joanna Das [de Souza]). In a full solo, the dancer commonly would continue in slow *vilambit laya* performing *ṭhāṭ*, a "stylized 'tuning of the body, mind and spirit'" that draws attention to subtle movements of the eyes, eyebrows, neck, and wrists; and by presenting *āmad*, deliberate and refined compositions utilizing dance *bols* that include "tā theī tat" (C. Das 1986a, 9–10; Maharaj 2002, 80). In *Twelve Minutes*, Pandit Das hinted at a *ṭhāṭ* just forty-four seconds into the performance by moving relatively slowly into five different stances. However, he immediately shifted into footwork, building speed through an abbreviated *kramalaya*, or stepwise increase in rhythmic density. While also a common component of *ṭhāṭ*, in other performances Pandit Das might demonstrate eight or more different speeds of the same footwork pattern. On this occasion, however, he demonstrated only three speeds (of *tatkār*), embellishing them, as is typical, with different movements of the arms and hands, interspersing other patterns of footwork in improvisation, and in this case, inserting a brief composition. After concluding this section with a short *gintī*, a composition recited using numbers rather than *bols*, he launched into an abbreviated performance of "Hindol Tarānā"—a characteristically lively piece in the *tarānā* song genre whose music was composed by Ali Akbar Khansahib in *rāg* Hindol (▶ see video 3.2, cue point 2:05).[20]

Between the few repetitions of the *tarānā*'s main melody, on this occasion Pandit Das interspersed *nṛitt* or "pure dance" compositions, which he sporadically recited while dancing. During these compositions, the melodic line dropped out and the two accompanying drummers simultaneously played compositions as Pandit Das danced. A traditional solo typically includes similar *bol-paran* sections, in which the dancer might present rhythmic compositions by reciting, then dancing. Not knowing what compositions to expect, and perhaps hearing some for the first time, tabla players are challenged to absorb them while the dancer recites, then play them back immediately as the soloist dances. Despite the complexity of this call and response, dancer and drummer might not even rehearse together before the concert. In this regard, *Twelve Minutes* was not a "traditional" solo as Pandit Das would commonly use the term; the synchronization of dancer and percussionists in performing each composition indicated a greater level of planning than typical for his longer solo performances. In moments between these compositions, the *jal taraṅg* performed "Hindol Tarānā's" principal melody, during which Pandit Das was always in motion, alternating between choreographed movements and spontaneous "fillers" discussed above.

After a *nṛitt* section of nonnarrative dance, kathak performers typically turn to *nṛitya*. This style combines rhythmic sophistication with storytelling through the recitation and enactment of *kavitās*, or poems; *gat nikās*, short depictions of anonymous character-types; and the more detailed storytelling, *gat bhāv*. After his "Hindol Tarānā," Pandit Das transitioned directly into a *gat bhāv* depicting the tale of "Madan Bhasma" (▶ see video 3.2, cue point 5:01).[21] Many members of an Indian audience would likely already know the story and recognize its various characters. In order for the largely non-Indian audience at the 1984 Olympic Arts Festival to quickly understand the underlying drama and recognize its distinct characters, Pandit Das began this performance of "Madan Bhasma" by narrating while enacting its various personae. In this tale, Madan, the God of Love, is sent by the gods to rouse Lord Shiva from his meditation and to encourage him to fall in love and conceive a son with Goddess Parvati, because only a son of Shiva would be able to defeat the demon Tarakasur. Madan is accompanied by his wife, Goddess Rati, who urges him on. After Pandit Das's narrated-and-danced introduction, the music swelled and he shifted fully into dance. As Madan, he approached Lord Shiva with great trepidation, eventually loosing an arrow of desire on the meditating God. With a quick turn, Pandit Das transitioned to the character of Lord Shiva, who opened his third eye, releasing a powerful beam of fire that burns Madan to ashes (*bhasma*).

As in many kathak solos, Pandit Das intensified his dancing as he reached the performance's conclusion, next displaying more footwork and a series of one hundred and eight *chakkars* (swift turns), which he announced "symboliz[ed] the *chakra*, the wheel of life." He concluded with a *savāl-javāb*, a "question-answer" section with the drummers. In *savāl-javāb*, the dancer typically begins by producing rhythmic phrases through footwork and one of the musicians responds by translating the same phrase with their instrument. Performers go back and forth in this manner gradually shortening the length of their traded phrases and ending together with a *tihāī*. In performances of Hindustani music as well, the melodic soloist will often engage in *savāl-javāb* with the tabla player; this section is a favorite of western audiences because of its overtly improvisational nature and because the unfolding structures are relatively easy to follow.

In *Twelve Minutes*, Pandit Das condensed and simplified the kathak solo, showcasing the faster, flashier aspects of the dance form, including footwork, *chakkars*, and *savāl-javāb*. In an interview three years before this performance, he highlighted these aspects of kathak as facets that the "layman" could appreciate: "One can't always expect the layman to appreciate the traditional *bols*, which are sometimes very complicated in composition and *laya*. What the layman does go in for is the footwork, the pirouettes, the *sawaal-jawaab* and *ladai* [from *laṛant*: battle] with the Tabaliya [tabla player]. He enjoys the excitement, the speed. Naturally, I have to keep his interest in mind, also" (quoted in Ghosh 1981, 6).

While Pandit Das experimented with radically abridging his material in *Twelve Minutes*, in performances of his most well-known work, *The Train*, he learned to expand on his presentation in various ways in order to educate audiences and to garner further support for the innovative and challenging piece.

Introducing *The Train*

Unlike the "onslaught" of complex compositions he displayed in early performances, *The Train* showcased technical prowess without requiring much understanding of the structure or aesthetics of the art form. Although it was always a crowd-pleaser, over the course of his career he increasingly highlighted aspects of its technical sophistication and its similarity to past kathak innovations to advance audience and critical appreciation of the work.

The Train or *Relgāṛī* (lit. "rail car") was simultaneously the most popular and most controversial item from Pandit Das's repertoire. Presenting a steam engine's journey from one railway station to another, it evoked the nostalgic sounds of yesteryear. In 1981, journalist Anashua Ghosh described the performance's reception in India: "Chitresh Das has received plenty of criticism, perhaps more than his share of it. And about the harshest has been regarding his deviating from tradition and modernizing Kathak *that* bit too much. Temperatures have soared on either side of this criticism. . . . But," he asks, "must Chitresh bring Kathak down to the level of his 'popular' *railgaadi* dance steps?" (1981, 5–6). Ghosh quoted Pandit Das: "It's the sound of a railway carriage leaving the station, changing tracks, gathering speed, crossing a bridge, passing open fields and trees, slowing down, changing tracks again, and finally, reaching its destination and coming to a halt at the platform. It's all a gamut of sound and speed variations and the whole thing is just footwork'" (6). As Pandit Das suggests, his feet and *ghuṅgharū* were the piece's sole instruments; he felt this lack of accompanying tabla or melodic instruments drew the most criticism. Sushil Kumar Saxena may indeed have been commenting on *The Train* when he wrote a decade later that "in good Kathak the element of sounding rhythm *never appears, on the whole, to dominate visual appeal*" and "it is, in fact, common for our *gurus* in this field to emphasize the thematic and expressional aspects of the art, as against mere footwork, by pointing out that the very word Kathak *means* 'one who tells a story'" (1991, 17, original emphasis).

Of course, these two elements are not mutually exclusive; while *The Train* privileged the sonic element, it also very explicitly told a story. In a November 1999 concert in Toronto, for example, Pandit Das's brother Ritesh Das introduced the piece, encouraging the audience members to "close your eyes and listen to the sound of the train from his feet," an unusual request for a dance performance (in C. Das 1999).[22] Sound was clearly central to his evocation of *The Train*; however, Pandit Das also made use of visual cues to highlight and clarify the sonic world being portrayed: pointing to the ceiling of the train station where the initial sounds of his steam engine train echoed in response, quickly moving his hands back and forth across the profile of his face as an electric train passed, and indicating the train's passage over the horizontal beams of a bridge by sweeping his arms downward and to one side as the beams were quickly left behind.

In Pandit Das's repertoire, *The Train* held a special place; because of its unique nature and longstanding popularity, one can trace its mention over time, thereby gaining a sense of the changes in Pandit Das's manner of presentation. At the beginning of his career, Pandit Das was adamant to differentiate his performance of *The Train* from traditional kathak: "I don't call it kathak. I warn my audience. I deliberately step out of the classical tradition. Then I can experiment. But it is not Kathak" (quoted in Suraiya 1970, 19). In subsequent years, however, he altered his stance radically, couching the piece within the context of tradition in two main ways: by performing *The Train* alongside other mimetic compositions preceding it historically, and through the use of South Indian rhythmic theory, described further below.

"The Innovations of the Gurus"

A central issue for detractors of *The Train* was its literal rendering of an inanimate aspect of the modern world, as opposed to more common depictions of characters from India's ancient epics. Later in his career, Pandit Das responded to critics with extended introductions to the piece that recast it as one within a history of compositions mimicking the outside world. For example, at the 1999 Toronto concert already mentioned, Ritesh Das introduced *The Train* at length; but when Pandit Das reappeared on the stage, he launched into what seemed to be a different repertoire entirely, announcing, "Ladies and gentlemen, I present to you 'The Innovations of the Gurus'" (▶ see video 3.3).

Pandit Das continued this presentation by invoking two names significant to kathak's history: Wajid Ali Shah, a renowned patron-practitioner of kathak and the last Nawab of Lucknow (from 1847 to 1856); and legendary kathak guru Thakur Prasad-jī (touching his ears in deference on saying Thakur Prasad's name).[23] "In his own way, [Wajid Ali Shah] would say, 'Today Guru-jī, I would like to hear the sound of the cannon.' So the Gurus would come up with [a] beautiful composition on tabla, a *top* [cannon] *paran*—pure traditional." His mention of these notable figures was key in arguing for the authenticity of this composition and subsequent ones—the dancers at Wajid Ali Shah's court in Lucknow included the brothers Durga and Thakur Prasad, who with Durga Prasad's sons Kalka and Bindadin are credited with shaping the Lucknow *gharānā* of kathak (see, e.g., Kothari 1989, 24). Pandit Das proceeded to recite the *bols* of a composition imitating the sounds of a cannon and paused before dancing to reiterate, "so I present to you, old compositions."

After demonstrating the sound of cannons, Pandit Das next imitated Rajput warriors on horseback, drawing laughs of recognition from the audience when his feet mimicked the sound of galloping horses. Transitioning to a third composition, he declared, "My guru-jī comes from Rajasthan, very warrior-like, very Rajput-like. So my guru-jī taught me a composition. [The] peacock is the national bird, and Rajasthan is full of peacock[s]." Pandit Das's recitation of this composition was marked by a high "coo-coo!" and he brought the peacock to life through a suggestive walk and quavering fingers placed at his hips to portray the rustling of the bird's tail feathers. Again, at moments of recognition, the audience responded with laughter and applause. Introducing the penultimate composition, Pandit Das continued his story: "And the mother hen heard that peacock. [It was] a little cloudy [and the mother hen was] very annoyed. The little chicken[s], they were right [next to her] and when the cloud came, the mother hen cackled at the cloud." With this composition, Pandit Das demonstrated what he called a "new technique" in which he produced five distinct sounds with his heel while making two full spins on that foot.[24]

After this litany of revered kathak gurus and demonstrations of compositions depicting cannons, peacocks, and chickens, by the time Pandit Das finally announced "the journey of the train," audience members had no reason to imagine it unacceptable or untraditional. But to drive the point home, Pandit Das told the audience that tabla players also created compositions based on the sounds of the train, suggesting that *relā* (a common type of tabla composition) derived from the word *relgāṛī* (train), and that this composition was taught to him by his guru when he was nine years old.[25] Pandit Das subsequently shared with me that his guru had first taught *The Train* to his guru-sister, a *ṯavā'if* known to him only as Baby Rani, who danced it along with tabla player Akbar Husain "Ballu" Khan.[26] It was later taught to Pandit Das without tabla, which proved to be a significant aspect of the piece's success and its notoriety.[27] Although the mimetic compositions he first presented would most likely be performed by other dancers with musical accompaniment, his performance without accompaniment likely led less knowledgeable audiences to believe that this was the way they were typically performed.

The *Jātis*

Pandit Das's use of *jātis*, specific rhythmic groupings common to South Indian Karnatak music, also was crucial in garnering support for the piece—particularly from Indian audiences.[28] In utilizing aspects of South Indian rhythmic theory, Pandit Das and other North Indian classical artists have drawn on the symbolic importance of South India as a source of (specifically Hindu) tradition and antiquity.[29] During a 1981 interview for the Indian newspaper the *Telegraph*, Pandit Das described *The Train* as being based on *khaṇḍa jāti*, a pattern of five beats grouped as 2 + 3 or sometimes 3 + 2 (see table 3.1). With this revelation, the interviewer writes, "the theme is modern, but the treatment is very much classical" (Ghosh 1981, 6).

By the late 1990s, Pandit Das's performances of *The Train* utilized not just five-beat *khaṇḍa jāti* but also the other four most common *jāti* groupings. He described a "great commotion" regarding *The Train* when performing at a Calcutta festival in 1996: "As soon as I came on stage the people howled for *The Train*" (interview, August 17, 2005). As he indicated he would oblige the request, a noted female kathak dancer in the audience stood and publicly challenged the validity of the piece, saying, as Pandit Das recalls, "'What is this *Train*? Who taught you this?'" He responded: "Well, my guru-jī taught me this." When she further challenged him to justify the piece, he explained that it involved the *pāñcha* [5] *jāti*. Pressing him yet further, she reportedly replied, "show us *pāñcha jāti*." In response, he performed variations of a *paran* (a well-known type of composition utilizing the *bols* "dhā ta ke thungā") by transforming the *bols* of the *paran* to fit the rhythmic structures of each of the five *jātis*.

In later years, rather than giving audience members a chance to challenge his work, he preemptively described the *jātis* and demonstrated each one through several footwork variations exploring its rhythmic possibilities (▶ see video 3.3, cue point 2:49). *Jātis* include the units 3 (*tiśra*), 4 (*chaturaśra*), 5 (*khaṇḍa*), 7 (*miśra*), and 9 (*sankīrṇa*). Pandit Das and his students often utilized them in this ascending order; however, South Indian music theorists most commonly list these *jātis* in the order of 4, 3, 7, 5, and 9 (Viswanathan and Allen 2004, 35–36). These five groupings "permeate Karṇāṭak rhythmic thinking, both at a macro level as building blocks out of which lengthy improvisations are structured and at a micro level as the five ways in which an individual beat may be internally subdivided" (35). Each of these groupings is based on the patterns for three (expressed by the syllables "takiṭa") and four ("takadimi"). Five is usually made up of 2 ("taka") + 3 (together: "taka takiṭa"); seven is 3 + 4 ("takiṭa takadimi"); and nine is 4 + 2 + 3 ("takadimi taka takiṭa") (table 3.1).[30]

While the *jāti* system is sometimes used by Hindustani musicians, in North Indian practice, "divisions into 5 or 7 parts (*khaṇḍa* and *miśra jātis*) are somewhat rare, and those into 9 (*saṅkīrṇa jāti*) exceedingly so" (Clayton 2000, 157). Pandit Das cited his father, Prohlad Das, as his primary influence for using the *jātis*: "In kathak we always had *chhands* [rhythms, grooves], and some of them were in *miśra jāti* [7], some were even in *saṅkīrṇam* [9], but we didn't call it that. My father was a dance scholar so he looked into these things, and I was surrounded by these ideas from childhood, because my parents' dance school was in our house, so I grew up with [South Indian] bharatanatyam and kathakali dancers around" (C. Das interview, November 14, 2005).

Table 3.1. The five (*pāñcha*) *jātis* as taught by Pandit Chitresh Das

Tiśra (3)	ta ki ṭa
Chaturaśra (4)	ta ka di mi
Khaṇḍa (5, here 2+3)	ta ka, ta ki ṭa
Miśra (7, here 3+4)	ta ki ṭa, ta ka di mi
Sankīrṇa (9, here 2+3+4)	ta ka, ta ki ṭa, ta ka di mi

In the 2000s, Pandit Das typically contextualized *The Train* with a demonstration of "The Innovations of the Gurus" similar to that described above, followed by an explication of *jātis* and a display of rhythmic possibilities for each grouping. After this elaborate and lengthy preface, Pandit Das finally performed *The Train* (▶ see video 3.3, cue point 4:41).

Jātis in *The Train*

Analysis of a 2008 San Francisco performance of *The Train* provides greater insight into the rhythmic techniques Pandit Das utilized. In music examples 3.1 through 3.4, I transcribe footwork techniques, tempo, and rhythmic groupings using a modified form of western staff notation.[31] This transcription reveals that Pandit Das indeed made use of each of the *jātis*, though some at a breathtaking speed that renders them almost indistinguishable.[32] He also included groupings that fall outside of the five-*jāti* framework; at times he only hinted at rhythmic ideas before shifting to others; and he accelerated or decelerated at will, all to serve his sonic portrait.

At the beginning of the performance, Pandit Das made use of *khaṇḍa jāti* (5) to evoke the sounds of a train's engine as it starts up and begins to move (▶ see video 3.3, cue point 5:20; and music example 3.1). Full slaps of the foot on beats 1 and 3 (measure 1) represent the train's engine; these are followed by lighter taps of the toes (m. 2) to indicate its sounds echoing off the train station's vaulted ceiling. As the train accelerated, Pandit Das added percussive footfalls for the rest of the beats of each phrase, still accenting beats 1 and 3.

As Pandit Das's train left the station, it crossed other train tracks, which he represented by performing purposely irregular patterns of footwork grouped mainly into sevens and sixes (▶ see music example 3.2 and video 3.3, cue point 6:18). Following a transitional two-step phrase (m. 5), Pandit Das provided this section's clearest articulation of *miśra jāti*'s typical three plus four subgroupings by accenting the first and fourth steps. He performed the pattern first beginning on the right foot and then on the left but interrupted his clear statement of the *jāti* even before completing the second iteration (see m. 7), subsuming the last footfall in the next grouping of six bass sounds produced primarily with his heels. By measure 14, Pandit Das introduced footwork groupings of eight (*eṛī tatkār*, see chapter 4) that would be repeated several times, communicating that the train had established a steady forward momentum. The way Pandit Das arrived at that steady pace, however, was irregular and complex. Three quick accents that begin the phrase in measure 11 initiate the first eight-beat grouping of the performance; he echoes that rhythmic motif in measure 12, but leaves the idea only seven beats into its second iteration. In the immediacy of performance, the next phrase (m. 13)

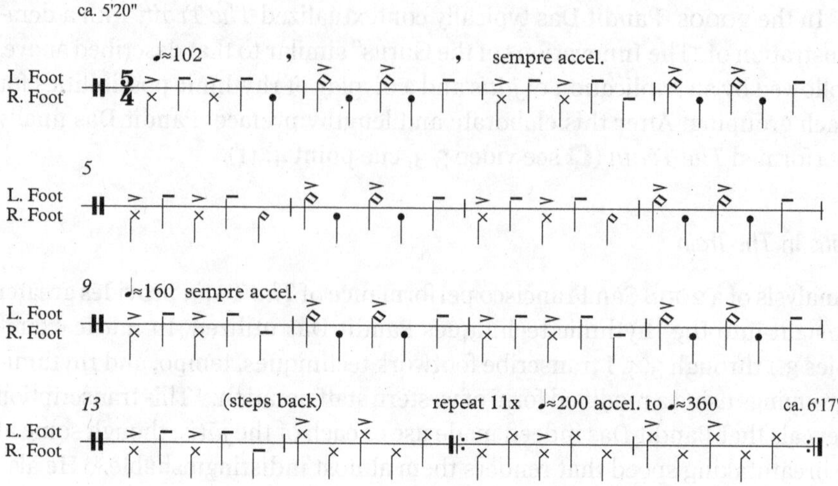

Key:

× Full foot slap

– Full foot step without producing sound (if followed by same, foot then a "brush")

◈ Ball of foot slap with heel planted

◇ Ball of foot step with heel planted without producing sound

● Heel strike

• Heel strike without producing sound

✱ Full foot slap producing bass sound with heel

MUSIC EX. 3.1. *The Train,* leaving the station: *khaṇḍa jāti* (5)

sounds like a standard grouping of seven-beat *miśra jāti*. The last step of measure 12, however, serves dual roles as part of the phrase that preceded it and potentially as the first step of a regular eight-step pattern, which appears in the following measure (m. 14) and repeats for several measures to follow as the train settles into a steady rhythm.[33] While the regular footwork pattern begun in measure 14 and continued in music example 3.3 is generally perceived by kathak dancers as groups of eight, its special emphasis on footfalls 1 and 5 (with slaps of the full foot instead of the heel) also audibly divides the phrase into groupings of four, *chaturaśra jāti*.

Not to rest long in any regular pattern, after "crossing the tracks" Pandit Das communicated to the audience that an electric train was about to pass his steam engine train, going in the opposite direction at full speed (▶ see music

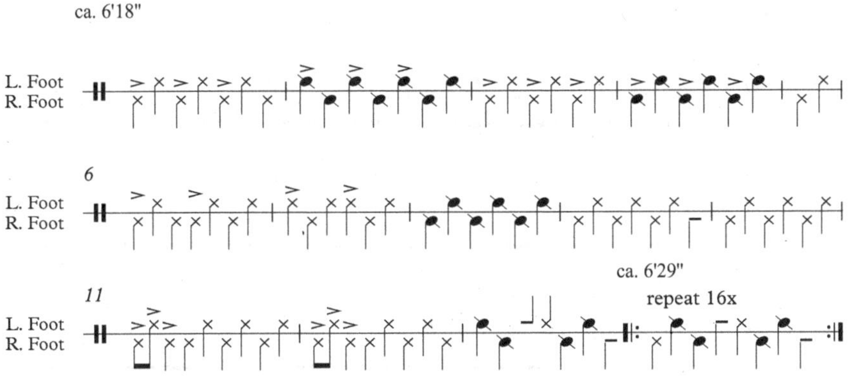

MUSIC EX. 3.2. *The Train,* crossing tracks: *miśra jāti* (7)

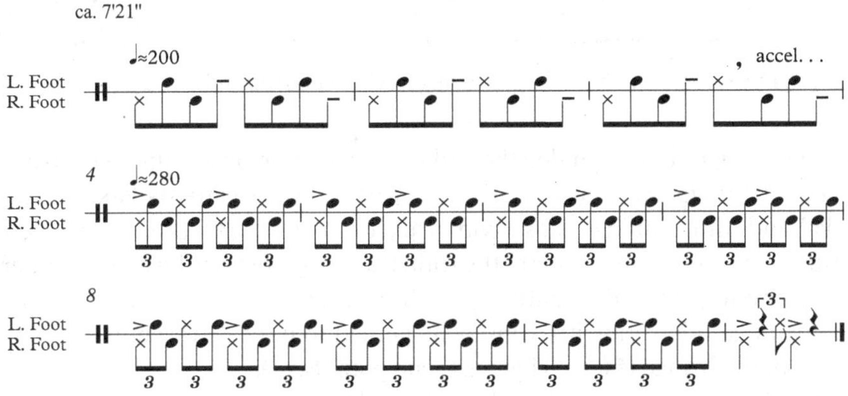

MUSIC EX. 3.3. *The Train,* passing an electric train: *chaturaśra* and *tiśra jāti*s (4 and 3)

example 3.3 and video 3.3, cue point 7:21). After a slight pause followed by rapid acceleration of his heelwork at the end of measure 3, Pandit Das launched into fast "dhingṛa dhāngṛā" triplet *tiśra jāti* patterns produced so rapidly that the heelwork was almost indistinguishable. Its dense sound effectively evoked the clacking sound of trains passing one another; however, this section's performative success also relied on Pandit Das's use of upper-body movements. Pandit Das turned his body sideways to highlight his arm motions. Then, with palms facing one another, he rapidly moved his forearms to and fro in front of him to show the passing of the newer, faster train, and swept his arms down and away with two final accents of his feet to emphasize that the train had passed, even looking behind him as it disappeared in the distance.

The next two events in the train's journey did not utilize new *jāti* patterns, but instead made use of footwork patterns in novel ways to conjure specific

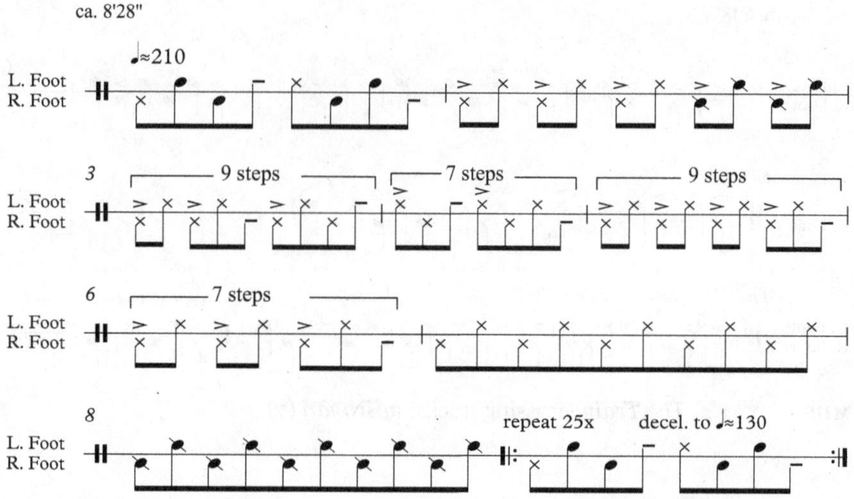

MUSIC EX. 3.4. *The Train*, ending, crossing tracks: *sankīrṇa* and *miśra jātis* (9 and 7)

imagery as Pandit Das guided the audience. The train picked up speed, passing small bridges and houses, performed with footwork patterns "takiṭa takiṭa taka" and "dhina dhina" (see video 3.3, cue point 7:43). Crossing a larger bridge, he evoked the sounds of the train traveling from one beam to another by combining atypical accenting, jumping up slightly in the midst of his fast footwork, and lowering his arms as he landed to indicate reaching the next beam of the bridge (see video 3.3, cue point 8:14).

Approaching its destination, the train again crossed over sets of tracks that would lead other trains to and from the station (see video 3.3, cue point 8:59; music example 3.4). He approached the tracks with the now-familiar *chaturaśra jāti* (*eṛī tatkār*) footwork (m.1), performed a quick set of six slaps followed by four bass sounds, and transitioned immediately into the performance's only two groupings of *saṅkīrṇa-miśra*, paired groupings of nine followed by seven.[34] In measures 3 and 4, *saṅkīrṇa-miśra* is presented with nine steps grouped as 2 + 3 + 4 ("taka takiṭa takadimi") and seven grouped as 3 + 4 ("takiṭa takadimi"). In measures 5 and 6, he reproduced the same number of footfalls, but did not group them into their smaller increments, instead differentiating his footwork groupings with only a "brush" step on the final ninth and seventh steps of the phrases. Pandit Das ended this section with two groupings of ten steps each, the first with full slaps of the feet and the second with heelwork, before returning to the *chaturaśra jāti* regular motion of the train. Pandit Das finally slowed as if a train braking to approach the station, reprising footwork patterns used at the beginning of the performance.

In *The Train*, Pandit Das highlighted the *jātis* in order to provide a theoretical basis and technical grounding to this evocative piece.[35] Controversies surrounding *The Train*'s reception, while partially indicative of more specific political rifts, also reveal overarching tensions in the kathak world between sight and sound, or storytelling and musicality (see, e.g., Saxena 1991). Although these aspects of kathak can be mapped onto different parts of the body—with storytelling generally associated with the upper part of the body, and musicality with the lower—*The Train* manages to accomplish both almost entirely with the feet. As Pandit Das declared in the introduction to *The Train* during the 2008 performance analyzed above, "Now you *hear* dance" (▶ video 3.3, cue point 3:00).[36]

Like many South Asian performing artists who preceded him in the United States, Pandit Das necessarily developed sophisticated techniques for dealing with the expectations of new audience members. These techniques, including demonstrating the "Innovations of the Gurus" and the *jātis*, also served to legitimize *The Train* in India, where he was considered an outlier until his senior years. And his demonstration of each rhythmic grouping before performing *The Train* helped spectators better understand the piece's technical virtuosity, which proved beneficial in both the United States and India. The next chapter continues to explore how Pandit Das adapted kathak for new and different audiences by focusing on interactions with students during his first phase, of approximately seventeen years, of teaching in the United States.

4

Teaching in a New Country

When Pandit Das arrived in the United States, his performances were much longer and rhythmically denser than his new audiences could appreciate or absorb. As discussed in chapter 3, he learned that he needed to shorten, simplify, or more thoroughly contextualize his performances in various ways; however, in his performing and his teaching he worked to maintain a high level of *taiyārī* ("readiness," but also agility in this context) and *layakārī* (rhythmic virtuosity), which he considered foundational skills. As he noted, "first my emphasis is on *taiyārī* and *layakārī*" (interview, June 25, 2002). This quote aptly summarizes the training philosophy Pandit Das employed throughout his teaching career, but perhaps particularly applied to his early years of teaching in the States, during which he and his students engaged in a variety of cultural and stylistic negotiations. The period was marked by culture clashes generally deriving from conflicting approaches to the teacher-student relationship: Pandit Das's desire to train for excellence and to replicate the strict discipline he received in training with his own guru as compared to his students' relatively easygoing attitudes and desire for cultural exploration. Emphasizing technical virtuosity proved a successful strategy in competing for dance audiences and funding sources, and partially satisfied the need for objective, quantifiable means of proving the skills of his early, non-Indian students; but this push came at an emotional cost for some students who perhaps got more than they had signed up for. This chapter focuses on the first approximately seventeen-year period of Pandit Das's teaching in the United States, examining societal expectations surrounding the transmission of knowledge, the challenges he and his fledgling dance company faced in becoming recognized in the States, and the methods by which they worked to achieve technical excellence.

Riyāz: Disciplining the Artistic Body

The lore surrounding many dance cultures is filled with stories of dance masters' harsh methods for disciplining students' bodies. This may especially be the case in India, where both dance and music gurus are remembered, and often lauded, for their strict teaching methods and unwavering commitment to practice. In this tradition, with a long history of both Muslim and Hindu practitioners, the idea of practice is expressed as *riyāz*, from Arabic, or as *sādhanā*, from Sanskrit.[1] The terms are roughly analogous, implying labor with devotion; however, George Ruckert distinguishes the two, noting, "a regular practice (*riyāz*) . . . can develop into a spiritual practice (*sādhanā*)" (1991, 12). Daniel Neuman writes that *riyāz* implies "abstinence, devotion, discipline, and hard labor" ([1980] 1990, 42). He further describes it as "a means of devotion and a measure of dedication . . . an explanation of success, and . . . a pedagogical device with a moral" (42). Pandit Das succinctly refers to *riyāz* as "a way of life" (2001).[2]

The concept of practice with devotion is so central to Indian artistic practice that Pandit Das titled his 2001 autobiographical production *Sadhana* (discussed in chapter 2). As he told the audience during the performance, "*sādhanā* isn't just me practicing my dance, but . . . how to practice . . . how to go through the journey of life." In one section of the production, the daily effort involved in becoming a kathak performer was illustrated through video montage (▶ see video 4.1). Close-ups on the feet of several Chitresh Das Dance Company members displayed the repetitive practice of *tatkār* footwork. As execution of this eight-step pattern accelerated, Pandit Das (in a recorded voiceover) spoke of "becoming one with the divine force" through one's dance as embodying the "essence of Indian tradition and Indian civilization." The video footage featured scenes of dance company rehearsals interspersed with clips from a solo performance by disciple Jaiwanti Das Pamnani as Pandit Das contrasted a sense of spirituality with the immediacy of physical practice: "So in one hand you're speaking of becoming one with everything, but it is another thing going through the practice, the rigors. . . . At that time, you don't think spiritual at all. You feel your breathing—you can't even breathe; you can't even move; you can't do things. You know, you're trying to save your breath, save your muscles. You're feeling your sweat—your blood, sweat, and tears. You're in pain!"

In close-up video clips, the audience heard dance company members' fast footwork and saw it reflected in slight vibrations distorting the skin of their sweat-covered faces. Pandit Das's voice continued: "But what happens is, over a period of time—practicing and practicing and practicing *and* practicing *and* practicing—that your pain becomes very secondary. You overcome that, but you don't even realize you're overcoming it. It becomes a routine; you get used to it, and then that's how you achieve skill—the technique of what you pursue."

Long hours of rigorous practice are a vital part of Hindustani musical training as well. Musicians will often praise their seniors by remarking on the number of hours spent in practice and will even discuss radical methods employed to stay awake. Stephen Slawek notes that "most musicians claim to have endured a period in the early years of their study during which they would practice as many as fifteen hours each day" (2000, 464). In enjoining his students, including myself, to practice more, Ali Akbar Khansahib often related that he spent "twenty years practicing eighteen hours a day" (Winnig 1999, 13) or some variant thereof, and recalled that his father, the celebrated Ustad Allauddin Khan, sometimes practiced for twenty-three hours a day (13; Ali Akbar College of Music 2006). Ust. Allauddin Khansahib's most noted method for keeping himself awake was to tie his hair to a rope attached to the ceiling, so that when his head nodded, the pulling of his hair would jerk him back to attention (Shankar [1968] 2007, 51; Worth 1991).[3] Whether or not such tales are hyperbole is not the point. "We learn not only that a musician *becomes* great by submitting himself to a very rigorous practice schedule, but also that, in part at least, the evidence for his genius lies in this very rigor" (Daniel Neuman [1980] 1990, 34).[4]

While some musicians stayed up all night in practice, as a young dancer, Pandit Das often began his training early in the morning. A fellow student who had lived upstairs from their guru animatedly described hearing "the sound of [Pandit Das's] footwork and bells starting from five in the morning—and for so many hours he would dance!" (anonymous interview, August 3, 2003). To communicate the rigor of *riyāz* to his serious students, Pandit Das often recounted the austerities of practice in his guru's flat, which included not being permitted to stop for a drink of water or to run a fan, even in Calcutta's intense summer humidity and heat that sometimes exceeded 100° Fahrenheit. Though the climate might have been more temperate, Pandit Das did what he could to replicate those conditions in his California classes and elsewhere by not allowing students to drink water during class and by keeping the windows closed.

It is perhaps not surprising, however, that Pandit Das encountered difficulties reproducing the strict training he had experienced for the predominantly white female students he taught in the San Francisco Bay area in the 1970s.[5] As he recalled several years later:

> This was the beautiful age of the flower children—the hippie generation. . . . I was trying to reinforce an achievement oriented discipline. The concept, which at that time, had lost its popularity. A path to mutual understanding was going

> to be rough. At times the obstacles seemed insurmountable. They were looking toward the East for answers, but I did not fit their idealized image of an Indian guru. I would tell them to be quiet, dance hard, and show respect—just as my guru and gurus before him had told their disciples.
>
> Caught between two cultures, I had some difficulty with the informal lifestyle and egalitarian classroom banter that American students were accustomed to. Having been schooled in the old world traditions—to respect and obey my teachers and elders, and to assume a secondary stance in their presence—my amused bewilderment at my students' behavior never ceased. Daily they would appear with bare feet, men with long hair, women adorned with garlands of flowers in their hair, and bearing the names of Hindu goddesses and nature. My sometimes caustic objections aside, I was going through a tremendous learning process to understand the psychology of these young Americans. (C. Das 1986b, 32)

Pandit Das was not the only Indian artist to face difficulties in teaching students abroad. His experience in some ways paralleled that of Smt. Tanjore Balasaraswati, who began teaching bharatanatyam in the United States in 1962. In subsequent decades, Balasaraswati encountered, as one student put it, "strong-willed women" (quoted in Cowdery 1995, 55). This student relates her attraction to bharatanatyam to an impulse to resist "the conformity and culture of ballet life" (55). Similarly, many US students found that Indian classical dances—indeed all things Indian—represented the newfound freedom of the era. But what these early students encountered was a training style that was in many ways as strict and rigid as ballet.

In the West, both Pandit Das and Balasaraswati found it difficult to replicate the pedagogical methods typically employed in the intense, one-to-one *guru-śiṣya* (teacher-disciple) style of training. James Cowdery writes of Balasaraswati, "In addition to adapting *what* she taught, Bala felt the need to adapt *how* she taught. Her *guru* had often used strict discipline, even humiliation, to make her try harder. She occasionally used such tactics with her American students . . . but Bala realized that most Americans would not respond well to this teaching style, however traditional it was in India" (52).

Thus, Balasaraswati adjusted her methods, and it was some years before she realized her students might be future carriers of the tradition. When she did, she reverted to pedagogical methods she used for students in India. While in India most beginning students were children, in the United States at that time, students of Indian dance were more often adult women. These differences were considerable: young pupils in India generally lived with their parents or sometimes with their guru, particularly if the guru was a family member, whereas adult students in the United States usually had to support themselves by working jobs with enough flexibility to allow for their continued training. Most young students in India would be supported by parents and extended community—people who were at least somewhat knowledgeable about the tradition and typically placed some value on the child's training. In contrast, adult students in the United States often had to educate their friends and family about the dance form and explain why they were engaged in such demanding practice.

Although in his early years of teaching in the States his students were not much younger than he was, Pandit Das was not willing to give up the discipline he considered to be a key aspect of the training. His classes often lasted over three hours and were nicknamed "the torture chamber." As these students were starting later in life than students in India, Pandit Das's goal was to train them in as little time as possible, so classes were as intense as any he would have taught in India, with perhaps an added sense of urgency. "'The flower children were all over the place then,' he said. 'I had nine students. I used to teach a three-hour class. I did not understand my students, they didn't understand me. They were free souls, and here was I, a conservative Indian who had brought his art from India. "You can't take dope and learn dance," I used to say. I used to yell a lot. It was very difficult for me in the beginning. Very difficult'" (C. Das quoted in Swapan 1996, B1).

According to Bonnie Wade, "For a time, everything about Indian music was dwarfed beside its association with drugs" (1978, 36). Pt. Ravi Shankar expressed dismay at the drug use he saw in his audiences in the West. At times, he lectured the crowd and even "said that he would refuse to play for audiences that preferred to 'get high' on drugs rather than on music" (36). While drug use was also an issue at the Ali Akbar College of Music (AACM), Khansahib seems to have been more lenient, except toward more serious students, many of whom approached their study with not just determination and effort but also appropriate sobriety. Pandit Das recalled occasions teaching at the AACM in the 1970s when Khansahib would ask him to go easier on his students. Khansahib expressed the same tolerant encouragement to Smt. Chetna Jalan, who briefly taught at the AACM before Pandit Das's arrival: "At that time, it was also pretty difficult because lots of hippies were there. I used to constantly run back to Khansahib, 'Look, their hairs disturb me' and 'They are sitting with their babies,' and 'What am I to do?'[6] And he said, 'Just let it happen naturally.' You know? 'Just do not have any preconceived ideas that *this* is how it should be. And you just continue. You see, the art will finally win'" (Jalan interview, July 31, 2003).

Pandit Das and his early students recall confronting issues similar to those expressed by Chetna Jalan, particularly dealing with hygiene. There are colorful stories about various dancers from the time; for example, one student practiced "urine therapy," and Pandit Das would force other dancers to stand behind her as punishment.[7] Pandit Das additionally became stressed over students' attire. Gretchen Hayden recalls: "Things that came up then would

FIG. 4.1. A kathak class at the Ali Akbar College of Music, then housed at the Arequipa Girl Scout Camp in Fairfax, CA, fall 1972 or 1973. *Left to right*: Mary Khan (seated), Julia Maxwell, Lee Anderson, James Pomerantz (seated), unknown dancer, Michele King, Chitresh Das, Deborah Wolf. Photo courtesy of the Ali Akbar Khan Library.

never come up now, like bras! That was a big one. And if you can imagine, he was so shy about saying anything. He would tell Julia [his wife at the time] or one of the advanced students to tell [the offending student] she must wear a bra. . . . People were coming in halter-tops, shorts—all kinds of strange outfits. Then it became understood that you need a bra and you need to put more modest clothing on at least . . . so the classes looked quite different visually" (Hayden interview, January 18, 2003). As a dress code was established, dancewear became more modest. Students typically wore dresses, or tunics with skirts, pants, or leggings for class until the late 1980s, when it became easier to purchase Indian clothing in the Bay Area (figure 4.1). Until then, even students who had been to India and owned more traditional kathak dance attire generally did not wear it to class. While these aspects of teaching in the 1970s certainly make for entertaining tales, also at play were significant issues rooted in culturally specific ideas about discipline and the role of the teacher.

The difficulties in Pandit Das's classroom were not limited to minor cultural differences or long hours of dancing; he also deliberately generated psychologically tense situations for his dance students. In recalling those early days, dancers report sometimes being locked out of dance classes, being told that they were not going to perform on the day of a performance, or being given the silent treatment for weeks on end. Julia Maxwell adds that "he sometimes linked . . . criticism of a student's weakness to a personal trait, thereby making it a character flaw" (2012, 135). These experiences were accompanied by promises that "going through the fire" would prepare them for anything. The metaphor of the guru as fire is a common one in discussing the *guru-śiṣya* relationship: get too close to the fire (guru) and you'll be burned, but stay too far away and you won't get any warmth (knowledge). Thus, in the midst of the physical exertion of kathak training, the very concept of a guru and the challenge of engaging in a *guru-śiṣya* relationship in US society led to adversities extending beyond the physical rigors of practice.

Examining the *Guru-Śiṣya* Relationship

Many scholars have described the *guru-śiṣya* relationship's central importance to Hindustani music pedagogy (see, e.g., Kippen 2008; Daniel Neuman [1980] 1990; Nuttall 2007; Schippers 2007; Slawek 2000). In both music and dance, a student should follow only one guru who embodies the tradition, teaching by example as well as through formal and informal lessons meted out and absorbed over a long period of time. "Students depend on their guru, not only for his teachings, his love and care, but for a sense of approval, and recognition of their own legitimacy as artists. The very conditions of their ongoing existence rely on their own subordination within this relationship" (Dalidowicz 2012, 241). In this hierarchical relationship, ideally the guru commands utter respect and the disciple demonstrates unquestioning loyalty and devotion: "The attitude to the guru in Indian cultures is one of extreme reverence. Respect for the guru has evolved into a kind of devotional form similar to that held toward God. . . . As gurus are the mediums through which God speaks, or communicates, there exists a belief that the guru provides a path to spiritual or divine knowledge and experience" (Nuttall 2007, 325).

The relationship of guru and God is described in a well-known verse by the Bhakti poet Kabir (ca. 1440–1518), which begins *gurū gobind dou khaḍe, kāke lāgū pāy*, "If both my teacher and God are standing in front of me, who should I bow before first?" (Devidayal 2007, 56). Devidayal expounds on Kabir's next line: "The obvious answer would be God. But Kabir suggested that it should be the teacher, for it was he or she who showed the way to God . . . and wisdom. The teacher in traditional India was considered an avatar of God" (56).[8] Reverence is sometimes accompanied by an element of fear, as expressed in this reminiscence by Pt. Ravi Shankar, speaking of his guru, Ustad Allauddin Khan: "*Bābā*, my music guru. Whenever I think of him, I have a mixture of fear and awe. For us, [one's] guru is sometimes greater even than God. He is the teacher through whom all knowledge is passed on" (Worth 1991).

Ravi Shankar-jī's emphasis on *all* knowledge reflects the widely held ideal that a guru transmits much more than artistic knowledge, training disciples spiritually and psychologically, in manners and etiquette, and in developing an ability to respond appropriately in a range of settings and situations. Pandit Das recalled coming to this realization as a child: "The first time I ate lunch at my guruji's house I spilled rice on the floor. 'This is not your parents' house,' my guruji said to me, 'pick up every grain and eat it.' I was deeply embarrassed and began to realize that my training would affect my entire behavior. I was to learn to be alert at all times—when I ate, when I spoke, and when I sat quietly. My awareness expanded further into everyday life" (C. Das 1986b, 29).

Gurus often have a level of authority in their disciples' lives that in the West would be reserved only for parents—if that. For example, an Indian musician once confided in me that he wanted to get married, but that his guru would not yet give his approval. This *śiṣya*, who was in his early thirties at the time, said his guru felt he should invest his energy in performing, teaching, and recording in order to establish himself as an artist before shifting some of his focus to marriage and children. Although he was unhappy about the situation, this musician communicated no ill will toward his guru. In some respects, this episode represents a relatively mild example of a guru exercising authority; many musicians and dancers, particularly of older generations, privately discuss more severe examples of their gurus' methods of control or physical punishment. Despite such experiences, successful artists generally emphasize the positive results of their gurus' strict methods. For example, Pandit Das wrote that "although my guruji was extremely stern he also showed his affection from time to time . . . I realize now that the severity of his training, as prescribed by ancient tradition, helped me to develop, from a very early age, the psychological strengths I would need for performing, and for dealing with daily life" (29). As Denise Nuttall notes, "Disciples often struggle physically and emotionally as they learn a tradition in this way" (2007, 325). However, many believe that "If the teacher is good, no obstacles will be thrown in the learner's way which are beyond his slowly unfolding powers to overcome" (Chattopadhyaya 1967, 18, quoted in Kippen 2008, 135).

While widely celebrated, even in India a *śiṣya*'s experience often may not match the ideal. As James Kippen writes, "less scrupulous teachers have taught 'with a closed fist' (Slawek 2000, 463) and have engaged in wily games of *ustād-bāzī* in which they affected sincerity but exploited students' loyalty to their own social and economic advantage" (2008, 134–35). He further asserts that, "in the case of some female disciples, it has been sickeningly common to learn that sexual and emotional advantage had also been taken" (135). As the #MeToo movement gains momentum among classical dance and music communities in South Asia and beyond, there will undoubtedly be more literature on this subject (e.g., Bhattacharya 2018; Nathan 2018). But heretofore, as Huib Schippers notes, critique of this pedagogical system has rarely found its way into public discourse surrounding the tradition:

> Critical reflections on the guru are virtually non-existent from Indian sources, as they are socially unacceptable in music circles. Although it is common to think of the guru as a person who generates divine musicianship in his pupils as a matter of course, most gurus find it understandably difficult to live up to this profile. In public and writing, students generally exalt the source of their musical skills and understanding. From private, oral reports . . . one learns that many gurus may act like demi-gods, but in fact, they have changing moods, weaknesses, and oversights. They are, in effect, human in addition to being sublime musicians. . . . Although gurus are idealized in public, on closer examination, not all appear to be ready or capable of assuming the full onus the position implies. (2007, 124)

Critical writings on music or dance gurus are also uncommon in western scholarly sources. As scholars engage in participant observation in various parts of the world, they often adopt the role of student and absorb cultural expectations that come with that social position (Witzleben 1997, 236, and 2010, 144). Fieldworkers studying many South Asian music and dance practices (especially "classical" ones), like other students of these traditions, will often learn from one guru and will adopt deferential attitudes in their studies. Regula Qureshi suggests that "any critique of this ideology, or detachment from it, tends to be resisted by the ethnomusicologist who, as a musical participant, is protecting the productive arrangements of art music in order to protect a powerful source of her personal satisfaction" (2000, 20). Like fellow students who owe their performing careers to their gurus' blessings, ethnographers generally pay homage to their teachers, who provide artistic training as well as a window into the art form's broader cultural complex—knowledge on which to build their careers as scholars and teachers.[9] It is unwise for professional performers to openly criticize their gurus, whose authority usually continues to influence their students' success. To some extent this is also true of scholars, whose "personal satisfaction" and continued research is often dependent on maintaining positive relationships with their gurus (20).[10]

Studying Hindustani music or kathak dance outside of the *guru-śiṣya* pedagogical system potentially brings greater breadth to a scholar's perspective, as he or she may more easily interview, observe, or learn from any willing teacher. However, like any other would-be student, they "must be accepted as an insider to a significant degree in order to be permitted access to the rarefied training whose purpose is to make him a fully functional representative of the tradition" (Kippen 2008, 133). Thus, while engaging with one guru, his or her students, and artistic world for an extended period of years or decades opens the scholar to a depth of training and understanding that is not possible without the commitment of discipleship, it also often brings with it complex challenges of balancing the responsibilities of discipleship and academic integrity (see Kippen 2008).

On Mainstream American Understandings of Gurus

Despite the paucity of insider criticism concerning gurus of music or dance, in the West, the role of guru (often spiritual gurus as opposed to artistic gurus) has been subject to scrutiny in both published accounts and mainstream media productions. For example, in an episode on India of the PBS program *Adventure Divas*, tabla player Smt. Anuradha Pal is interviewed by Holly Morris, a US documentary filmmaker: "Tell me about your gurus. The concept of a guru is—I think it means something different to me than it does here [in India]" (Morris 2001; cf. Morris 2006, 115). Wisely, Pal turned the question back on her interviewer, asking her what guru means to her. "Well, guru in my mind is sort of a blind devotion," Morris says, adding, "and my sense of what it means here is more of a teacher." Her impromptu response is telling of the perspective of many westerners, in which blind devotion entails a suppression of the individual voice and giving up of personal agency. The interviewer's inflection projected a negative quality onto this devotion, which Pal immediately addressed: "Well actually, it is blind devotion. In the case of a guru, what we—what our Indian tradition tells us to do is a surrender, which I think is just alien to [the] Western rational mind." Indologist Georg Feuerstein echoes the sentiment that "blind devotion" to a guru irreconcilably conflicts with the psychological makeup of many westerners, here discussing his own extended experience of spiritual discipleship: "Among other things I realized that the autocratic way of teaching favored by most gurus is ultimately alien to my being. Indeed, I believe that it is alien to the being of most Westerners, and for very good psychohistorical reasons: Our postmodern world is a world of intense individualism" (1991, xxi).

Binary and essentialist discussions such as these of "Indian" versus "western" concepts and ways of being leave little room for diasporic, postcolonial, bicultural, multicultural, or otherwise cosmopolitan perspectives. As a dance company with members possessing a range of ethnic, racial, and national identities, particularly in the early 2000s when I was engaged in extended fieldwork, the Chitresh Das Dance Company resisted such easy oppositions. However, group discourse here too was often based on broadly constructed notions of western and Indian cultures. Below, Pandit Das's disciple Seibi Lee emphasizes individualism in western approaches to learning. Like Pal, she casts the *guru-śiṣya* relationship in a positive light; however, she downplays the role of devotion and surrender—which she refers to more negatively as acquiescence and passivity—and depicts the pedagogical process between guru and *śiṣya* as far-reaching and dynamic:

> In the western context, the teacher student relationship tends to be compartmentalized; there is a time and a place for teaching and learning. In the eastern sense, one takes on a teacher and the subject becomes a way of life. . . . The western idea is much more individualized. You learn something from someone and then go on to do your own thing. Often westerners think of the idea of *guru-shishya* as very acquiescent and passive but it's absolutely not that. It is an exceedingly active process for both the *guru* and the *shishya*. It is the most active relationship there can be, because . . . the relationship the *guru* takes on with the *shishya* encompasses that of a teacher, a parent, a guide, and embodies so much more. (Lee in Desai et al. 2010)

In addition to the tension of reconciling an ethos of individualism with hierarchical *guru-śiṣya* relationships, an added challenge in the West involved mainstream society's narrow familiarity with guru-based religious traditions. Diana Eck writes: "During the 1970s and early 1980s there was a great deal of attention and concern about what were called 'cults,' some of them being new guru-centered religious movements from India. When young people, Protestant, Catholic, and Jewish, followed enthusiastically after Hindu gurus or new-style Tibetan Buddhist teachers, it was newsworthy and, to some, alarming. An anti-cult movement complete with 'deprogrammers' was mobilized" (1993, 40). In 1985, sociologist James Beckford described the media representation and public response to cults in the United States, Britain, France, and West Germany: "Many books and articles about religious cults begin with stories about the painful or embarrassing incidents that first brought to their authors' attention the fact that young people had begun to experiment with novel and often frightening forms of religion in the 1960s and 1970s. . . . Readers could be forgiven for thinking that the very fabric of society was being rent asunder by invading hordes of insidious cult recruiters. . . . the idea was quickly created in the early 1970s that recruitment of youth on a massive scale had already taken place" (5).

While these fears were exaggerated in the mass media, several Indian gurus did develop large followings, often including celebrities and other wealthy patrons. Some of the best-known of such leaders included Maharishi Mahesh Yogi, the "giggling guru," who in 1958 began a series of world tours in which he taught his Transcendental Meditation technique and developed centers throughout Europe and North America. A. C. Bhaktivedanta Swami Prabhupada first traveled to the United States in 1965 and subsequently founded the Hare Krishna movement. Bhagwan Shree Rajneesh, sometimes called the Sex Guru, built a large community in Oregon and became known for his "crazy-wisdom shock tactics" and collection of as many as ninety-three Rolls-Royce cars (Urban 2005, 169). While these and other gurus actively taught in the United States, some, such as Sathya Sai Baba and Swami Muktananda, became influential without ever setting foot on US soil.[11]

Beginning in the late 1970s, the cultural climate in the United States shifted again, resulting in "a powerful backlash against forms of dissent and non-conformity which flourished in the 60s and early 70s" (Robbins 1978, 180). New religious groups from a variety of spiritual backgrounds were weakened by scandals associated with their charismatic leaders. Bhagwan Shree Rajneesh (later known as Osho) was deported in 1986 amid allegations of sexual, financial, and political abuses; and Maharishi Mahesh Yogi's organization suffered from accusations of fraud. Similar scandals disrupted American Buddhist communities founded by Suzuki Roshi and Chögyam Trungpa Rinpoche, although their biggest problems involved the US man each had designated as his successor (see, e.g., Downing 2001; Eldershaw 2007). In these and other instances, leaders of some new religious movements took financial, psychological, or sexual advantage of their followers. Public opposition to cults, however, solidified in 1978 after the mass suicide by members of Jim Jones's quasi-religious cult called the Peoples Temple—a tragedy about which 98 percent of the American public was aware, according to one Gallup Poll (Barker 1986, 330).[12] Such factors resulted in an "active and vociferous anti-cult movement" (Wallis 1988, 355).

More recently, documentarian Holly Morris voiced similar suspicion when visiting one guru's ashram in the Himalayas frequented by western seekers: "In my albeit limited notion of ashram, I have this image of middle-class kids who padlocked their trust funds and come here to find themselves. And swami and guru? Those terms to me? Jim Jones" (2001). The backdrop of mainstream societal distrust of gurus and cults, reflected in such statements, influenced both the experiences of Pandit Das's kathak students and his approach to teaching them.

A "Modern-Guru-in-Training"

Pandit Das refrained from calling himself a guru for many years. While partly in response to the term's negative stereotypical implications in the United States, this also had to do with his relative youth. When Pandit Das began teaching in California in 1971, his students often called him by his first name, Chitresh, or *Dādā* (older brother). His students were not much younger than he, making for a complicated dynamic that one former dancer described thus: "He . . . was acting like he was one of us, very casual on one hand, but inside, his expectation of everybody was still based on that other [*guru-śiṣya*] system" (anonymous interview, November 2, 2004). As this quote suggests, there was a tacit expectation that his students would assume the roles of disciples as best they could. For example, for his first sixteen years in the States, until 1986, Pandit Das did not know how to drive and was most often chauffeured by students. He recalls, "When I was fresh from India, I did not know—I thought the guru should be taken care of" (interview, July 12, 2002). Eventually, he adapted his expectations, learned to drive, and by the turn of the century drove hundreds of miles each week to teach at the branches of his school located throughout the Bay Area.

Only in his fifties did Pandit Das slowly adopt the term *guru*, and then only in the modified version, *modern-guru-in-training*. Coined by a Bengali American student, Sushmita Banerjee, this relatively unthreatening, even humorous appellation stuck for many years and was an effective way to communicate his guru-like status while mitigating negative associations that might derive from the unmodified title. It was also a catchphrase used to explain ways that Pandit Das refrained from following some of the rituals associated with gurudom. For example, he refused to allow anyone else to carry his tabla, although it is common practice for students to carry their guru's instrument and, according to Daniel Neuman, is "the sure sign of a disciple" ([1980] 1990, 46). Pandit Das also discouraged others from touching his feet, a customary Indian gesture of respect to gurus, teachers, or other elders.

While I was in California conducting fieldwork in 2002, an incident caused Pandit Das to more explicitly express his desire not to be called a guru. His school had for a number of years held *ghuṅgharū* ceremonies. This formal ritual, presenting newer students with their first set of dance bells, was held to mark their transition from taking introductory classes to becoming somewhat more invested in their study. Because Pandit Das did not hold *gaṇḍā bandan* ceremonies (which formally mark the guru-disciple relationship) with students at an early stage of their study as his guru did with him, this ceremony created a similar ritualistic experience for newer students without the accompanying responsibilities of officially becoming guru and disciple. This particular *ghuṅgharū* ceremony, attended by approximately fifty people, was held at the Mahea Uchiyama Center for International Dance in West Berkeley. Almost immediately upon his arrival for the ceremony, Pandit Das began speaking on a seemingly peripheral topic: "Especially in this culture, some parents might think, 'Oh, no! My children are joining a cult.' No, it's not like that at all. On the contrary, everything is a cult. Football is a cult, people in churches, Wall Street is a cult, business people . . . so please don't have any false notions of this" (fieldwork video, October 2, 2002).

Only later in his lecture did we learn what had provoked these remarks. To decorate the space, a senior student had strewn flowers along the path to the door of the dance studio, a gesture that apparently symbolized cultish behavior to Pandit Das, and an impression he sought to rectify:

> So then why do we perform this [*ghuṅgharū* ceremony]? Because you have to feel good about receiving bells and knowing what it means. You should not feel that I am some "baabaa" or someone. . . . I am not some cult guru. In Europe they used to have apprentices—it's the same thing. But as soon as you say the word *gooroo*, uh-oh! They don't understand what the word *guru* means. The word *guru* is very simple: one who removes the darkness . . . one who really goes with you through the ups and downs for the rest of your life. But I'm not a guru to you, I'm a stepping-stone, and this ceremony is given to you so that you respect the *ghuṅgharū* . . . It is as simple as that. So, next time don't have flower petals on the ground. I am not some "gooroo"; I am just a modern-guru-in-training.

The spelling of *gooroo* in the above quote reflects a common American pronunciation of the word *guru*; Pandit Das employed both variants to differentiate typical Indian and US understandings of the term.

As in his *gooroo* pronunciation, Pandit Das emphasized the word *baabaa*, overly stressing the long vowels, speaking in a low voice with mock reverence, referring to "cult" gurus. While they might carry negative connotations in such contexts, *bābā*, like *guru*, can also be used with genuine reverence to refer to Indian master-teachers, as in the quote by Pt. Ravi Shankar earlier in this chapter.[13] Literally meaning father, the term *bābā* is also applied to Hindu ascetics known as sadhus, and to specific spiritual leaders such as Sai Baba of Shirdi (ca. 1838–1918), Meher Baba (1894–1969), and Sathya Sai Baba (1926–2011) (Hausner 2007, 2). The latter two attracted large followings of western disciples, and Pandit Das was likely alluding to them.

Given the history of mainstream western suspicion of gurus and cults outlined above, and indeed, the close connection between the two concepts in the American imagination, it is not surprising that Pandit Das would be careful to distance himself from actions that felt overly cultish. This sensitivity was again demonstrated when one of India's more prolific dance critics described Pandit Das's popularity in the United States: "Barring Chitresh Das, by now a cult figure in Kathak in the U.S., there was none else whose Kathak performances Americans had seen regularly, except occasional visits by Birju Maharaj and his troupe" (Kothari 2004). Although this wording suggests a more benign usage of the word *cult*, akin to common phrases like "cult classic" and "cult following," the term's use drew strong reactions within this kathak community's internal discourse. Understanding and articulating the roles and responsibilities of guru and *śiṣya* remained a central concern for the Chitresh Das Dance Company, which published an interview with their senior dancers titled "What Is a Shishya?" in 2010 (Desai et al.).

Educating the broader public on their views of the *guru-śiṣya* relationship was important both to Pandit Das and to his serious kathak students, who struggled to navigate their duties as a student or disciple and their roles in work and family life. Often dancers' difficulties reconciling conflicting demands on their time were paired with a general resistance to the guru-disciple relationship coming in part from family and friends. Again, this problem may stem from the age at which many American dancers began their training. Pandit Das became ceremonially tied to his guru from a young age with the full support of his parents, and his most intense years of training occurred before the age of twenty-five. Because many of his serious students in the United States began as adults, their increasing connection and commitment to the dance often coincided and conflicted with romantic relationships, marriages, families, and outside careers. Recall the Indian musician, trained from childhood, who waited for his guru's approval before getting married. Although to my knowledge nothing so extreme was experienced in this kathak community, there remained concern that romantic relationships might interfere with a dancer's training, and some dancers worried that dedicating such a large percentage of their energy to kathak would hinder their ability to find a suitable life partner, start a family, or develop a career outside of dance.

Dancers' intense commitments of time and effort combined with the hierarchical structure of the *guru-śiṣya* pedagogical system tended to encourage outside perceptions of cultishness. However, as Pandit Das's disciple Charlotte Moraga describes, these perceptions were apt to change based on positive media exposure and the financial well-being of the organization:

> People who don't know anything about the dance say, "Oh you devote so much time; do you get paid for this? Oh, you *don't* get paid for this?" People definitely don't understand that. And there's just a cultural difference in terms of respecting your teacher in a certain way, and always being a learner. I know that there are some people . . . in my extended family [who] were curious about it. Now *eleven* years into [my training] . . . I've done a solo, [the dance company has] been getting grants, and we are starting to get paid better; [my family] reads the reviews and they're like, "Wow you've really accomplished something," so they don't think like that anymore. In the beginning that [perception] was definitely there. (Interview, October 2, 2002)[14]

The Ethnicity Issue: Negotiations of Style

Despite the physical and psychological difficulties encountered by Pandit Das's early students, many remember Marin County of the early days as a kind of sheltered enclave. South Asian immigration to Marin County was still relatively minimal in the 1970s but included performing artists from India teaching under the auspices of the Ali Akbar College of Music. Within that environment, Pandit Das's mostly white students could almost ignore issues of ethnicity inherent in the performance of this visual art form by dancers who looked so obviously different from the South Asian norm (figure 4.2). On this topic, Gretchen Hayden reflected: "I think that within our little sphere we all felt at home doing it. Largely because Chitresh-jī was quite clear to us: 'Stop worrying; that's ego. Just dance.'" But she continued: "I do think that because dance is so visual, on a basic level it does look different. You see a westerner doing it; it does *not* look the same as Indians doing it. When you get past a certain level of development, somehow it doesn't matter as much. . . . [But] I know he struggled with . . . how to [work with] these western-looking bodies, visually so different." Hayden felt "his answer was to go to the core—the core of the study does not have to do with whether you are western or Indian, really" (interview, January 18, 2003).

What was the core of the study, and how did this young teacher drive his new students to reach that "certain level of development" as quickly as possible? Michele Zonka recalled: "At the time, he wasn't so concerned with perfect body alignment. He didn't care where your elbows were; he didn't care

FIG. 4.2. Early students of Chitresh Das perform at Stern Grove (Sigmund Stern Recreation Grove), San Francisco, 1972 or 1973. *Left to right*: Michele King, Deborah Wolf, Antonia Minnecola, Gretchen Hayden. *Background*: accompanying musicians from the Ali Akbar College of Music. Photo courtesy of the Ali Akbar Khan Library.

where your eyesight went. His focus was on getting you dancing as fast and strong as you could, so the emphasis was footwork speed and technique—*only*. Because he wanted to build you up as fast as possible . . . to stand as a soloist" (interview, November 14, 2005). Going to the "core" of kathak in this context meant emphasizing footwork technique over the form's softer, subtler upper-body motions and narrative aspects: emphasizing the aural over the visual.

This strategy to circumvent the issue of ethnicity became increasingly necessary when the CDDC was founded in 1980, and Pandit Das's predominately white female students began performing with him on stage: "If I look back at the selling of himself with westerners, I think it was difficult for him. People *did* want to see 'authentic Indians'" (Hayden interview, January 18, 2003). Julia Maxwell describes the perspective she encountered when beginning to promote the fledgling dance company in California: "Where or how might our company fit in? We were considered an 'ethnic' dance company. At that time, dance was divided into 'ballet,' 'modern,' and 'ethnic' genres, and were valued and funded in that order. Our Company was also comprised of fair-skinned, American women, several of whom were blonde. Even though ballet companies already had prominent dancers of different ethnic backgrounds,

FIG. 4.3. Chitresh Das and early members of the Chitresh Das Dance Company, ca. 1983. *Left to right*: Marni Wieser Ris, Michele King, Chitresh Das, Julia Maxwell, Jane Simmons.

we were still an oddity, making it difficult for American presenters to sell us to their audiences" (2012, 115–16).

From Pandit Das's perspective, the rejection of his students was a criticism of him and his work: "When I created a company of blondes and brunettes, I thought I was doing something very noble, but to my astonishment, I was really discriminated [against] very subtly, by one group [who] wrote about Indian dance and music. They are the first people I thought would help me and support me—the Americans [earning] PhDs and writing books—but when another American was dancing or singing or [playing] the music, it was not kosher. But that was in the early '70s and it changed later" (C. Das interview, June 17, 2004).

Even though he felt they experienced prejudicial treatment in the United States, Pandit Das continued to perform with his students and to market the dance company there and on occasional tours to India (figure 4.4). Their reception in India was markedly different; Pandit Das's "American danseuses," as they were described on a Calcutta billboard in December 1981, were a sensation. "We were treated like celebrities," then CDDC member Marni Wieser Ris recalled (pers. comm., August 9, 2015). A former student of Pandit Das's parents' Calcutta-based school describes the perspective of Indian audience members at that time: "They were very exotic. It became his signature in India: people would go out of curiosity to see what Americans can do" (pers.

FIG. 4.4. Chitresh Das taking students to perform in India for the first time, December 1977. *Left to right*: Chitresh Das, Marni Wieser Ris, Elizabeth Ingraham.

comm., March 11, 2015). There, Pandit Das promoted and profited from his dancers' relative exoticism. In the brochure for a 1986 festival in India, for example, he was the only guru to include a photograph of himself with his students. However, Pandit Das wanted his protégées to be accepted both in India and the United States as serious dancers, not just as novelty. The dance company seemed to be a liability to his own growing renown in the States, where, in the same year, one finds this distinctly color-conscious review: "Chitresh surrounded himself with a company of six female dancers, all westerners. They offer a seductive, colorful and friendly background. . . . [T]heir performance is distinctly pale alongside the powerful Chitresh. It was as though their main purpose were [*sic*] as decorative objects" (Tucker 1986).

It was suggested that members of the dance company wear black wigs in performance in an attempt to pass as Indian onstage. Gretchen Hayden recalled, "The AMAN Dance Company in LA was helping Julia [Maxwell] with promoting the Chitresh Das Dance Company, and they suggested we wear wigs—do *that* look. I remember talking to Julia about it and us both saying 'No way. I am what I am and this is the dance.' It had come up in terms of promoting us, but Chitresh-jī wouldn't have liked that idea either" (interview, January 18, 2003). Julia Maxwell responded to this suggestion in a letter to Pandit Das's AMAN-affiliated booking agent: "I believe deeply that for Chitresh to perform with wigged dancers would be extremely detrimental to his artistic stature, and also to his marketability" (J. Das 1986b). Perhaps responding to the above review, printed only four months earlier, she also proposed separating Pandit Das's solo performances from those of his company: "This will allow you to market the very best that there is, to sponsors who want the 'real' thing from India. Also it allows you to offer the Chitresh Das Dance Company as Chitresh's extraordinarily unique experiment in the West." In an interview with me, another dancer from that time elaborated on the effort to find a niche for the dance company:

> It was always a struggle in him: how much to perform, how much to teach—he knew he needed to bring the students along, but he needed to move so fast on the stage in order to reach his goal. . . . He wanted to bring the whole company along with him on stage, but he knew we weren't anywhere near ready to perform on the same level with him. We weren't really the main product, but we had to come along somewhere. It created a lot of inner tension and frustration that he couldn't make it happen as fast as he hoped. And so there was no peace, no balance. (Zonka interview, November 14, 2005)

Also in 1986, the CDDC performed *Class Tech* at Forest Meadows, an outdoor venue at Dominican College in San Rafael. This choreographed work attempted to resolve the dance company's "identity problem" through carefully

FIG. 4.5. Promotional photo for *Class Tech*, 1986. *Left to right*: Michele Zonka, Noelle Barton.

selected choreography, music, and costuming (J. Das 1986b). Rather than relying exclusively on traditionally showcased compositions, the performance used "all the footwork components of class," employing various rhythmic patterns or *chhands* (Barton, pers. comm., July 7, 2006). The organization's promotional literature describes this piece as comprised of "purely classical technique" with an "energetic, fast-moving modern theme" (J. Das 1986a, 21). Sarod and tabla accompanied the performance along with the saxophone, which the group justified by noting that "the use of Western instruments as accompaniment to the dance was pioneered by Allauddin Khansahib in the early 1900s" (21). The costuming, however, was more clearly and unabashedly divorced from tradition. Although the dancers still wore *ghuṅgharū*, their costumes consisted of leotards, sweatpants, tights, and headbands—dancewear more commonly used by modern, jazz, and ballet dancers (figure 4.5).[15] In the case of *Class Tech*, both the use of western dancewear and choice of title communicated that the company, at the time, was not promoting itself as a group of fully developed kathak soloists.

By the 1990s, US reviews of the dance company improved considerably. Perhaps the cultural climate had changed enough that the company members' ethnicity was not such an issue. Possibly by then the dancers had attained that "certain level of development" at which ethnic identity no longer mattered as much (Hayden interview, January 18, 2003). Or perhaps Pandit Das and his dance company members had learned how to preemptively shape the attitudes of their reviewers:

> His two leading soloists . . . are American—both blond, both subject to what he considers petty criticism for not being "ethnic-looking" in this exotic art form. "Americans should also dance these beautiful Asian art forms," Das says, mentioning the two American dancers, Marni Ris and Michele Zonka, and one of his [sarod] players, Christopher Ris. "The prejudices come from Americans, not the Indians." . . . And taking on the purists whom he considers reverse racists, he says, "I'm very tired with the ethnomusicologists, who are all white and are making these rules about who can do what. My dancers are not a bunch of fly-by-night hippies studying with a guru and smoking pot. I was in Marin County in the 1970s. I know who those people were. I refuse to have these women wear dark wigs. I want them to be blond. That's what America is all about, about assimilating influences." (Welsh 1994)

As mentioned at the outset of this chapter, Pandit Das's focus on teaching *taiyārī* and *layakārī* (physical "readiness" and rhythmic virtuosity) was also a key factor in the growing acceptance of his students by US audiences.

Developing Speed and Athleticism: Focus on Footwork

While Pandit Das's emphasis on athleticism and agility grew out of his own dance inclinations, it was also profoundly influenced by teaching non-Indian students in the United States. Gretchen Hayden reflected: "I don't know how it must have been for him to look at these very different bodies and try to make them work. So, I think he thought, 'Technique—they can do this and look good'" (interview, January 18, 2003). Pandit Das employed a "drill-drill-drill" method with her and other early students, and only later came to develop a teaching style that incorporated greater musicality, variety, and flow (Hayden interview). One element that remained consistent throughout his teaching career, however, was his emphasis on *taiyārī* through intensive training in the physicality of the dance, grounded in footwork practice that began from the very first classes.

For beginning dance students at Chhandam, the school Pandit Das founded, the first classes might often have felt overwhelming. Because the precise, staccato movement qualities kathak dancers employ with the lower body are so different from the relatively fluid and delicate movements of the upper body, absorbing and producing both at once requires a great deal of practice and coordination. By 2000, several exercises were developed to allow students to focus on one part of the body or type of movement at a time.

These sequences, focusing on *hastaks* (hand positions), *kharants* (stances), neck exercises, and basic footwork, were followed by exercises in which the hands and feet move simultaneously, gradually progressing in speed and complexity.[16]

If students began taking classes at the beginning of a session, they would be led through progressive stages of kinesthetic complexity in a fairly systematic, measured way.[17] If they began mid-session, however, they would likely be placed at the side or back of the room and enjoined to do their best for the first several lessons as their minds and bodies absorbed and adjusted to the many actions they were being asked to perform simultaneously. Often teachers of these beginning classes, members of the CDDC, would tell those students not to worry too much as they worked to grasp the various interrelated movements and to just "flail." "Flailing" applied primarily to the upper half of the body; regarding the lower half, expectations were more exacting. Teachers emphasized that the most important thing a new student should take away from their first classes is the basic *tatkār* footwork pattern.

Tatkār steps become second nature for a kathak dancer. This pattern consists of eight steps that can be thought of as two sets of four: right left right left (with corresponding *bols* "tā theī theī tat"), then left right left right ("ā theī theī tat") (table 4.1).[18] A new student will often first learn the style of *tatkār* known as *āṭh śabd* ("shabd"), literally "eight sounds." In this manner of producing *tatkār*, the whole foot is lifted from the floor so that sound can be produced by striking the foot on the floor. Through practice, students learn to hold their weight as they shift from one foot to the other and to keep their knees loose. They also begin to find that this striking is actually more akin to a slapping motion. As beginning kathak students become more proficient at *tatkār*, they are taught different styles of *tatkār* and are pushed to achieve progressively faster speeds.

Tatkār can be executed in a variety of ways; in *panje tatkār* (from "toes"), the heels remain fixed on the ground while the rest of each foot lifts and taps the floor lightly (▶ video 4.2, table 4.2). The most commonly practiced technique outside of Pandit Das's school is *eṛī* (lit. "heel") *tatkār* (▶ video 4.3). In this technique, the first and fifth steps (*bols* "tā" and "ā") are produced with the full foot as in *āṭh śabd* and the rest are articulated with the heels. On the fourth and eighth steps, often a quick "brushing" motion accompanies the heel strike to the *bol* "tat."[19] In *āṭh śabd*, each footfall entails lifting the

Table 4.1. *Tatkār bols* and corresponding steps

Bols:	tā	theī	theī	tat	ā	theī	theī	tat
Steps:	right	left	right	left	left	right	left	right

Table 4.2. Styles of *tatkār*

Bols:	tā	theī	theī	tat	ā	theī	theī	tat
Panje:	toes	toes	toes	toes	toes	toes	toes	toes
Eṛī:	slap	heel	heel	brush	slap	heel	heel	brush
Aṭh śabd:	slap	slap	slap	slap	slap	slap	slap	slap

full foot and returning it to the floor with a loud slapping sound, a technique requiring more energy than *eṛī tatkār* (▶ video 4.4). Pandit Das most often demanded *āṭh śabd tatkār* of his dancers. Whereas in both *panje* and *eṛī tatkār* styles some part of the foot is always on the ground, at faster levels of *āṭh śabd tatkār* the feet lift off the floor in such rapid succession that dancers do not rest their weight on one foot or the other. They learn to lift the weight of their torsos up off the pelvis to leave their legs free and loose enough to strike with greater speed. When this is done correctly, the dancer experiences the seemingly contradictory sensations of hovering above the ground while remaining heavy and grounded in executing footwork.

Tatkār, Speed, and Technique

New dance students would also learn how to fit this footwork into a specific rhythmic framework, or *tāl*. Speeds of *tatkār* are almost always performed in relation to the *tāl* and are defined according to the number of sets of *tatkār* completed within one *tāl* cycle. These speeds are expressed with derivations of Hindi numbers and the suffix *-guṇ* (lit. "quality" or for numbers, "-fold, times" [McGregor 1993, 269]). For example, *diguṇ* derives from *do* (two) and can indicate two sets of *tatkār* within one cycle of the *tāl*; *tīnguṇ* from *tīn* (three) indicates three sets of *tatkār*; *chauguṇ* from *chār* (four) refers to four sets, etc.[20] This method of defining rhythmic density requires maintaining awareness of an entire cycle of *tāl*. For example, in *tīntāl*, *diguṇ*—two sets of *tatkār* with eight steps each, totaling sixteen steps—fits into *tīntāl*'s sixteen-beat rhythmic cycle by executing one step for each count of the cycle.[21] In the moment of execution, however, dancers will focus less on the time span of an entire cycle of the *tāl*, concentrating instead on the *mātrā*, the temporal interval between one count and the next, and focusing on how many steps should be evenly placed within that *mātrā*. For *diguṇ*, for example, dancers are less likely to concentrate on completing two sets of *tatkār* than they are to think to themselves "one step per beat." Similarly, while dancing *chheguṇ* (six), the dancer will be more aware of the immediate need to fit three steps of *tatkār* evenly within one *mātrā* than the broader perspective of performing six sets of *tatkār* within one cycle of the *tāl* (music examples 4.1 and 4.2).[22]

+ first set

|Tā — theī — theī — tat — Ā — theī —|

2 second set

|theī — tat —' Tā — theī — theī — tat —|

o third set

|Ā — theī — theī — tat —' Tā — theī —|

3

|theī — tat — Ā — theī — theī — tat —|

MUSIC EX. 4.1. *Tīnguṇ tatkār* in *tīntāl*

Ṭhā (1)

|Tā — — — theī — — —|

Diguṇ (2)

|Tā — theī — theī — tat —|

Tīnguṇ (3)

|Tā — theī — theī — tat — Ā — theī —|

Chauguṇ (4)

|Tā – theī – theī – tat – Ā – theī – theī – tat –|

Chheguṇ (6)

|Tā theī theī tat Ā theī theī tat 'Tā theī theī tat|

Āṭhguṇ (8)

|Tātheītheītat Ā theī theītat 'Tātheī theītat Ā theī theī tat|

Bārahguṇ (12)

|T t t t Ā t t t' T t t t Ā t t t' T t t t Ā t t t|

Solahguṇ (16)

|T t t t Ā t t t'T t t t Ā t t t'T t t t Ā t t t'T t t t Ā t t t|

MUSIC EX. 4.2. Speeds of *tatkār* within four beats of *tīntāl*

The suffix *-guṇ* also can be used in Hindustani music and kathak to describe the number of notes or footfalls performed at a constant speed within the space of one *mātrā*. In this case, *tīnguṇ* (three) would indicate the speed of three articulations within one *mātrā* and there is no need for cognitive shift, such as when dancers performing six sets of *tatkār* per cycle (*chheguṇ*) need to remember to produce only three footfalls per *mātrā* as above. In this second way of using the term, what Pandit Das and those he trained called *solahguṇ* (sixteen sets of *tatkār* per cycle, or eight steps per *mātrā*) is referred to as *āṭhguṇ*. Reginald Massey uses this second definition of *-guṇ* when, writing on kathak in India, he suggests, "sometimes even *aṭhgun* (eight times the speed of tha) is used" (1999, 34).

Massey's use of "even" suggests that for most dancers, this speed represented the upper limit of rhythmic density. However, in Pandit Das's school, this speed (eight steps per *mātrā*, which they call *solahguṇ*) was quite common. It was taught in the second year of study and much of the repertoire students learned and practiced thereafter utilized *solahguṇ*. Many advanced students and CDDC members pushed to attain even greater footwork densities; after *solahguṇ*, faster speeds are often differentiated by the terms *ḍeṛhī* (one and a half times the speed of the last), and *barābar* (lit. "even"), here meaning twice the speed. Between 2000 and 2003, many members of the Chitresh Das Dance Company executed *tatkār* in the *ḍeṛhī* of *solahguṇ*, more precisely called *chaubīsguṇ* (twenty-four sets of *tatkār* within a cycle of *tīntāl*) (▶ see video 4.4, cue point 0:38). During subsequent years when I visited periodically, it became apparent to me how steadily Pandit Das and his dance company pushed their limits for speed. I returned in 2006 to find CDDC members working to produce thirty-two sets of *tatkār* within a *tīntāl* cycle: *battīsguṇ*. Of course, the *laya*, or speed, of the *tāl* was set slower as the dancers pushed to attain such levels of rhythmic density; nonetheless, the dancers' footwork was becoming faster.

The development of speed and athleticism in Pandit Das's style of training seemed to be in keeping with a more general trend in the development of dances in the United States. For example, in 2006 the director of grants at the San Francisco Arts Commission described a conversation she had with a recently immigrated Korean dancer who stated that she felt her dance had to become "more American." Asked to clarify, the dancer responded, "it has to be faster; it has to be flashier; there has to be more lights" (S. Wong 2006). Pandit Das also partly credited his development of a strong athletic component in kathak with the economic realities of competing with other dance styles for US grants: "When grant writing came in, I was in competition with ballet, jazz, hip hop, flamenco, and many other dance forms. Because I was,

I had challenges from both ends [India and America]. It was not very easy for me. I had to build up the technique in my students far more in order to survive" (interview, February 26, 2003).

Developing the "California *Chakkar*"

In addition to competing with the levels of athleticism found in other dance forms in the United States, Pandit Das cited sports—including ice skating—as influential to his vision of kathak. However, he expressed frustration at the lack of understanding of kathak in comparison: "[Kathak technique] is not understood. How can they understand it? It's very easy for figure skating because the commentators will say, 'now watch—can they do a triple loop? Let's see if they can do it!' Someone on the sidelines is saying 'that's incredible' and the people on the sidelines get excited; but do they really know what a triple loop is or what it takes?" (interview, April 22, 2002). Ice skating influenced his development of what Pandit Das labeled the "California *chakkar*," a dynamic style of turn in which both arms and feet blur in motion (▶ see video 4.5, cue point 0:20). In the technique for this turn, the dancer's feet push off the ground in a rapid succession of right-left pairings, creating the appearance that the feet are hovering off the ground as in ice skating. Its effect is enhanced by the height difference between performer and audience in most contemporary performance venues; with a more direct sight line of the feet, such theaters provide an ideal perspective from which to appreciate this innovation.

While ice skating was the inspiration for the California *chakkar*'s floating footwork, Pandit Das credited windmills with shaping the upper half of the body—in particular the thousands of wind turbines dotting the Altamont Pass that he watched as he drove weekly to Stockton to teach in the late 1980s. In executing California *chakkar*s, the arms seem to flow in succession diagonally across the body. From the perspective of the audience (the direction in which the dancer is spotting), the right hand draws upward in a scooping motion from the lower right to the upper left while rotating left. At approximately 180 degrees, or halfway through a full rotation, she raises her left arm, closely following the same path from lower right to upper left. As the front of her body nears completion of the full rotation, the left arm appears to crown the head.[23] The California *chakkar* is one of the more obvious instances of Pandit Das incorporating influences from his US experience into kathak technique. As this chapter details, his broader drive for technical and rhythmic virtuosity was grounded in rigorous *riyāz* instilled in him as a child, encouraged in the American context, and imparted to his own students.

Of his fourfold categorization of kathak elements, Pandit Das clearly emphasized *taiyārī*, technical speed and power, in his early years teaching in the United States: "In the world of art, *taiyārī* and *layakārī* is first . . . achievement of technical virtuosity. And *khūbsūratī* and *nazākat*, the beauty and the subtlety and delicacy of the beauty is like a matured wine. It didn't come to me overnight. How do you expect young Americans to understand that?" (interview, June 25, 2002). As he suggests, *khūbsūratī* and *nazākat* take time to develop. While he continued to emphasize technical excellence in training dancers, Pandit Das increasingly highlighted "the beauty and the subtlety" of kathak in his artistic creation and training methods during the 1980s, as his senior students were developing as mature artists and as he gained new students with familial ties to South Asia. Questions of how these demographic shifts and other life experiences influenced Pandit Das's relationships to masculinity and femininity, to *khūbsūratī* and *nazākat*, and to the practice of narrative *abhinaya* are explored in the following chapter.

5

Dancing Gender

August 20, 2005: Śiṣyas, *dance company members, and serious students gathered with Pandit Das for an annual multiday retreat at a camp nestled in the redwoods of northwestern Sonoma County, three hours north of San Francisco. After waking to the call of a conch shell at six a.m., we dancers sweated through morning footwork and composition (*bol-paran*) sessions. We then changed into dry* śalvār qamīzes, *shared lunch, and prepared for our next dance lesson:* bhāv *or* abhinaya, *the expression of character and emotion.*[1] *Instead of standing behind his tabla where he would typically dance and play at the same time while leading classes, Pandit Das reclined gracefully on the floor.*

"In my guru-jī's time," Pandit Das reminisced, "all the ṯavā'ifs *came [to Calcutta] from Lucknow, Benares, and Rajasthan. The* bhāv *was mostly sitting down—what you must have seen in the movies. But times have changed, and now we stand or sit, it depends. But if you sit and do it, then you take one line and show it in so many ways."*[2] *Leaning on his left arm, with his left knee tucked under and his right toe out to the side, he began singing one of his favorite* ṭhumrīs*:* Kahe rokata dagara pyāra nanda lāl mero *(Braj Bhāṣā: "Why do you block my path, my beloved son of Nanda?") (▶ see video 2.3 for a staged example). As he sang the line over and over again, Pandit Das took on the persona of Radha, devotee and lover of Lord Krishna, enacting some of the many possibilities of expression and intention contained in its words. With some of these iterations he displayed various shades of* śarm *(bashfulness) or* lajjā *(shyness), a stylized mode of female behavior typically expressed in kathak and other classical dance forms. In one variation, Radha was too timid even to glance toward Krishna, covering her face with*

a veil. Several interpretations later, he explored the other side of the spectrum: a worldlier Radha was annoyed at the impropriety of Krishna's public displays of affection but welcomed the intention. In yet another variation, Pandit Das suggested that "she found out something from the grapevine" and portrayed the anger of a betrayed lover. He also presented what he called a "spiritual" interpretation, explaining that although it could be perceived as sensual and seductive, "in the Indian context, always there is a double meaning."[3] *In this iteration, he sang the lines with his hands behind him, gesturing with movements of the head and facial expression only. Sitting with an arched back, this Radha accentuated her chest but seemed neither to notice nor to care, so lost was she in her need for communion with the divine.*

After quiet observation, the students, also seated, were encouraged to imitate Pandit Das's gestures. As we joined in singing, the melody shifted from free rhythm to a variation in dādrā tāl, *a cycle of six beats (see music example 5.1). Similarly, while Pandit Das's gestures had been spontaneous in his own demonstration, he next loosely fixed a set of movements for us to learn. The motions were deceptively simple; we raised our palms up to the right for* kahe *("what, why") and turned them over to indicate* rokata *("stop, block").* Dagara *("road, path") was subsumed by gestures for* pyāra *("dear, beloved one"); with our arms wrapped around our own bodies, we each threw a glance to the right, toward Krishna. As we tried to absorb these motions and make them our own, Pandit Das occasionally added narration to support our actions, such as "My beloved, you hold me like this sometimes," or he gave quiet verbal suggestions, like "Use your eyebrows subtly to give him the hint." Making his meaning explicit, he added, "You're using your feminine power."*[4] *Pandit Das encouraged us to go deeper into our own expression, saying, "Real* abhinaya *comes from an inner place." As we students began to feel comfortable with this particular set of movements, he added, "This is to give you an idea; in* abhinaya *nothing is fixed."*[5]

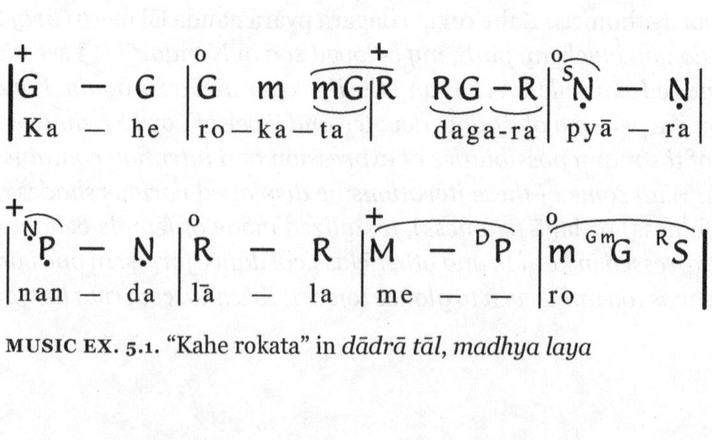

MUSIC EX. 5.1. "Kahe rokata" in *dādrā tāl, madhya laya*

While narrative enactments by solo kathak dancers are not uncommon, the preceding vignette might have been surprising to those familiar with Pandit Das's public persona; such audiences often knew of his speed and power as a dancer and did not associate him with a softer style of kathak. Although Pandit Das continued to emphasize physical and rhythmic prowess (*taiyārī* and *layakārī*) as the foundation for kathak training, grace and delicacy (*khūbsūratī* and *nazākat*) grew to become more central to his style of kathak in the 1980s and 1990s, beginning with a period in his life of change and increased introspection. At that time, his senior students were mature dancers, ready to delve yet more deeply into *abhinaya*, or expression of characters, which is considered by many to be kathak's pinnacle practice (Chakravorty 2008, 109) and one of its "most potent attractions" (P. Shah 2008, 3). Pandit Das's increased emphasis on *khūbsūratī* and *nazākat* also coincided with and was further influenced by the addition of South Asian and South Asian American students who joined his classes in increasing numbers beginning in the late 1980s. These new students possessed greater familiarity with characters from Hindu mythology and with culturally-specific body language, both providing some advantage in the challenging process of depicting characters through *abhinaya.*

This chapter considers the practice of *abhinaya* as well as other ways Pandit Das and his students performed gender through their dancing. By examining key examples of their repertoire from three different periods of Pandit Das's teaching—the first from 1971 to the late 1980s, the second from the late 1980s into the 1990s, and a third beginning in the late 1990s and continuing into the 2000s and 2010s—this chapter considers certain changes to the ways they moved, which marked a general shift from a more "masculine" (*tāṇḍava*) to a more "feminine" (*lāsya*) style over the course of several decades. These changes had kinesthetic and philosophical implications, as well as effects specifically relating to gendered interpretations of the dance. The chapter concludes by examining some of the overtly masculine aspects of Pandit Das's performance of kathak that endured or were even augmented over the course of his career. First, however, it will be useful to orient readers to ways in which dance terminology has been gendered in scholarly discourse and among dancers themselves.

Gender and Dance Terminology

As discussed previously, kathak involves two basic types of dancing: non-narrative movement (*nṛitt*) and that which explicitly tells a story (*nṛitya*). For both *nṛitt* and *nṛitya*, movement quality may be gendered as *tāṇḍava* (strong, masculine) or *lāsya* (soft, feminine). These terms for portraying style are regularly applied to various dances of South Asia, and appear in foundational Sanskrit treatises: the Nāṭya Śāstra, dated between the second century BCE and fourth century CE, and the Abhinaya Darpaṇa, from about the thirteenth century CE. Mohan Khokar clarifies: "*Tandava* is masculine, robust, expansive, *lasya* tender, graceful, lyrical. Evidently *tandava* is nearer to men and *lasya* women, but this does not mean that men alone can dance *tandava* and women *lasya*. The two aspects refer simply to the style of rendering the dance, not to who is qualified or privileged to do the rendering" (1979, 49–50).

In storytelling (*nṛitya*), each dancer is expected to utilize *tāṇḍava* and *lāsya* movement qualities to portray various types of characters, though these characters often represent "idealized versions of masculinity and femininity" (Dalidowicz 2010, 216). When a solo dancer portrays all the characters of a story, the practice can be called *ekāhārya abhinaya* (Shah, P. 2008; 1998, 12). As Pandit Das often told his students, "*you* are the masculine; *you* are the feminine. As you dance, you become Krishna; you become Radha" (field notes, April 8, 2003). He took this concept further by connecting performance of gender fluidity to Sanskritic culture and history, highlighting the image of Shiva/Shakti known as *ardhanārīśvara* (figure 5.1).[6] The deity's body is half male (Shiva) and half female (Shakti or Parvati), symbolizing, at the most basic level, a complementarity or interdependence of the masculine and feminine and representing for Pandit Das, the masculine and feminine energies residing in each individual (Kinsley 1986, 50; E. Goldberg 2002).

While the image may reify essentialized categories of male and female, for advanced Hindu practitioners the form symbolizes the "perfect symmetry of transcendence" in which gender identification falls away at higher levels of nondual understanding (E. Goldberg 2002, 3).Purnima Shah further notes "several sects within Hinduism hold that one can realize the spiritual essence within oneself only by transcending the social constructs of gender" (1998, 9). Following this concept, kathak dancers work to portray masculine and feminine characters with equal credibility. Shah describes a sense of "oneness" that may arise when mature performers engage in fluidly shifting characters and gender identifications (9).

In my observation, Pandit Das most frequently invoked the symbol of *ardhanārīśvara* to proclaim a general ideal of gender balance that could be cultivated through the practice of kathak. However, his early style emphasized angularity and other "masculine" elements of kathak described by Anashua Ghosh in 1981: "Chitresh amplified that he concentrated on the Tandav Ang [branch] of Kathak which one could loosely call the 'masculine' *ang*. It involves tremendous speed, power—not forgetting, of course, the clarity of movement." Pandit Das clarified: "Not that I don't do the Lashya [*lāsya*] Ang which entails the softer aspect of grace and expression. My Guruji used

FIG. 5.1. *Ardhanārīśvara*, drawn by Uday Sen Gupta and commissioned by Chitresh Das, San Francisco, 1970s.

to train his disciples according to their temperament and encouraged me to concentrate on the Tandav Ang. I prefer that, too" (quoted in Ghosh 1981, 5). Although he concentrated on the *tāṇḍava* elements, Pandit Das commissioned the image displayed in figure 5.1 for a brochure promoting his kathak classes in the San Francisco Bay Area in the mid-1970s, communicating, even early in his career, the value of integrating masculine and feminine energies.

Changing Demographics, Softening His Style

During the 1980s several personal and professional changes encouraged a shift in Pandit Das's attitude toward what he called "the softer aspect of grace and expression" (quoted in Ghosh 1981, 5). Leading up to and following the end of his marriage in 1988 to Julia Maxwell, who had been with him even before he moved to the United States, Pandit Das refrained from traveling to India for approximately eight years, describing this period as one of intense personal reflection. Grants for the arts were becoming more difficult to obtain, and the South Asian population in the Bay Area was growing dramatically. Pandit Das recalled seeking counsel from modern dancer Murray Louis, who had helped him twenty years earlier in India and when he first arrived in the United States. "[Louis] said, 'I cannot help you now. My best advice is to go to your Indian community; they are the ones who will support you'" (C. Das interview, June 19, 2006).

Taking Louis's advice, Pandit Das shifted his attention from his dance company of "blondes and brunettes," whom he praised as a "serious group of Pioneers who are helping preserve our Art form in America," to his Chhandam school. He observed that "a new generation of Indians is coming forth with their children to establish their heritage in the land of the immigrants" (C. Das ca. 1988). Indeed, following the Immigration and Nationality Act of 1965 that reopened Asian immigration to the United States after more than forty years of almost complete exclusion, the number of "Asian Indians" counted in the US census doubled in the 1980s to more than 800,000 in 1990 (Mann et al. 2001, 66). Recognizing the potential of these changing demographics for his school and dance company, Pandit Das began teaching classes specifically for children and adults of the *desī* (South Asian) community in San Francisco's South and East Bay regions, where the number of white-collar professionals coming from South Asia for study, research, teaching, and work opportunities was fairly high compared to Marin County, where he lived and primarily taught.

In approximately 1987, Pandit Das began teaching kathak classes in Fremont, in the South Bay; he began a similar class in 1989 at Ashkenaz, a center for world music and dance in Berkeley where he had been teaching intermittently since 1978.[7] Classes for the South Asian community began in both locations at the prompting of members of that community. Labonee Mohanta, who began studying kathak in the first Berkeley children's class, recalls: "He would tell us that after one of his concerts in the 1980s, a member of the Bay Area Indian community came up to him and complimented him on his performances, but asked, 'What are you doing to educate our children?'" (pers. comm., July 14, 2016). In Fremont, the students came from a variety of regional backgrounds within the broader South Asian American community. In Berkeley however, his students were, like Pandit Das, all members of the Bengali community, and they shared a common cultural framework that seemed to put Pandit Das at ease: "He had fun with us, the 'Bengali class,' and he wasn't super rigorous with us. We would do Bengali songs and things like that. He was still teaching the core kathak material, but we were going at a slower pace" (pers. comm.; figure 5.2). Despite the lighthearted

FIG. 5.2. Chitresh Das with members of the first kids' class in Berkeley following their *ghuṅgharū* ceremony, 1990. Photo courtesy of Labonee Mohanta.

nature of his teaching in Berkeley, classes did not flourish there as they did in Fremont, which had a larger South Asian population. After four years, Mohanta shifted her study to the Fremont location and realized how much more rigorously classes there were being taught (pers. comm.).

How was the demographic shift to teaching students of South Asian descent reflected more generally in Pandit Das's teaching and repertoire? The fast, strong footwork (which some critics glossed as "male") emphasized during his early years when teaching primarily white students remained a consistent feature of Pandit Das's kathak style throughout his career. However, the carriage of his students' upper bodies went through noticeable transformations. In this new phase, his style "softened" dramatically, resulting in different hand positions, upper-body movements, and repertoire. The relatively rigid, angular style that characterized the first decade and a half of his teaching in the United States gave way to rounder, smoother movements, sometimes gradually, and sometimes with dramatic abruptness as in the case of *hastak*s, or hand positions.

Changing Hands

When I asked about his own training in *hastak*s, Pandit Das responded, "my guru-jī never showed us; he would just say, '*hāṅ, aise karo*'" (Hindi: "yes, do it like this") (interview, May 11, 2006). Similarly, Pandit Das's early students were given little direct instruction. "We used to just look at his hands and wonder how we could make ours do those same beautiful movements" (Hayden interview, August 3, 2004). *Hastak*s were later set and standardized for his teaching in California and simply numbered "first *hastak*," "second *hastak*," and so on. While the use of defined *hastak*s helped maintain uniformity across Pandit Das's school, he still rejected a certain level of exactness in the details of these basic hand positions. In contrast to his precision in teaching footwork, Pandit Das preferred to let each hand position fit the individual dancer. In this way, he felt he was remaining true to his guru, who taught according to what looked good for a particular student's form and way of moving.

By 2000, the beginning of my extended period of fieldwork and training, a choreographed flow transitioning through several different *hastak*s was practiced in beginning classes, but the most basic position used—the one to which dancers most commonly returned—was second *hastak*. Until the late 1980s, however, the primary *hastak* used was what was later called first *hastak*.[8] In practicing first *hastak*, hands may be placed in front of the chest with palms down and elbows out. The top of each hand should be flat; the "pointer finger" is bent at its larger knuckle (the proximal interphalangeal joint) and curved slightly at the smaller knuckle so that the fingertip joins with the tip of the thumb (figure 5.3). In comparison to the angularity and rigidity

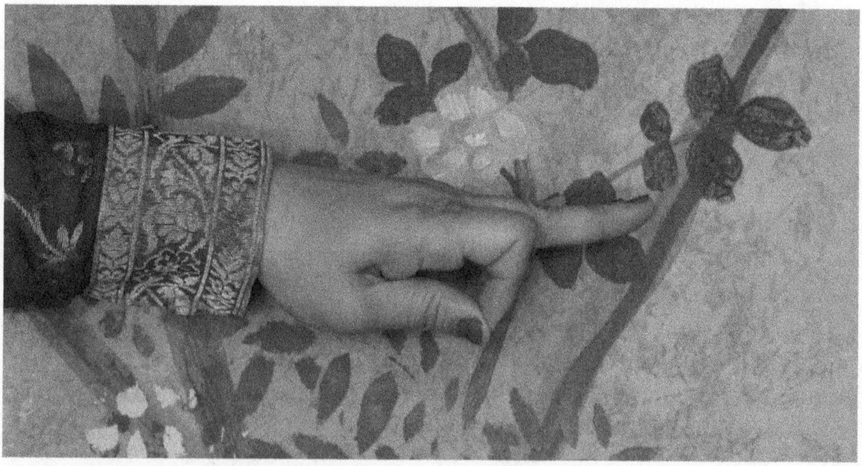

FIG. 5.3. First *hastak*. Photo by Rucha Chitnis. Courtesy of Seibi Lee.

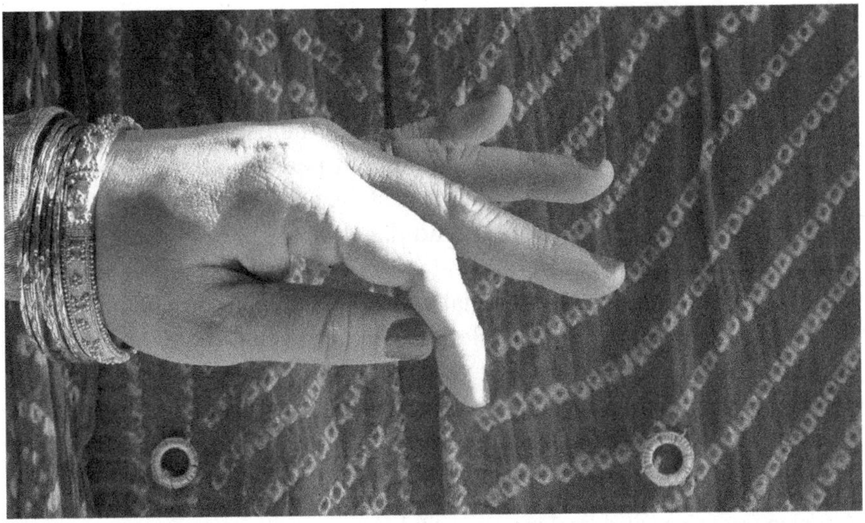

FIG. 5.4. Second *hastak*. Photo by Rucha Chitnis. Courtesy of Seibi Lee.

of first *hastak*, second *hastak* is more relaxed and delicate. The pointer finger, bent sharply in first *hastak*, is eased into a gentle curve; the tip of the thumb touches the forefinger between the finger's two knuckles (the middle phalanx), with the rest of the fingers fanning out above (figure 5.4).

A senior disciple describes the shock of transitioning from first to second *hastak*: "The 'first *hastak*' that he hardly uses now: he did not change from that until the late '80s. To me it was all of a sudden that he was using all second *hastak*. . . . [First *hastak*] had been in place for so long—let's say more than 15 or 17 years, and suddenly we had to change to this 'second *hastak*.' We wondered why for all those years we had to do first *hastak* with elbows up, and suddenly he softened everything and used second *hastak*? We thought, 'well, why did we have to go through that angularity?'" (Hayden interview, January 18, 2003). This shift from first to second *hastak* included a slight dropping of the elbows and signaled a more profound transition from a style of teaching relatively rigid movements and stances to a softer, more graceful style.[9]

Although the shift from first to second *hastak* took place rather quickly, most changes to the style Pandit Das taught involved a more gradual process of input and feedback within the shared space of the dance studio. While teaching, Pandit Das gave verbal and nonverbal cues and occasionally demonstrated movements, but he rarely danced in the front of the room for others to follow. In his earlier years in the United States, he often sat playing tabla as he taught; in later years, he regularly stood playing his tabla and performing footwork while leading classes. Even when he was dancing in later years,

Pandit Das's hands were still occupied by playing tabla, and thus he was not regularly modeling upper-body movements in classroom practice. Younger dancers instead primarily learned by watching and imitating the movements of more senior students positioned in front of them. In my observation, if Pandit Das liked the way a particular student performed a series of movements, he would highlight that dancer's style, sometimes by bringing that person to the front of the room to lead the class in those movements or by telling others to stop dancing and watch. Inevitably, we would try to imitate what we saw. In this way, small variations in movement accumulated to form larger stylistic changes. Thus, while some of the changes that took place over the years were abrupt and instigated by Pandit Das, more often changes happened gradually, and while guided by Pandit Das, they could not be attributed to a single dancer or event.

Altering Exercises and Performance Style

Along with changes to and greater standardization of hand positions, full movement sequences were altered in both minor and more substantial ways. When I asked senior dancers for examples of the angularity they described in early classroom materials, they often brought up an exercise danced to the *bols* "theī tā theī tā theī, theī theī tat tat."[10] During the first phase of Pandit Das's teaching in the United States, dancers performed the first part of this exercise, "theī tā theī tā theī" by pivoting their bodies 180 degrees to the back of the room for each "theī" (first turning to the right, then left, then right again), and turning to the front of the room again on each "tā." When turning to face the back of the room for "theī" (as pictured in figure 5.5), one leg supported the body with a bent knee; the other leg slid behind the body, with the ball of the foot planted on the floor. The torso tilted forward slightly over the front leg and the corresponding arm was held in front of the body at a 45-degree angle to the floor. In moving into this position, the other forearm circled in toward the neck and then out behind the body at a 45-degree angle toward the ceiling. In this position, the arms formed a relatively straight line, with both hands held in first *hastak* (▶ see video 5.1 and figure 5.5). Dancers stressed how difficult this exercise was to perform: "Today you dancers do it the easy way, but we used to have to face *all the way* to the back of the room on each "theī" . . . and we used to do it over and over!" (Barton interview, June 20, 2004).

In the late 1980s, the exercise changed somewhat, becoming less angular. The body still pivoted on "theī," though not as far to the back of the room, and the torso no longer tilted forward. The dancers' arms, more similar to later renditions of the exercise, moved in and away from the body in a swooping,

FIG. 5.5. Gretchen Hayden teaching the early version of the "theī tā theī tā theī" exercise to kathak retreat attendees, Craryville, NY, July 2015. Courtesy Gretchen Hayden.

curvilinear motion (▶ see video 5.2). By the late 1990s, each "theī" involved an even gentler 45-degree shift of the body. The arms pressed away from the center of the body with hands in second *hastak*; the front arm and corresponding leg extended to one of the front corners of the room, with the opposite arm forming a relatively straight line to the back corner, creating a set of movements quite different from those of the 1970s and 1980s (▶ see video 5.3 and figure 5.6).

The second half of the exercise, accompanying the *bols* "theī theī tat tat" also changed over the years. In the 1970s and 1980s, dancers bent their torsos far forward on "tat tat"; their arms dropped and fingertips almost swept the ground before circling out to the sides of the body and returning to first *hastak* (and later to second *hastak*) in front of the chest. By the late 1990s, this large, extravagant motion became smaller and subtler, with the dancers leaning forward only slightly and arm movement mostly confined to below the elbow. In this style, the dancers' forearms drop as the wrists bend, leading the movement; both palms are revealed to the viewer as their fingers gently straighten one by one before the hands and forearms circle around to return to the basic second *hastak* position in front of the chest (▶ compare videos 5.1, 5.2, and 5.3).

Another general shift in performance style involved the relationship of dance compositions (recited with *bols*) and the way they were expressed in the body. Dancer Noelle Barton reminisced, "Everything that we recited

FIG. 5.6. Seibi Lee performing a contemporary version of "theī," 2015. Photo by Rucha Chitnis. Courtesy of Seibi Lee.

came out of our feet, whereas now they're doing more arm [movements]" (interview, November 14, 2005).[11] As Pandit Das's style developed, he placed relatively less emphasis on precisely replicating the spoken *bols* of a composition through footwork—what was considered *tāṇḍava*-style interpretation. In this shift, percussive sounds produced by the feet became somewhat less important as greater emphasis was placed on *lāsya*-style interpretations involving flowing, rounded upper-body movements, on song and melody, and on *abhinaya*.

"Subtleties Come with Maturity"

The late 1980s and 1990s were a time of remarkable creative output for Pandit Das, reflecting his general embrace of *lāsya* ways of moving and working in kathak. "In the early period, I focused on power and the grace in power; it was no compromise. Strong, fast, and furious, not tempered. In the '80s, that started changing. Internally, that change came in me when I stopped going to India. I became more refined. That's the period when [the dance pieces] 'Hara Hara Mahādevā' and 'Sharpa Shirsha' developed" (C. Das interview, May 11, 2006).[12] While *lāsya*-style portrayal is more often associated with female characters, the two pieces Pandit Das mentions here involve depictions of the male Lord Shiva. With these two pieces, he broadened his approach to depicting Shiva—whose vigorous cosmic dance is itself the source for the word *tāṇḍava*. More generally, in this period, Pandit Das expanded his vocabulary for portraying masculinity beyond his earlier "fast and furious" *tāṇḍava* style, to incorporate "tender, graceful, lyrical" *lāsya* qualities (C. Das interview; Khokar 1979, 49–50).

Performances of "Sarpa Śīrṣa" by Pandit Das and his students generally portrayed Lord Shiva with a grace and quietude reflected in movements and in music. Sung in *rupak tāl* (seven beats) in *madhya laya* (a medium tempo), the melody he and his students often practiced centers on *Sa*, *Re*, and lower *ni* (tonic, the major-second degree and minor-seventh below, respectively, see music example 5.2). The song's weighty, dignified quality is emphasized by *āndolan* (a slow oscillation) on *ga* (the minor-third degree) appropriate to *rāg* Darbari Kanada, in which this version of the song was set.[13] Its lyrics and corresponding movements describe Shiva's attributes—"serpents and the crescent moon as his head ornaments, playing the *damarū*"—and praise him as lord of dance (*nāṭarāja*), lord of fire (*agnipati*), and lord of destruction (*dhangśapati*) (table 5.1).

These aspects of Shiva can be portrayed in various ways. For example, in the piece "Madan Bhasma" (described in chapter 3), Pandit Das depicted Shiva in his destructive form (*dhangśapati*) opening his third eye to burn Kama, the God of Love, to ashes by shooting a tremulous right hand out, away from the middle of the forehead repeatedly (▶ see video 3.3, *Twelve Minutes*, cue point 8:15). Performing "Sarpa Śīrṣa," Pandit Das and those he trained portrayed *dhangśapati* more reservedly through a strong sweep of the arms downward and away from one another, symbolizing not just material destruction, but also breaking the bonds of attachment and egoic identification (▶ see video 5.4, cue point 2:03). Lord Shiva, here, is presented as "benign yogi," "showing mercy."

Whether depicting male or female characters, the *lāsya* aspects of *khūbsūratī* and *nazākat* are, in Pandit Das's words, "like a matured wine" (C. Das interview, June 25, 2002). At a gathering in the spring of 2005, he described his own process of maturation in understanding and portraying female characters with *khūbsūratī* and *nazākat*. Pandit Das sat with his disciple Gretchen Hayden's older students and their parents in the Boston suburbs, getting to know them and, through his stories, allowing them to understand him better as well: "My guru-jī used to say that this is very good—all speed

Table 5.1. "Sarpa Śīrṣa": lyrics and translation (adapted from Das et al. 2001, 52)

sarpa śīrṣa ardha chandra	With serpents and the crescent moon as his head ornaments,
bājave damarū nāṭarāja	playing the *damarū* [drum]: the Lord of the Dance
agnipati dhangśapati	Lord of Fire, Lord of Destruction,
deva deva paśupati	Lord of Lords, Lord of Animals,
girijāpati mahādeva	Parvati's Husband, Great Lord,
karata dayā sada shiva	showing mercy, the benign yogi is Shiva.

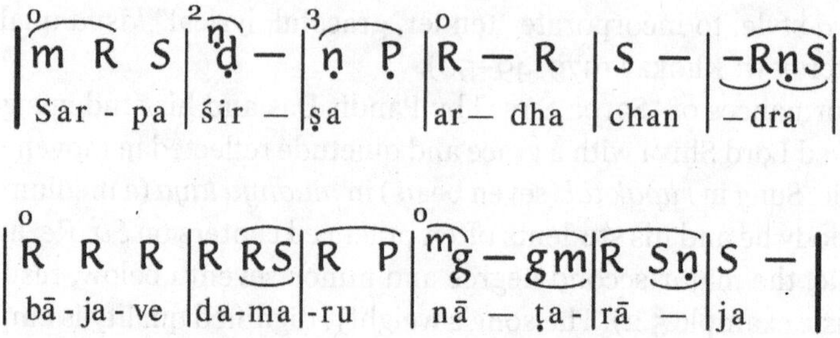

MUSIC EX. 5.2. "Sarpa Śīrṣa" in *rupak tāl, madhya laya*

and power and strength—but to portray *khūbsūratī* and *nazākat*—beauty and grace and subtlety—is the essence also. [For me] the portrayal of women, of female energy, was developed much later. As the story goes . . ." (field recording, April 10, 2005).[14]

Launching into one of my favorite stories, Pandit Das described the day when his father visited dance class at his guru-jī's house and young Chitresh was told to demonstrate Radha. "I was very angry. [I thought] my father has no business here. . . . So I started being Radha: 'Tā theī theī TAT ā theī theī TAT.'" As he recited the *bols* in a sharp, staccato voice, he demonstrated how he must have pulled Radha's veil (a movement representing feminine modesty) in a stilted, rough manner, getting lots of laughs from his informal audience. "I danced totally like a monster. My father looked at my guru-jī, '*Arre, yeh kyā hai*?' [Hindi: 'Hey, what is this?']" His guru consoled his father, who was appalled at how clumsily and resentfully young Chitresh portrayed Radha. "My guru-jī was—you know, Capstan cigarette in his hand—he'd sit like this." Pandit Das straightened his back, demonstrating his guru-jī's self-assured dignity. "He said to my father, '*Dās, usko zarā muhabbat kare, to milegā usko—rādhā kyā hai.*' 'Das, [as he translated it] let him make love first, and then he will know what Radha is.' Although," Pandit Das exclaimed, "then it *still* didn't happen!"

In this iteration of the story, Pandit Das said that he did not come to understand Radha through his first sexual encounter. Instead, he described learning about "Indian classical sensual art" by watching the renowned Odissi dance guru Kelucharan Mohapatra perform in the early 1980s: "And then I saw the great Kelucharan Mohapatra. [He was] fifty-five or fifty-six at that time—totally bald, slim, and wearing a dhoti.[15] He put a veil on his head, and walked out as Radha." Guru Kelucharan Mohapatra began singing a song from the Gīta Govinda, twelfth-century verses, which Pandit Das explained typify the conflation of sensuality and spirituality that is the hallmark of Bhakti literature. "Kelucharan Mohapatra sat there as Radha, and Radha was singing, 'Come Krishna, I am making *chandanan* [sandalwood

FIG. 5.7. Chitresh Das as a young man portraying Radha with her veil.

paste]. I want you to come here. Put this *chandanan* on my ear . . . on my forehead . . .' and finally she says, 'on my breast.' And we were sitting like this [with mouths agape], stunned. I have never seen anyone perform so erotically. This is not pornography; this is an Indian classical sensual art. That hit me very hard. I said, 'as a kathak dancer, I must do this,' and then I began to see."

Pandit Das also acknowledged the impact of changes in his personal life to this development in his dance style: "What happened also was that my life was changing. After my divorce, my next partner straightened me out a lot. She started making me realize what women are, actually. And I began to understand the sensitivity that we men lack. Lucky for me that I have the Indian dance with me, the *ardhanārīśvara*."

Abhinaya and Self Expression

Just as Pandit Das drew from his own experiences to depict various characters, he often encouraged his students to go into their "inner qualities," as he did in the vignette at the outset of this chapter. However, there is a distinct difference between inner emotion and culturally specific ways of expressing that emotion. Our kinesthetic repertoire, informed by daily ways-of-being in the body cannot help but inform the body in dance. As Cynthia Cohen Bull writes, "*how* any individual moves, speaks and symbolizes emerges from the intricate process of living in society" (1997, 270). And in kathak, the expression of characters (*abhinaya*) draws particularly from observation, mimesis, and embodiment of daily movement vocabularies. Pandit Das encouraged his students to pay attention to any and all nonverbal interaction taking place around them, and he even sometimes imitated "American" styles of flirtation in his performances. However, this directive was somewhat more useful for his students of South Asian descent, who were more familiar with routinized movements and gestures typical in South Asia, with common Hindu stories, and with the personalities and portrayals of various Hindu figures such as Radha and Krishna. While experience with particular cultural modes of expression varied among students who grew up outside of India, those connected to a South Asian diasporic community generally absorbed and could draw from specific embodied cultural experiences. By contrast, those who did not grow up in a South Asian community often felt they lacked some of the kinesthetic language required for the dance, leading in many cases to insecurity surrounding *abhinaya*.

Many of Pandit Das's female students, regardless of background, took issue with stereotypical portrayals of the feminine. One particularly clear expression of this sentiment came from Marni Wieser Ris, a member of the Chitresh Das Dance Company from 1976 through the mid-1990s, who told me, "The thing was that I could never relate to Radha; I would often get cast in these one-dimensional, soft female roles and I would say defiantly under my breath, 'Women aren't really like that!' . . . So I had a hard time with a lot of the traditional stories; I liked the pure dance, and I just wanted to be *strong*, and do all the technical stuff. And that's how my *Kali* piece began, because I wanted to express what felt vital and authentic to me" (interview, July 5, 2003). As she notes, Ris responded by choreographing and periodically touring (1994–2001) a performance depicting the goddess Kali, a female character with remarkably different attributes than Radha (figure 5.8).

> When I started researching Kali I was familiar with her as the fearsome goddess of legends, but I came to find there are many people who worship her as *Shakti*, the creative power of the divine, and see her with broader attributes—including an ability to take in the poor, sick, and helpless and administer to them in her compassion. . . . I depicted her drinking the blood of demons, [as] this was the only way she could defeat the demonic armies that continued to spring from the drops of blood shed from the wounded demon Raktabija. She drinks his blood to vanquish evil; she transmutes it; and this is how she restores equilibrium to the world. My intention for this performance was to show her breadth as well as to highlight the power of the feminine as it can be expressed through kathak. (Pers. comm., January 7, 2015)

FIG. 5.8. Marni Wieser Ris performing *Kali*, Berkeley, August 20, 1994. Photo by Lawson Knight.

Unlike stereotypical portrayals of Radha as demure and devoted, Kali is generally portrayed as fierce but compassionate in her strength, embodying attributes Ris respected.

Other dancers trained by Pandit Das also developed solo performances based on female characters they admired. These included *Meera* (2013), Rachna Nivas's depiction of radical Bhakti saint and princess Meerabai, and Rina Mehta's *Chandanbala* (2011), based on the story of the Jain *sādhvī* (nun) who, as she reflected, was "the kind of person who endures trauma but emerges with phenomenal grace on the other end" (pers. comm., February 3, 2017). In her production, *The Twentieth Wife* (2015), based on the novel of the same name by Indu Sundaresan, Farah Yasmeen Shaikh portrayed Empress Noor Jahan, the twentieth and last wife of Emperor Jahangir, believed to have been the power behind the throne of the Mughal Empire for many years.

Once reaching a requisite level of proficiency and creative independence, these artists at times judiciously selected the types of femininity they chose to portray, such as in the solo examples above; nevertheless, they also continued to portray a wide range of characters. Students from the span of Pandit Das's career spoke about the gamut of *abhinaya* required in kathak—and the dance form more generally—as a healthy means to access and express the full range of one's internal landscape. For example, Rina Mehta juxtaposed the confines of what is considered "appropriate behavior" in everyday life with the freedom of expression available in dance:

> I think [kathak] is one place in my life that I feel free. . . . I have the freedom to be who I want to be, what I want to be, all the different, millions of parts of me. . . . Growing up in India I am always aware of what is and is not appropriate behavior. And I can be appropriate in kathak *and* be pissed off. . . . I can push myself physically; I can be strong, but I can also be soft. . . . It gives room for every part of who I am. (Interview, June 18, 2004)

While I posit that the increased participation of South Asian American students beginning in the late 1980s helped encourage Pandit Das to emphasize a more fluid, *lāsya* style of kathak, this period resulted not simply in a more feminine style, but more generally, an expansion of his and his students' movement vocabulary and possibilities for gender expression. Though Pandit Das began privileging the refined elements of *khūbsūratī* and *nazākat*, the disciplines of *taiyārī* and *layakārī* continued to hold a prominent place in his training and performance. Prior to these shifts, which took place in the late 1980s, Pandit Das experienced an eight-year period of "intense personal reflection" during which he did not visit India. During that time, he began running several miles a day and to play tabla or hold weights, or both, while dancing. While shepherding his students into the realm of fluid *lāsya* and narrative expression, Pandit Das simultaneously was moving further into masculine performance realms.

Dancing Masculinity

In the summer of 2003, I accompanied Pandit Das on a visit to Kolkata's elite Calcutta Club. He greeted various wealthy and influential figures gathered there as quickly as possible without seeming impolite, eager to reach his chosen destination: the workout room. Stepping into the gym, we were met with air suffused with testosterone, sweat, and Hindi film songs accompanying twentysomethings pumping iron. Pandit Das was recognized by one of the young men, who was quick to offer a tour of the equipment. Stopping at the free weights, he deferentially demonstrated what kinds of exercises the dumbbells could produce, showing him front and side raises and overhead triceps extensions. Pandit Das politely watched the demonstration and asked if he could test out the dumbbells for himself. The young man handed one over and then quickly took it back. "One more thing you can do is this exercise," he said, showing him the all-important biceps curl.

I noticed Pandit Das suppress a grin as he waited for this final demonstration to be completed.

As Pandit Das slowly began to turn the dumbbells in his hands, testing their weight, he suddenly, confidently lifted both over his head in one hand and began to slap his feet against the floor using "takiṭa takiṭa dhina" and other patterns of kathak footwork.[16] *As he started singing in accompaniment to his feet, someone turned off the background music. With the attention of the entire room of muscle-bound Indian men, the then fifty-eight-year-old dancer in bare feet and a white cotton* kurtā *pushed himself to produce faster and more vigorous footwork. He variously held the dumbbells high over his head and moved them about in graceful patterns, culminating his demonstration by throwing one dumbbell into the air and catching it on* sam*—beat 1 of his self-accompaniment. After some stammering exclamations of respect by the young fitness buffs, Pandit Das took his leave. Several paces away, he flashed me a smile and half-jokingly asked me not to tell his wife about the episode.*

It was not only out of fear for his safety that Pandit Das's wife disapproved of his throwing dumbbells above his head. She understood that public presentations of his "dumbbell-dancing" risked damaging his reputation as an artist. In an art form in which, by Pandit Das's own declaration, dancers must master the four elements of *taiyārī*, *layakārī*, *khūbsūratī*, and *nazākat*, it was unwise to be stereotyped as all beauty or all power. Yet, throughout his career, the softer, more feminine aspects of Pandit Das's dancing were overshadowed by his flamboyant displays of speed and power. His dance persona was commonly perceived as possessing an overt, almost dangerous machismo, as demonstrated in headlines such as, "Chitresh Das—A Volatile Kathak-Dancer" (Panchali 1977), "A Hurricane-Force Explosion of Artistry" (Moore 1979), and the "Mohammad Ali of Kathak" (Abdullah n.d.). Dance scholar David Gere described his dancing as "a kind of divine madness" (ca. 1988), and another critic portrayed him as "virile, explosive, [and] volcanic" (Kothari 2004). While article titles from the late 1970s suggest that his style of performance was already considered masculine, Pandit Das further augmented this aspect of his dancing in later years, particularly by including tabla and dumbbells into his dance practice, and slowly incorporating them into his public presentations.

At a lecture-demonstration in 2003 organized for athletes and press in Kolkata, Pandit Das briefly displayed his practice of dancing with dumbbells for what he told us was the first time in a public forum. As he performed, variously holding the dumbbells in front of his body or pressing them above his head, Nimai Goswami, former captain of one of India's top soccer teams, discussed the mechanics of his dancing.[17] Goswami particularly emphasized the power generated from Pandit Das's hips and abdomen, as well as the lung capacity and physical endurance required. Though this particular demonstration utilized nonnarrative dancing (*nṛitt*), in other situations Pandit Das also held dumbbells while portraying characters (*nṛitya/abhinaya*), for example, as he delicately mimed pulling aside Radha's veil (the very portrayal he so resented as a young man). The challenge in that practice, as he reported, was not to let the additional labor of carrying weights diminish one's expressive depiction of the character (pers. comm., March 28, 2007).

While dance and sport often are positioned as "opposing, gendered, and often hierarchically related genres," Pandit Das worked to connect the two (Spielvogel 2004, 943). The following section explores Pandit Das's unique merging of dance, drumming, and athleticism as a manifestation of a masculine (or even hypermasculine) identity. However, it is first useful to situate this style vis-à-vis gender politics within the transnational kathak and Hindustani music communities.

Gender and the South Asian Dancer in Transnational Perspective

In its athleticism, Pandit Das's style was reminiscent of Gopi Krishna (1935–1994), whose "quantifiable virtuosity" as star of the popular 1955 film *Jhanak Jhanak Payal Baje* was "the instrument by which his character overcomes all obstacles" winning both his romantic interest and prestige in the dance world (Booth 2005, 60). Sunil Kothari describes Gopi Krishna's movements as "broad, virile and vigorous" with "bravado, bravura and showmanship" (1989, 190). In independence-era India, such male virtuosity was lauded by dance scholar Projesh Banerji, who criticized most male kathak performers of the time, stating that they had "mixed up the two [male and female] styles and [that] the modern spectators laugh behind their handkerchiefs, when they see a male dancer with his gorgeous dress attempting to show 'Lasya Nritya' with the crude gestures of a female" ([1942] 1947, 155). For much of the last fifty years, however, a more feminine style of kathak became the norm in India, led by the doyen of the Lucknow *gharānā* of kathak, Pandit Birju Maharaj.

Because of his energetic style, Pandit Das was often assumed to be an adherent of the Jaipur *gharānā*, which is characterized by its "fast tempo and vigor" rather than the Lucknow school, typically described as embodying "'femininity,' elegance and grace" (Natavar 1997, 213).[18] Pandit Das's stylistic lineage, however, was mixed. His guru, Pandit Ram Narayan Mishra, grew up in Rajasthan, home of the Jaipur *gharānā* of kathak, where he studied with his father, Pandit Gobardhan Prasad, until the age of ten. Pandit Mishra later settled in Calcutta and was accepted as a student of Pandits Shambhu and Acchan Maharaj, renowned exponents of Lucknow *gharānā* kathak and

Pt. Birju Maharaj's uncle and father, respectively. Although he mainly taught Lucknow-style kathak, Pandit Mishra also taught elements of the Jaipur style, particularly to students for whom the style was well-suited. As Pandit Das stated, "My guruji was greatly renowned for his *bhāo* [*bhāv*], the dramatic expressive aspect that is the forte of the Lucknow *gharana*. Having come from Rajasthan, however, where the dance is more vigorously technically oriented under the Jaipur *gharana*, he was committed to developing more power and speed in his disciples than is normally stressed in the Lucknow variety, to complement a strong foundation in *bhao*" (C. Das 1986b, 29).

The styles of kathak practiced by Pandits Das and Maharaj were often contrasted, by journalists and critics, scholars and students, and even by Pandit Das himself. Dance critic Sunil Kothari wrote that "today in the U.S., Kathak has two distinct faces," citing Pandit Das and his dance company on one hand, and on the other, the "Lucknow *gharana*, as perpetuated by Birju Maharaj and his disciples like Rita Mustafi and Anuradha Nag" (2004). In many ways, Pandits Das and Maharaj's styles seemed easy to compare, and located at opposite extremes of gendered movement.[19] Whereas Pandit Das was known for the speed and virtuosity of his footwork, in a style viewed as *tāṇḍava* or "masculine," Pandit Maharaj was known for the subtlety and refinement of his *abhinaya* (and particularly his portrayal of female characters), embodying the "feminine" or *lāsya* aspects of the dance. In a comparison of workshops led by each, Chakravorty encapsulates their differences by stating that where "Birju Maharaj emphasized the beauty of the form, Chitresh Das emphasized strength" (2000, 141).

These gendered distinctions can be read into various aspects of these two artists' approaches to kathak, which were of course also transmitted to their disciples. For example, Pt. Maharaj's female students more often wore costumes obstructing the view of their feet—a less common choice for dancers trained by Pandit Das, for whom showcasing movement of the feet is considered a more essential facet of kathak aesthetics. One might infer that the emphasis for Pandit Maharaj was on the upper half of the body, whereas for Pandit Das it was the lower half. In a comparison of workshops taught by each, Chakravorty notes that differences between the two gurus also extended to their affinity and affiliation with specific Hindu deities: Pt. Maharaj's "version of Kathak articulated the versatile splendor and beauty of lord Krishna, whereas [Pandit Das] attributed his dance to goddess 'Kali'" (2000, 142).[20] Pandit Das's spirituality was largely mother goddess-focused, and it is worth noting that in this dichotomy, Pt. Maharaj's "feminine" style of kathak is associated with a male god, whereas Das's "masculine" style is linked to a goddess.

These gendered differences are not simple dichotomies, and distinctions between these two artists' work do not fall along two-dimensional axes.

However, given the differences between these two artists, can we further deduce any relevance to their physical positioning on either side of the globe? Based in India, Pt. Maharaj was able to assert his style as the national standard, whereas Pandit Das was able to create a style of kathak outside of that framework. As discussed in chapter three, Pandit Das's positioning in the United States allowed him to develop his own style while distanced from the hegemonic structures influencing kathak in India. Undoubtedly, a more *tāṇḍava* style of dancing appealed to Pandit Das from early childhood and was encouraged in the United States, where athleticism was considered an important element in dance. But in further developing a masculine dance persona, he could look to other South Asians who had successfully represented their traditions in the West.

Of Pandit Das's three primary influences in this realm, Ustad Ali Akbar Khan, Pt. Ravi Shankar, and Swami Vivekananda (see chapter 3), Vivekananda provided a particularly compelling model as "a hypermasculine Indian/western male" (P. Roy 1998, 10). Credited with bringing Hinduism to America, Vivekananda loomed large in the consciousness of many Bengalis, including Pandit Das.[21] Did Swami Vivekananda's gendered positioning act as a blueprint for Pandit Das's construction and presentation of the self? Searching through archival materials in 2005, I came across a letter from Pandit Das's mother dated 1988 and written on stationery with Swami Vivekananda's image. Having similar ideas already in mind, I asked him why his mother would have selected that particular stationery. Pandit Das's answer was surprisingly precise: "Because he showed the way out—to the world" (pers. comm., August 16, 2005).

Like Pandit Das, Swami Vivekananda first traveled to the United States as a virtually unknown figure in his own country. However, Vivekananda's success was almost immediate and was trumpeted in India as a victory for the country:

> Vivekananda returned to hero's welcomes of a tremendous magnitude in Colombo, Madras, and Calcutta. The word of his triumphs had spread throughout India, and he was widely acclaimed as one who had vanquished the West. *The Indian Mirror* of July 18, 1896, had quoted an English newspaper, "The Swami boasts of having converted nearly 4000 persons to Hinduism in the States." An editorial on January 21, 1897, in the same journal offered this enthusiastic estimate: "The tide of conversion seemed to have rolled back from the East to the West—the tables were completely turned—and the Hindu mission to the West was crowned with a greater and more glorious success than what has ever been vouchsafed to Christian mission in the East." (French 1974, 69)

These quotes from the *Indian Mirror* at the end of the nineteenth century illustrate Vivekananda's significance in India as a figure who conquered the colonizers. But the West was also integral to both Swami Vivekananda's and Pandit Das's process of self-discovery. Parama Roy argues that Vivekananda discovered himself as "the swami . . . as Indian, as Hindu, and as male, an implicitly heterosexual male, in the west, outside the Indian nation-space," and that he "discover[ed] India in Chicago" (1998, 114). So too, decades later, Pandit Das's mother pushed him to leave India, telling him, as he often repeated, "only by leaving India will you understand India."[22] Swami Vivekananda's identity as "a hypermasculine Indian/western male" was developed in reaction to colonially derived perceptions of Indian men (and particularly Bengali men) as effeminate. While these stereotypes certainly informed and influenced Pandit Das, he also cultivated his "exorbitant masculinity" in response to tabla players, who represent the epitome of masculinity in the world of Hindustani music (P. Roy, 1998, 115).

Gender and Accompanying Instruments

One can extend this reading of gender to a discussion of musical instruments, for which gendering depends largely on cultural context. For example, flutes (and transverse flutes in particular) are usually considered the quintessential feminine instrument in western art music, but the shakuhachi, a vertical flute, is seen as a phallic symbol and is gendered male in Japan (Hahn 2005). Drums, on the other hand, are less often the sites for such differing gender interpretations. In many societies drumming has been the preserve of men; in some cases, women have been banned from or refuse touching or playing drums (Hagedorn 2006; Nketia 1963; Vosen 2001). In northwestern India, the *dhol* (a double-headed barrel drum) has such a strong association with men that "*dhol* player" is used as an epithet for "husband" in some Punjabi songs (Shelemay 2001, 190).

Just as instruments can be gendered, so too the broader categories of dance and music. As Foster states, "Music's visible abundance of 'structure,' its close alliance with mathematics, and the viability of its notation system carried a masculine valence that contrasted with dance's feminine ephemerality and bodiliness. . . . Enjoying the full range of stereotypic attributes associated with the feminine, dance was often viewed as ornamental or sensual, chaotic or emotional, fecund but insubstantial" (2002, 30). Pandit Das often worked to counteract perceptions of dance as effeminate or chiefly the province of women. For example, at a 1996 performance in the courtesan quarters of Kolkata's Bow Bazaar, when the son of the accompanying tabla player got up to leave the room, Pandit Das stopped dancing mid-performance and told him to sit back down and watch, stating in no uncertain terms that "dance is for men too." Further, the development of his technique of playing tabla while dancing—which Pandit Das developed to an exceedingly sophisticated level—seemed in part a strategy to prove his rhythmic virtuosity to male tabla players who had, in his mind, been unwilling to acknowledge the difficulty of kathak technique and the potential of the art form.[23]

After his impromptu performance in 2003 at the Calcutta Club, Pandit Das explained his actions to me: "The boys of the younger generation [in India] have to see that this dance is not a joke. They think that kathak is just about learning to pull a veil—and why shouldn't they think so? It's all they see" (interview, July 20, 2003). While such demonstrations were used as an explicit message to men in India, Pandit Das also made overtures to the South Asian American male population. For example, in a 1993 article in the Bay Area's popular periodical *India Currents*, he announced that he "would like to encourage a class only for men" (Zonka 1993). Despite this sentiment, Pandit Das did little to actively recruit male students until 2007, when an all-male class was organized, which Pandit Das proclaimed "the beginning of his[-]tory" (S. Roy 2007). This all-male class did not last long, however; indeed, over the course of his career, very few men studied with him, and even fewer reached even an intermediate level of proficiency.[24] Although male students of Indian classical dances are heavily outnumbered by women even in India, their scarcity was notable in Pandit Das's US school. What accounted for their absence? Was this simply due to a more general aversion to dancing, common for many US males? Was this a symptom of middle-class South Asian parents' attitudes that daughters should study dance and sons should drum?[25]

Again, a turn to Vivekananda and his relationship with his disciples provides a provocative viewpoint. Parama Roy suggests that "in order to identify as a masculine and heterosexual Hindu subject," in the international arena, Vivekananda had to "interpellate a fit female audience" and found western women the most suitable (1998, 114). Although most *guru-śiṣya* relationships in religious communities were traditionally male to male, Roy demonstrates that, for Vivekananda, western female disciples were "solicited as central to the project of imagining India/Hinduness and imagining Hindu masculinity" (92). In this light, the disparity between Pandit Das's enthusiasm as a kathak preacher to men and ambivalence as their teacher becomes more comprehensible.

As a teacher, Pandit Das's hypermasculine, heterosexual stance also perhaps served to deter male students (regardless of sexual orientation) uncomfortable with being subsumed in subservient, feminized student roles. Perhaps also, the fact that his students were overwhelmingly female left little social space for men to enter. A senior student recalls: "Kathak does demand so much *lāsya* and it might be hard; culturally I don't know if guys are ready to leap into that. I remember first seeing [Pandit Das] and it was amazing, but it looked really odd to me to see him pulling a veil. So I am sure that it would be difficult unless you're a man who knows something about theater or is drawn to this in a certain way" (anonymous interview).

As kathak dancer Vikram Iyengar notes, in India, "The male dancer—classical dancer—has been represented as effeminate to say the least" (2010, 229). In the United States, though relatively few openly lesbian, gay, bisexual, transgender, and queer/questioning students studied with Pandit Das at his Chhandam School, he regularly interacted with LGBTQ students in the kathak classes he taught at San Francisco State University (between approximately 1988 and 2005). Working with a number of LGBTQ-identified students and particularly with one student who was transitioning from male to female while taking Pandit Das's class, whom he mentioned often, prompted Pandit Das to problematize the heteronormative gender constructs he utilized in teaching kathak and to work to relate those concepts to his students' experiences. He later reflected: "How do you teach them *ardhanārīśvara*, which is a very masculine interpretation of male and female, right?[26] . . . I had problems. . . . I had to learn all these things 20 years ago in San Francisco State which I had *no idea* . . . what I used to say to them is this, 'if the two persons—if they're male or if they're women or anybody—if they feel that in their union they are becoming one, and they feel oneness, *that* is spiritual'" (Pai 2014).

While Pandit Das's experiences at San Francisco State University helped him develop a more inclusive understanding of and language for discussing gender and sexuality, the cis-gender heterosexual women who comprised the majority of Pandit Das's students over the years were, in this respect, relatively less challenging. Furthermore, their presence likely worked to augment Pandit Das's masculine, heterosexual, authoritative identity. But while it might be tempting to read his relationship with female students (and particularly white women) merely as that of a South Asian male guru reversing the pattern of colonization while maintaining patriarchal authority, this would be an injustice to the process at work.

Cultivating Strong Women

As dancer Rina Mehta stated, "He has had very strong women around him" and these "women *do* challenge him" (interview, June 18, 2004). One of Pandit Das's express goals was to draw out the strength in his students or, in his words, to create "a superior race of strong women" described in greater length in the next chapter. Pandit Das's focus on strength and power, while augmenting his own hypermasculine persona, resonated with US women of many backgrounds. Further, the strength he encouraged extended beyond physical abilities to include relative social autonomy and "self-assured femininity," although these goals were not always easy for his students to attain (Dalidowicz 2010, 207).

Many of the social issues navigated by women endeavoring to study kathak intensively with Pandit Das were similar to (though comparatively less challenging than) those often encountered by female artists in India. In discussing the study of music in university programs in northern India, Amelia Maciszewski notes that women were generally considered to be less serious in their studies because it was assumed that women were doing their degrees as a kind of "finishing school" unlike men, who were more likely to enter the profession (1998, 13 fn. 4). From interview responses and my own fieldwork experience, serious pursuit of the arts into adulthood was difficult for women in the United States as well. In choosing to train rigorously with Pandit Das, many women found themselves having to challenge expected roles in the home:

> [It's a] time commitment—in every which way. First of all [Pandit Das] is encouraging you to pursue something for yourself, because there's no other reason to do dance. It's not going to make you money; it's probably very likely not going to make you famous; it's not going to do anything for anyone else in your family. Purely the act of doing something that is your own for many women—and definitely for Indian women—is really revolutionary: to do something that is not for your husband, not for your parents, not for your kids . . . not for your family. So just the act of saying, "I want to pursue a hobby that is my own," becomes increasingly revolutionary as you commit—as you go from taking classes to being a student. As you go from taking one class a week to taking two classes a week, to taking three classes a week . . . then you start having to negotiate your roles at home. (Mehta interview, June 18, 2004)

In her fieldwork, which included taking classes with Pandit Das in Kolkata, anthropologist Monica Dalidowicz notes that Pandit Das communicated a similar vision of strong, powerful women, while modifying his message slightly for an Indian female audience: "He articulated a new ideal of a contemporary Indian woman as assertive and powerful and presented a lifelong path of Kathak that challenged the idea of dance as a mode of female refinement for marriage. He challenged the conventional patterns of female loss of autonomy and subordination of independence by teaching strength and perseverance in both dance and the everyday. In a creative move, Das uses his own version of traditional Kathak to counter the traditional ideals of femininity and women's role in Indian society, encouraging students to break with the traditional patriarchal model" (2010, 220). The "feminine power" Pandit Das championed involved not just the power to seduce (as described at the outset of this chapter), but also physical strength as well as emotional fortitude to withstand societal pressures and maintain one's dedication to dance. In US society (South Asian American and otherwise), where ambivalence surrounded the serious pursuit of dance, Pandit Das and his students supported one another in what was ultimately a solo practice and an individual path.

This chapter explores diverse ways Pandit Das and his students performed gender—through movements with specific gender qualities and associations and in their embodiment of gendered characters—as well as Pandit Das's gendered presentation of the self. Throughout his career, Pandit Das worked to subsume these varied gendered practices under one concept, *ardhanārīśvara*. Just as he developed his use of *ardhanārīśvara*, so he adapted his style of kathak in response to different generations of students and as he evolved as an artist over the course of his lifetime. The following chapter, situated in the 2000s, further examines how Pandit Das worked, both rhetorically and artistically, to create unity within this diversity.

6

Dancing Unity, Articulating Difference

This chapter brings us squarely into the period of my own field research; in the late 1990s and early 2000s, the Chhandam school expanded considerably in San Francisco's South and East Bays. The number of dancers studying kathak in Fremont, where classes began in the late 1980s, had grown significantly, and additional formal branches of Chhandam opened in Berkeley, Mountain View, San Bruno, and San Jose between 1998 and 2003 (table 1.1). While such changes facilitated an increase in the number of students of South Asian ethnic heritage, at that time, the Chitresh Das Dance Company (CDDC) consisted of dancers from a range of ethnic backgrounds—diversity that was the subject of intriguing discussion within the community. This chapter analyzes some of the creative and sometimes problematic ways Pandit Das manipulated concepts of race, difference, gender, and power to unify and catalyze this diverse group of dancers, and examines an innovative practice he cultivated during this period, called kathak yoga. In developing kathak yoga, Pandit Das drew on Hindu philosophy and his guru's teachings to bring together the musical, rhythmic, and kinesthetic elements of the dance in a new way. Sometimes translated as *union* (McGregor 1993, 845), the term *yoga* reflected the mechanics of the practice, and familiarity with yoga in South Asia and the West made "kathak yoga" an ideal phrase for appealing to and communicating his innovation to a broad audience.

Virtuosity, Spirituality, and Improvisation through Kathak Yoga

In "The Ecology of Indian Music in North America," Daniel Neuman cites several factors contributing to the West's interest in Indian classical music, including its technical virtuosity, improvisatory nature, and religious significance, exemplifying the "spiritual East" (1984, 13). Kathak, being the music's associated dance form, has also been distinguished by these features. This section of the chapter examines the technical aspects of kathak yoga and takes Neuman's insights as a starting point for exploring how technique, improvisation, and religious concepts served in marketing kathak yoga to a diverse population.[1]

The practice of kathak yoga developed in part from Pandit Das's real-world challenges as a member of the once relatively small South Asian diasporic population in Northern California. In Marin County, though in residence with some of the most elite artists from India, Pandit Das was removed from the support system necessary to sustain a professional kathak dancer, including a larger network of musicians with whom to regularly train. He recalls: "In the early days, sometimes the tabla players wouldn't be there. They would go away for concerts, because they were just at the beginning of their careers. So, I used to practice by myself . . . I started counting sixteen [*tīntāl*] with my tongue, humming the melodies of sixteen, and dancing. It was out of necessity that these things developed" (interview, June 25, 2002). The classroom context also required Pandit Das to provide instrumental accompaniment while dancing—formative experiences that provided the foundation for kathak yoga: "Also when I taught classes . . . there were no tabla players, so I used to play the *ṭhekā* and teach the class, and I would also hum the *nagmā* [or *laharā*], the melody of the sixteen beats. And sometimes I had to run the compositions that [my students] would be dancing. So, what happened was I had to maintain the *ṭhekā*, or how would they know? They wouldn't have the reference point" (interview, April 14, 2004).

Dancing Kathak Yoga

In practicing kathak yoga, dancers multitask within a set of integrated and complimentary practices, dancing while themselves producing the most basic musical elements necessary for dance accompaniment: *ṭhekā* and *laharā*. They recite the *ṭhekā* with syllables representing a tabla player's marking of the beats of a particular rhythmic cycle while singing a repeating melody, called the *laharā* or *nagmā*, that also serves to melodically indicate the passage of the time cycle.[2] Simultaneously, they produce all that may be involved in the dance, including footwork, turns, upper-body movements, facial expression, and sometimes even the portrayal of characters.

One of the first practices newer students will be asked to attempt using kathak yoga is *kramalaya tatkār*, progressing through various levels of footwork density while singing a *laharā* and enunciating the *bol*s of the *ṭhekā* for the *tāl* being used. A fundamental skill, *kramalaya tatkār* continues to be practiced and performed throughout a dancer's career with increasing

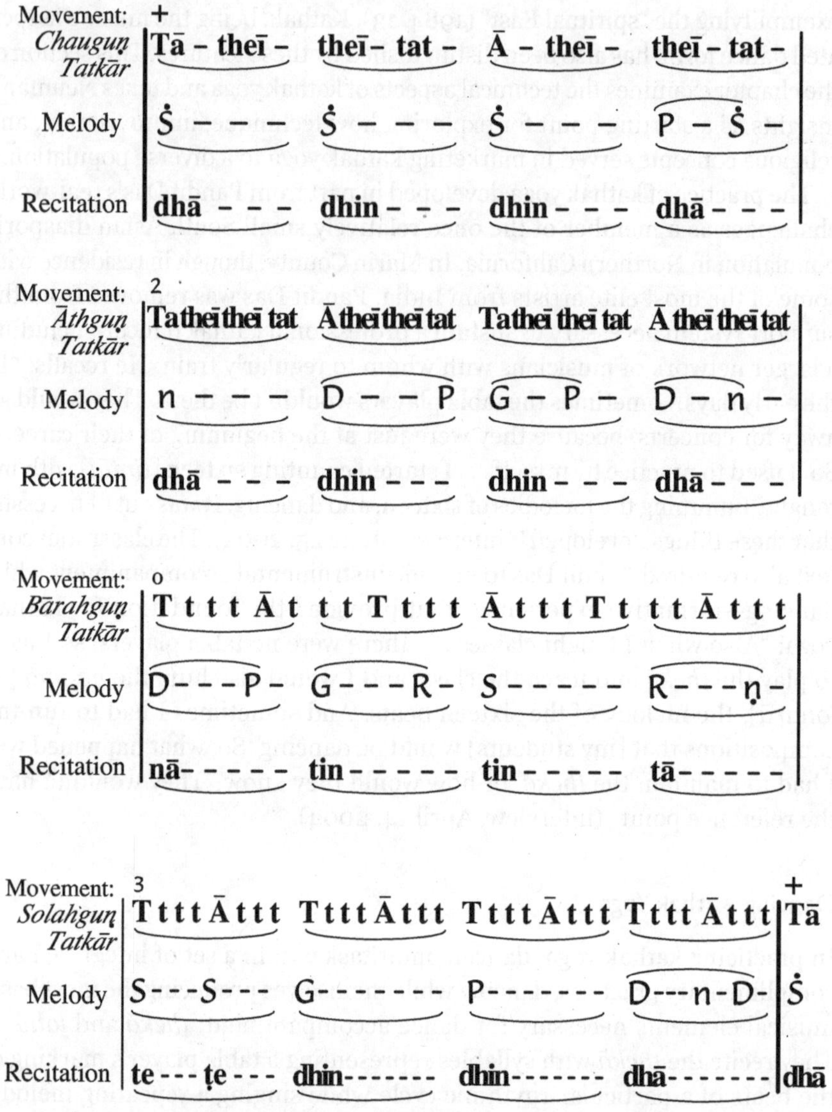

MUSIC EX. 6.1. *Kramalaya tatkār* with *laharā* and *ṭhekā* (kathak yoga)

complexity and sophistication, as can be seen later in this chapter. Music example 6.1 provides notation of this practice in an abridged version, including four possible footwork speeds (*chauguṇ*, *āṭhguṇ*, *bārahguṇ*, and *solahguṇ tatkār*) in one cycle of *tīntāl*, with a sung *laharā* (here in *rāg* Kalashri) and recited *ṭhekā* (▶ compare music example 6.1 with video 6.1, in which CDDC members perform a different, but also abbreviated *kramalaya tatkār*, and music example 4.2).[3]

Tihāīs, important cadential figures in both Hindustani music and kathak, serve as a productive tool for further appreciating the complexity of kathak yoga. Embedded within the overarching rhythmic cycle, a *tihāī* consists of a rhythmic phrase that is repeated three times. *Tihāīs* might begin at any point within a rhythmic cycle but typically end on beat 1 (*sam*) of a subsequent cycle (*avartan*). The *tihāī* to be considered here (in *tīntāl*) begins on beat 5, the fifth *mātrā*, of the rhythmic cycle and therefore is referred to as a fifth-*mātrā tihāī*.[4] Each iteration of a *tihāī*'s repeated phrase is called a *palla*, and each *palla* of this particular *tihāī* can be recited simply by counting from one to five. The first four numbers have a duration of three-quarters of a beat each, and the fifth number has a duration of only a half beat. Between each *palla* of this *tihāī* is a gap of a full beat during which dancers recite "one, two," each of which also has a half-beat duration (see music example 6.2, "Movement" notation). As with other *tihāīs*, dancers may execute this fifth-*mātrā tihāī* in a variety of ways. Those trained by Pandit Das typically performed it with swift turns (*chakkar*s) completed by a sharp slap of the foot coinciding with each number. In keeping with this *tihāī*'s construction, dancers must time each of their turns to have a duration of either one-half or three-quarters of a beat. And utilizing kathak yoga, one must keep track of the different timings of these turns while simultaneously singing a *laharā* and reciting the *bol*s of the *ṭhekā* (▶ see video 6.2, cue point 0:15, and music example 6.2).[5]

For both tabla players and kathak dancers, recitation is usually the first means of learning a new composition. Typically, a student vocally recites a rhythmic composition while counting the steady progression of *mātrās* with the hands. In kathak yoga, the oral and kinesthetic processes experienced in recitation are reversed: one tracks the regular pulse vocally and creates the composition's more complex rhythms with the rest of the body. Doing so serves to "get inside" of compositions, helping dancers develop a stronger sense of their place within the rhythmic cycle. Because this practice increases dancers' rhythmic awareness, ideally it also fosters the ability to dance in an *upaj*, or spontaneous, improvisational fashion (as discussed at greater length in chapter 7). In his own kathak yoga practice, Pandit Das typically danced in this spontaneous manner while playing the tabla (▶ see video 6.3, cue point 2:24). As a pedagogical technique, kathak yoga was first confined to singing, reciting, and dancing; however, as the practice evolved, his students also began utilizing musical instruments. Many learned to play *manjīra*—small cymbals that are used to mark time—while singing, reciting, and dancing. Some, following Pandit Das's example, practiced playing tabla, and others developed proficiency in playing the *laharā* on a melodic instrument (such as harmonium or bansuri) while executing the other elements of kathak yoga.

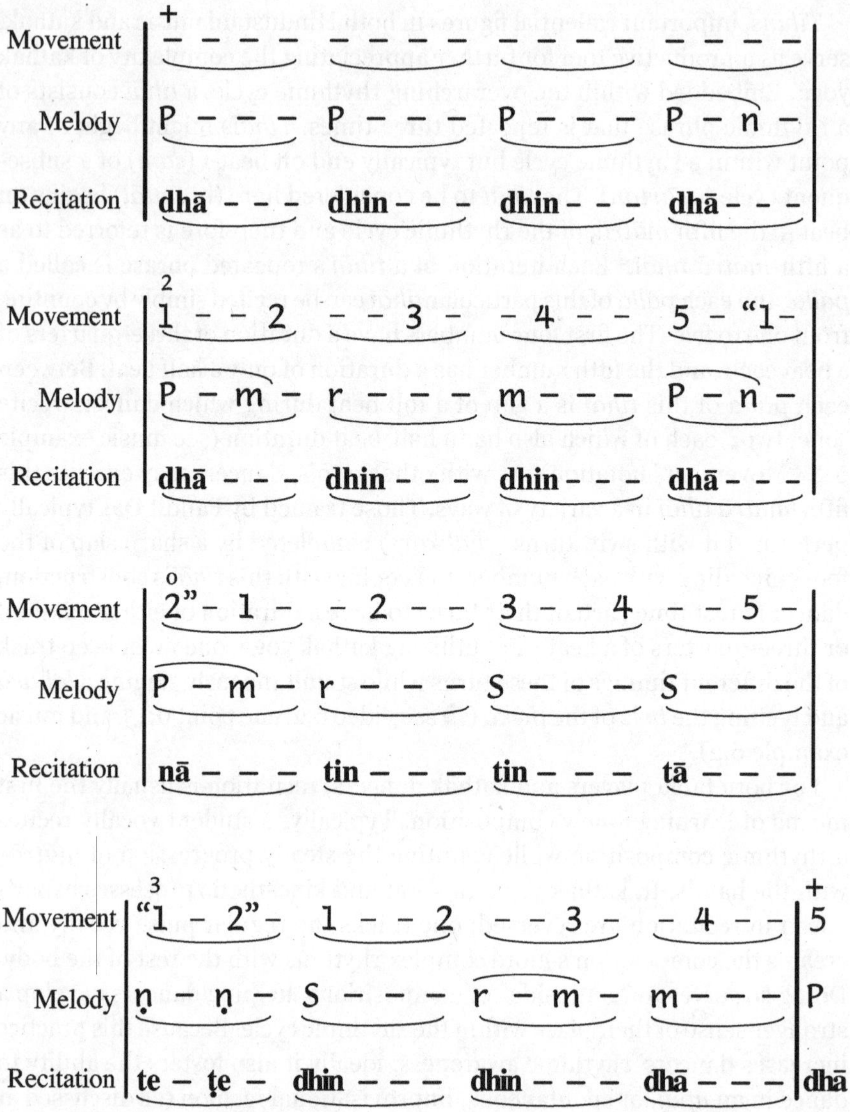

MUSIC EX. 6.2. Fifth-*mātrā tihāī* with *laharā* and *ṭhekā* (kathak yoga)

"Union," Yoga, and the Science of Dance

As kathak yoga was a new and complex technique, the term *yoga* served as a particularly effective one for communicating this practice to others. An internationally recognized practice, yoga was familiar to a broad populace and carried "prestige value" useful for conveying both the technical and philosophical intentions of kathak yoga (K. S. Joshi 1965, 53). In describing his experience of and inspiration for kathak yoga, Pandit Das frequently evoked images of sadhus or yogis, religious mendicants performing great feats with the mind and body (▶ see video 6.3, cue point 0:30). *Yoga* refers to a method of spiritual realization and—in its more globally recognizable contemporary manifestations—a system of physical postures, breathing exercises, and meditation techniques aimed at fostering mental equilibrium and physical fitness (Strauss 1997, 258; Van Ness 1999). Although yoga traditionally comprises several branches of practice, the goal is "union" through the "yoke" (another translation of the term) of disciplined practice. Connected to the philosophies of the Hindu school of thought known as Advaita Vedānta, or nondualism, the inherent unity of the individual self (*ātman*) and god, the highest reality (*brahman*), can be realized with the help of yogic practices (Pandit 1992, 80). A nondualistic sense of union can be experienced through kathak practices as well. For instance, Purnima Shah argues that through *ekāhārya abhinaya*, wherein one performer fluidly shifts between characters and genders, dancers experience a unified sense of self existing beyond gender identification (2008). But it is the rigors of *riyāz*, or concerted practice, that more directly informed the yogic path to union promoted by Pandit Das. The following passage, written by former CDDC member Michele Zonka, describes using kathak *riyāz* as a vehicle for experiencing a union of self and other:

> When I am deep into practice and the initial resistance of physical and mental exertion subsides, I enter a realm where there is no "other"—where time is no more . . . My body moves beyond its struggle with inertia and energy [emanates] from a well-spring beyond myself. Muscles relax into their disciplined patterns, and a fluidity of motion frees my body constraints. I have no wants, desires, preferences; all emotional requirements, responsibilities, and obligations cease. There is neither happiness nor yearning—neither going to nor fro. Every part of me is in motion and yet, paradoxically, there resides a continuous stillness, a centering that brings great confidence and harmony. Within this realm, I enter into a direct relationship with the Divine; a relationship in which my will is met in perfect union with Divine will. (Zonka n.d.)

Hindustani music practitioners also commonly use *riyāz* to facilitate connection with the divine, and an emphasis on the spiritual aspects of artistic practice is not unique to kathak yoga. In kathak yoga, however, the spiritual significance of physical practice manifests in the mechanics of the practice itself. Kathak yoga's assimilation of distinct strands of the art form—the melodic, rhythmic, and kinesthetic—within a single artist's practice reflects yoga's emphasis on union, and was so emphasized by Pandit Das. This relationship is also reflected in Pandit Das's oft-repeated phrase, "*lau ban jai*—make everything one," or as he commonly extrapolated, "dance in such a way that you become one with everything." Told to him by his guru, Pandit Ram

Narayan Mishra, this short phrase served to link the new and potentially controversial practice of kathak yoga not only to older and more widely accepted forms of yoga but also to Pandit Das's guru's philosophy, and therefore to the kathak tradition.

While Pandit Das spoke of the "oneness" generated through kathak yoga, his students filled in the blanks, couching the practice in the language of more mainstream yoga by variously discussing the mind-body connection facilitated by kathak yoga, or the detachment from ego investment the practice necessitates. Reflecting on the relationship between hatha yoga and kathak yoga, Pandit Das's disciple Seibi Lee contrasts the mental processes involved first when a dancer recites the *bols* of the composition they are dancing, and then when the voice and the rest of the body take on different roles: "When you recite the *bols* and dance the same *bols*, everything is in the moment. Your body and mind are in sync and are dancing to an [external] rhythmic source. But when you recite the *ṭhekā* instead, part of your conscious mind has to separate to keep the rhythmic cycle with your voice, and another part focuses on keeping your body dancing the desired *bols*. Keeping that rhythm along with the dance *bols* requires detachment" (Lee interview, July 24, 2004). Lee associates this experience with varying levels of attention to the breath in hatha yoga practices. "In yoga, when you are first learning, you are consciously thinking, 'I am breathing in. How am I breathing? Where is the breath starting from? Now I'm releasing the breath . . .' All this is in the moment; all your attention is fixed on the breathing process. As you let go—as you detach from the thought process—the breathing takes on a life of its own and your ego is no longer involved. There is no conscious, 'I am breathing in and I am holding to four'; it just happens and becomes a yogic practice." Finally, Lee relates the experience of simultaneously dancing and reciting the same material to "ego investment" and describes the challenges of maintaining a more expansive consciousness when performing several different but complimentary actions at once in the practice of kathak yoga.

> In a sense, you can loosely associate saying the *bols* and being in the moment with ego investment. And as the rhythmic cycle begins to take up part of your mind and your soul as you're dancing, the ego drops away. The yoga takes over and the feeling is something like an out-of-body experience. But it's a delicate balance to maintain and requires a lot of concentrated practice. Because there are too many things going on—the singing, counting, footwork, and sometimes wrists, neck and eyebrows, and breathing on top of that—once your ego gets involved, you screw up! (Lee interview, July 24, 2004)

While for some the relevance of yoga lies in its "ancient Hindu origins," some hatha yoga practitioners have also stressed its universality, emphasizing a "spirituality" seemingly not linked to specific doctrine (Van Ness 1999). Similarly,

Pandit Das's choice of the term *yoga* to identify this dance practice served to appeal to Indian, and particularly Hindu populations while also speaking to mainstream US understandings of yoga, thus bolstering his work to promote kathak as a practice with "universal" relevance.[6] As Dalidowicz suggests, the "intersecting cosmologies" of Hinduism and American "New Age practices" infuse kathak yoga with yet greater rhetorical potency (2015, 849).

Claims to yoga's universality were presented to Americans from the late 1800s onward, notably by Swami Vivekananda, who encouraged yoga's portrayal as a synthesis of the best of East and West, as a practice whose roots can be found in ancient Hindu wisdom, yet whose mental and physical benefits can be verified through modern science (Strauss 2005, 119–20). A century later, as Sarah Strauss notes, contemporary "presentations of yoga in Indian media . . . also tend toward use of Western ideas of 'science' to explain the value of yoga"; and the "theme of scientific validation" has been used for both Indian and western audiences "as a way of establishing credibility by showing that yoga is not simply 'traditional' and therefore irrational, but has the force of both time and rationality behind it" (120).

Interested in scientifically verifying kathak yoga's health benefits, in 2002 Pandit Das embarked on what he called a "kathak yoga experiment" with a lung specialist in Stockton, California. This series of tests attempted to assess his physical output when practicing kathak yoga.[7] Pandit Das and his students often stressed the benefits of kathak as a weight-bearing exercise, which, with the addition of the singing and recitation of kathak yoga, challenges the cardiovascular and respiratory systems, becoming a more effective workout. He hoped to prove kathak's efficacy as a long-term means of maintaining health in order to more broadly promote kathak in alternative health and fitness markets. Pandit Das was later the subject of a similar sports biomechanics study with Shayamal Vallabhjee, founder of Mumbai's HEAL Institute, which he optimistically pronounced, "will put kathak in the league of several aerobic sports and indicate the richness of ancient Indian arts in a global perspective" (C. Das quoted in Pawar 2014).

Kathak Yoga in Performance

Whether extolling the physical or the spiritual benefits of kathak yoga, Pandit Das emphasized its role as *sādhanā*—intense, solitary, devoted and devotional practice—often declaring that the technique was "not for the stage." However, as it developed, kathak yoga was increasingly included in public performances by Pandit Das and his students. At Chhandam's 2004 annual school show, for example, Pandit Das frequently stopped accompanying his students, prodding them—children and adults—to sing and recite the *ṭhekā* while they danced. He repeatedly described to the audience the difficulty and significance of what the students were doing, making kathak yoga a central feature of the concert program. Pandit Das first performed kathak yoga himself on stage in 2001 during the autobiographical production, *Sadhana*.[8] Conceived as an evocation of the history, memories, and experiences that influenced Pandit Das's daily dance practice, this was the ideal setting in which to present kathak yoga to the public.

After intermission, the lights came up for the second half of Sadhana *to reveal Pandit Das engaged in the mundane task of tuning his tabla. Unceremoniously dressed in athletic wear, with his set of 350* ghuṅgharū *wrapped over workout pants, he nonchalantly walked back and forth across the stage, occasionally launching into short bursts of rapid turns and footwork. After stretching his arms, adjusting his sleeves, and clearing his throat, Pandit Das closed his eyes and took a more serious stance. Singing a* laharā *in* rāg *Bairagi, he performed* pranām, *a short invocatory sequence to center and prepare the dancer for performance, typically completed offstage or at the beginning of practice. His melody then changed to* rāg *Kalashri; while reciting the* ṭhekā *and singing the* laharā, *Pandit Das launched into spontaneous footwork quickly culminating in a short* tihāī (▶ see video 6.4).[9]

Pandit Das's kathak yoga presentation continued for another eleven minutes, during which he showcased three variations of kathak yoga practice: the first involved singing, reciting, and dancing; in the second section, he additionally played *manjīra*; and in the third he exchanged his *manjīra* for tabla. As he moved through the initial section of his kathak yoga performance involving singing and reciting, Pandit Das performed an improvised *kramalaya*, incrementally but spontaneously increasing the rhythmic density of his footwork. A fundamental element of kathak practice and performance, this technique plays "an important role in the acceleration and performance process" for both Hindustani music and kathak (Clayton 2000, 157).[10] In this performance, Pandit Das explored various patterns of kathak footwork, including eight different speeds of *tatkār*, ranging from the spacious *ṭhā*, consisting of one set of *tatkār* (eight steps) for every cycle of *tīntāl* (sixteen beats), to dense *solahguṇ*, in which sixteen sets of *tatkār* are executed within one cycle of *tīntāl* (▶ compare video 6.4, cue point 1:58, with music examples 4.2 and 6.1).

Two years later, in a 2003 performance of kathak yoga, Pandit Das's disciple Charlotte Moraga briefly displayed *kramalaya* in *jhaptāl* (a rhythmic cycle of ten beats) before presenting various compositions in that *tāl*.[11] Her description of kathak yoga during that performance highlights a union of mind and body experienced in the practice: "Kathak yoga is something Chitresh-jī has been working on developing that requires intense focus and concentration. It requires bringing into harmony very different, contrasting and difficult elements. The dancer must recite this rhythmic cycle, while at the same time producing complex rhythmic patterns with the feet, blending and bringing into harmony breath, grace . . . it is a mind-body thing: mind, body, spirit, soul" (field recording, November 9, 2003). As Moraga performed kathak yoga in her "traditional kathak solo," the four accompanying musicians flown in from India and New York simply sat and watched. With arms folded or holding their instruments, they took in the performance, glancing at one another and Pandit Das, and shaking their heads in appreciation. After a particularly exhilarating *tihāī* performed with fast *chakkar*s, the most senior musician, sarangi player Pt. Ramesh Mishra stopped the concert and called Moraga over to the musicians' dais to simply and publicly state, "I am proud."

Since those early days of presenting kathak yoga, staged performances developed substantially in both difficulty and sophistication. In September 2007, the CDDC premiered *Shabd*, a thirty-minute piece entirely utilizing kathak yoga, in which all the dancers recited and sang. Each performer also played *manjīra* except for Rachna Nivas, who instead was featured playing harmonium (figure 6.1 and ▶ video 6.5, cue point 3:21). Over the following six years, the company performed variations of *Shabd* in the United States and India in which elements were added and subtracted while retaining the original concept and core piece. Pandit Das's disciples and other protégés continue to utilize kathak yoga in teaching, practice, and performance contexts; and a kathak yoga

FIG. 6.1. Rachna Nivas performing kathak yoga with harmonium in *Shabd* at the National Centre for the Performing Arts, Mumbai, January 29, 2010.

section has become a staple in "traditional kathak solos" by dancers in Pandit Das's lineage.[12] Though still not widely known, the practice was covered by the Indian media, including the *Economic Times*, which quoted Pandit Das: "I think it will be popular only 25 years after my death" (Molekhi 2010).

Diversity and the Dance Company

By 2004, when Pandit Das's Chhandam school show heavily featured kathak yoga, the school served approximately two hundred students per week, almost all of whom were "heritage learners" of South Asian descent.[13] The professional CDDC, however, consisted largely of dancers who first began their study of kathak in Pandit Das's courses at San Francisco State University; and this group, as might be expected, was more ethnically diverse.[14] Dance company members served as the public face of the CDDC and affiliated Chhandam school, performing as well as teaching classes.

The headline in the *Hindustan Times*, "In Perfect Harmony" (figure 6.2), was characteristic of the media's portrayals of the dance company as a harmonious assimilation of diverse individuals, united by their affinity for the art of kathak. Earlier, as the director of an all-white dance company, Pandit

FIG. 6.2. "In Perfect Harmony" from the *Hindustan Times*, January 25, 2004. Pictured (*left to right, top*): Joanna Meinl, Rachna Nivas, Anjali Nath, (*bottom*): Leah Brown, Farah Yasmeen Shaikh. Photo courtesy HT Media Ltd.

Das's attention had been focused on defending those students who did not look the part of Indian classical dancers, as demonstrated by his statement quoted in a 1994 article: "Critics have said: 'They're so white. They don't look ethnic.' When you say that you're not looking at the art, you're looking at the skin. These women have trained with me for 17 years" (Welsh). In less defensive moments, CDDC publicity conveyed similar sentiment under the rubric of US diversity. For example, a promotional pamphlet from the early 1980s depicts the States as a bouquet containing flowers of various colors, textures, and fragrances (figure 6.3).[15]

The use of the America-as-bouquet analogy by the CDDC carried into the next decade when, on the poster for a 1994 concert, members of the company were likened to flowers (figure 6.4). The poster's message can be read in two ways. The subheading, "Chitresh Das adds another flower to the American garland of cultural diversity," suggests that the garland in question represented America, and Pandit Das's company of US-trained kathak dancers collectively comprised one flower in that garland. Below, however, the phrase "Kathak Mala" evocatively dips to the bottom of the poster, visually connecting with the dancers' individual photos to form the shape of a *mālā*, or garland. This image suggests that the dancers each represented one flower in a kathak garland,

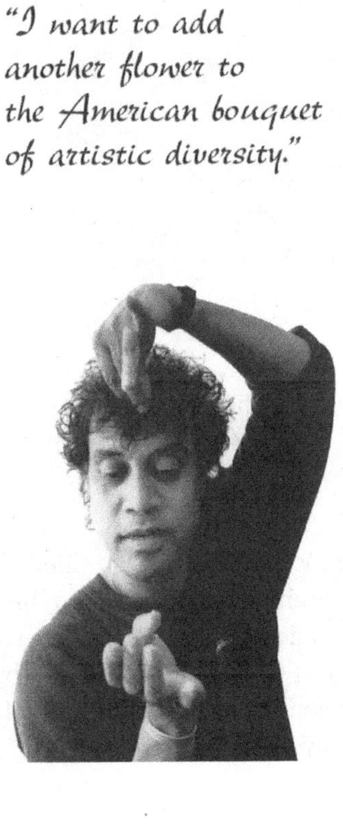

FIG. 6.3. Quote and photo from a promotional pamphlet, ca. 1981.

FIG. 6.4. Flyer for *Five Americans in Panch Tals* at St. John's Presbyterian Church, Berkeley, August 20, 1994. Pictured (*left to right*): Michele Zonka, Marni Wieser Ris, Gretchen Hayden, Jane Simmons, Joanna [Dunbar] de Souza.

seemingly one garland among the nation's many.[16] In the concert, titled *Five Americans in Panch Tals*, the five dancers presented five (*pāñch*) rhythmic cycles (*tāls*). Shared rhythmic foundations served as the basis for the performance's and performers' "unity" in *Pancha Jati* (2002), a production by a subsequent generation of the CDDC that was conceptually organized by five *jātis*—rhythmic groupings that might fit into any *tāl* (figure 6.5).[17]

FIG. 6.5. Image used to advertise *Pancha Jati*, 2002. Pictured (*left to right*): Charlotte Moraga, Jaiwanti Das Pamnani, Farah Yasmeen Shaikh, Seibi Lee, Leah Brown.

The five *Pancha Jati* (2002) performers in figure 6.5 include an Anglo American from Florida (Moraga), a Gujarati Fijian first-generation American (Pamnani), a second-generation Pakistani American who grew up in central California (Shaikh), a half-Japanese/half-Chinese Canadian American (Lee), and an African American dancer originally from the East Coast (Brown). Although in subsequent years this image was among the dance company's most popular and most often reprinted, the "cultural diversity" promoted in the dance company's 1994 performance was not explicitly referenced in conjunction with this 2002 image. Perhaps the company's discernible racial diversity meant that it no longer deemed it necessary to explicitly promote its contribution to US cultural diversity.

Racialized Discourse on Difference

Earlier, with a relatively homogenous, all-white dance company, Pandit Das confidently argued: "I refuse to have these women wear dark wigs. I want them to be blond. That's what America is all about, about assimilating influences" (Welsh 1994). The addition of South Asian American dancers helped to legitimize the dance company while they and other dancers of color also complicated Pandit Das's message. His subsequent phrase, "a superior race of strong, powerful women," initially used only in dance company rehearsals or other contexts with his senior students, notably succeeded in subsuming all these dancers' identities under the same phrase, acknowledging racial difference and dismissing it in the same breath.

During the years of my field research, Pandit Das would boldly assert phrases such as "I am creating a superior race of strong women!" so frequently that they became favorite refrains among his most serious students, all of whom were women. Pandit Das would recite these refrains day after day, playing with them, reworking and exploring their many facets, much in the same way as when performing *bhāv*, he might sing one line of poetry over and over, enacting the limitless emotions suggested therein. Just as the dancing portions of class were often a place for Pandit Das to work out kinesthetic ideas, his lectures acted as a discursive site in which to make sense of his and his students' unique place in the world of kathak.

The phrases "a superior race of strong women" and "a superior race of strong, powerful women" initially seemed to undermine mainstream notions of race, unifying these dancers not through shared racial identity but through their commonality as women and their shared commitment to artistic excellence. Common notions of gender were themselves reframed, as women were portrayed and defined by their strength and power. But while Pandit Das mapped meaning onto the group that was both universalizing and empowering, it was also problematic. He may have worked to redefine race in terms of gender identity and power, but the interpretation of power in this context was largely masculine. As discussed in the previous chapter, particular notions of power were manifest in Pandit Das's artistic expression. The style of kathak he promoted was distinctly fast and athletic, emphasizing footwork, swift turns, and improvisation. While in part due to Pandit Das's training and artistic temperament, this orientation also arose as a response to the challenges of teaching non-Indian students, for whom *taiyārī* and *layakārī*, agility and rhythmic sophistication, served as more objective measures of a dancer's skill than the subtleties of facial expression and storytelling. Additionally, Pandit Das's emphasis on speed and power may be interpreted as a response to the general American dance environment, in which many forms of dance and sport underwent "extreme" transformations in the last decades of the twentieth century (Rinehart and Sydnor 2003). Strength, in Pandit Das's "superior race of strong, powerful women" phrase, also suggested the emotional resilience and stamina necessary to persevere through grueling years of disciplined training. But just as this phrase seemed to praise his students on the grounds of their power, they remained in asymmetrical power relationships with him, demonstrated in this situation by the very fact that it was Pandit Das who held the power to name.

Another of his common refrains was to proclaim himself "guru of the *mlecchas*." Using a Sanskrit word for barbarians, Pandit Das reversed a colonialist construction of the Third World as heathen or barbarous by implying that it was the non-Indians who were barbarians. But he similarly challenged assumptions of what it meant to be Indian in diasporic contexts; on at least two occasions, I was in the classroom when he called himself "guru of the *mlecchas*" in the presence of South Asian guests—outsiders to his kathak community. He then would allow for a pause just long enough for grins to cross the faces of the guests before adding, "not just the Whites, the Indian-origins too—they are just as American as the others" (field notes July 27, 2003, and June 15, 2004).

Pandit Das's own means of self-identification similarly complicated assumptions; originally from Bengal with a Rajasthani guru, he described himself as "a Bengali Rajput Californian," a unique synthesis of multiple identities. Within the classroom, however, differences within and between groups were commonly expressed in the binary oppositions of "Indian" and "White," "Indian" and "non-Indian," or even more problematic, "Indian" and "American." Though I often heard these categories being used, they did not adequately represent the community's internal diversity or members' commonalities as citizens and long-term residents of the United States.

Deborah Wong reminds us that "to be American and to think about race means engaging with Whiteness and all its performances, yet this encompassing racialization is perhaps the most under-theorized embodiment of all, and therein lies its power" (2000, 58). Within this kathak community, whiteness became a marked category in the dialectical construction of "Indian" and "White" often used as shorthand in racial discourse. "Indian" sometimes rephrased as "Indian-origin" was a category subsuming all students of South Asian descent, including first-, one-and-a-half-, second-, and third-generation Indian, Bangladeshi, and Pakistani American students and students from the South Asian Caribbean diaspora. "White" in these instances indicated everyone else, including East Asian American and African American dancers. In this context, whiteness was constructed as an absence of South Asian culture or ancestry. For example, a fellow student of South Asian descent described a class in which Pandit Das asked us each to perform something one by one. When only non–South Asian dancers could accomplish the task to Pandit Das's satisfaction, he used racial difference to push his South Asian American students. As she recalled, "He said, 'The white women are doing it—why can't you *desīs*?'" This might have been unremarkable except that the two "white" dancers in the situation included me, a white woman, and an African American dancer.

Pandit Das's relative lack of distinction between different kinds of non-Indian-ness using the rubric of "whiteness" may derive from his early US experiences in majority-white communities. His students, however, did not always generalize whiteness in the same way, sometimes distinguishing between different kinds of whiteness in interesting ways. For example, in another conversation, a different dance-sister of South Asian descent reframed the category "white" to indicate a lack of Indian cultural knowledge when she said to me: "I hate when white people try to say—" and then stopped herself, saying, "I don't mean you, I mean *real* whites" (pers. comm., October 9, 2004). In other instances, whiteness indexed not just a lack of knowledge but a particular form of inauthentic knowledge associated with the hippie movement of the 1960s and 1970s.

On the Insecurities of Whiteness

In 2002, Charlotte Moraga discussed with me her perspective as a white person involved in kathak: "Actually that's my biggest issue—not being Indian, the ethnicity. Yeah, it's my biggest issue. Because . . ." Her voice trailed off, and when she began speaking again, it was on safer terrain: "Well, there are a lot of issues: there's family, there's having to make money, age, and all that" (interview, December 19, 2002). Later in the conversation she returned to the subject: "Kathak is not just [about] being pretty; it's being Indian. If you're not Indian, there are a lot of assumptions. People assume that if you're older and you're white, you must be some New Age hippie that's into the—I don't know, some kind of escape. . . . It's not really within you; it's not really authentic. You're trying to reach out and assume something else because you're unsatisfied." She then contrasted these assumptions with her own reasons for studying kathak: "I never felt that way about kathak. I've never done it because it's Indian. I've never done it because it's spiritually enlightening. I've just done it because it's *physically really cool*. It's really a challenge, and I just love to dance."

As she spoke, the initial discomfort I perceived in her voice faded, and in discussing the kinesthetic elements of the dance she conveyed yet greater ease and a positive tone. Like Das's construction of "a superior race of strong women," the power and physicality of the practice seemed to be her primary draw to kathak, and a defense against the negative stereotypes of hippiedom or New Age spirituality.[18] While spiritual connotations were a fundamental part of the appeal of Indian cultural practices for western seekers for decades, many serious practitioners I encountered sought to disassociate from the stereotype. In informal conversations I found that some older white students at the Ali Akbar College of Music similarly emphasized their interest in the "purely musical" aspects of their music studies and disengaged from more spiritual facets of the practice. I have not been immune from similar feelings of defensiveness, and I suspect that at some point in their careers many non–South Asian ethnomusicologists who study the region may have held concerns that a perception that their studies developed out of spiritual interests might diminish the legitimacy of their scholarship. For example, ethnomusicologist Stephen Slawek cites an instance of one scholar jokingly calling those attracted to Indian music people seeking "instant enlightenment" (1996, 31). Slawek suggests that this dismissive attitude affects academic writing in which "the ramifications of . . . the 'spiritual component' of Indian music remain understated" by western scholars who "felt compelled not only to distance themselves from the spirituality trope, but also to subvert the trope within their own discourse" (31).

Teaching "Indians" and "Non-Indians"

When I conducted fieldwork in the first few years of the twenty-first century, many dancers in the CDDC and the larger community felt that students of South Asian origin were pushed harder in class than were non–South Asians and were more readily called to task for mistakes in both dance and etiquette. In my presence, Pandit Das had often justified this approach as a means of breaking down any sense of entitlement South Asian American students might feel for the dance form. Were his comments in these instances influenced by aspects of my identity as one of his kathak students, as a researcher conducting fieldwork in the community, as a "non-Indian"? One evening during a 2004 trip to the Bay Area to visit Pandit Das and his students, I gained more insight into how his responses in discussions about training "Indians" and "non-Indians" might have been adapted to suit differing contexts and audiences. After we had dinner with a senior student and her husband (both Indian American), the husband began asking Pandit Das why—from the husband's perspective—he was so hard on his Indian students. This time, Pandit Das did not respond as I had usually witnessed; instead, his response focused on why he tended to ignore the "non-Indians."

> HUSBAND: "Is it not also true sometimes that non-Indians also are not doing as well, and you say something? Did that—"
>
> PANDIT DAS: "I don't say so much, but I kind of ignore them and they *fade out.*"
>
> STUDENT: "Who fades out?"
>
> PANDIT DAS: "They fade out, non-Indians. . . . They feel very sensitive that they are not Indians, so they cannot do this [or] that. But when they see a lot of Indians don't know to speak in Indian language[s], they find: OK, that is also there." (field recording, June 19, 2004)

Pandit Das's reply indicated that he expected non-Indians, who were then minorities in this kathak community, would give up on their studies of the dance form more readily. In this instance, he justified disparities in his teaching not by addressing why he was hard on Indian students, but why he was comparatively gentle with non-Indians who would tend to "fade out" unless they realized that some of the Indian students also lacked certain cultural knowledge, such as speaking an indigenous South Asian language. Although in that period, just after the turn of the twenty-first century, Pandit Das may have spent less energy on non-Indian students until they made a greater commitment to the dance, this certainly was not the case in earlier decades, when almost all his students were non-Indian. By the first few years of the new century, however, Pandit Das was investing more time and attention in understanding and articulating the dance's relevance for a growing population of South Asian American kathak students.

Negotiating South Asian Experiences and Identities

In Pandit Das's US kathak community, racial and ethnic categorizations played into dancers' experiences in ways that were complex, multifaceted, and changing depending on context. While non–South Asians contended with assumptions regarding their reasons for studying kathak and their level of expertise, South Asian American students—a newer demographic group for Pandit Das—experienced a different set of challenges. With non–South Asian affinity learners, Pandit Das's role as a representative of Indian culture was clear and uncontested; these students often took his perspectives on Indian culture at face value. Heritage learners, on the other hand, had more complex and subtle understandings of South Asian culture. Their families usually had ties to specific regions of South Asia; they sometimes spoke different languages and had religious and cultural practices that differed from Pandit Das's. They thus came into the study of kathak with their own, often competing beliefs and ideas about Indian culture. Rina Mehta, a kathak artist trained by Pandit Das described this complex relationship:

> Being a South Asian student in his classroom is difficult. I think there's much more that goes on between him and his South Asian students—him telling you to hold on to your cultural heritage, you [asking yourself], "What is my cultural heritage?" What I think my cultural heritage is [is] different than what he thinks my cultural heritage is. . . . It clashes because you have your own versions of what is Indian, and what it means to be Indian. And I think there's much more contention there . . . It's not an open dialogue, but it's definitely more of a conversation that's happening with him and his South Asian students . . . a negotiation. (Mehta interview, June 18, 2003)

Mehta also discussed the sometimes-fraught relationship between South Asian American family expectations and responsibilities as a dancer:

> As relatively new immigrants to this country, I think that there's a huge emphasis on making it financially—being successful. And people just don't think

> of dance as a viable profession. People cannot move past seeing dance as a hobby. In the Indian community dance is fine, [but only] as a hobby. Like, "it's, it's very nice that you're a well-rounded individual," and "oh how sweet, you're talented," but the minute that it starts to interfere with your roles . . . like [being a] mom, family obligations, making money for some people, [then] it's not cool anymore. So I do think that Chitresh-jī is creating—I mean, he pushes women, not only physically, but [also] in terms of women negotiating their roles at home. (Mehta interview, June 18, 2003)

Was Pandit Das indeed creating a unified "superior race of strong women" with the power to transcend externally imposed strictures of race and gender? And if so, is such female empowerment legitimate if created and maintained by a man—who had the power to name and bestow power, and also potentially to take it away? Ultimately, many dancers who continued to train with Pandit Das felt a measure of ambivalence in this arena, though most argued that he strategically employed these discourses to motivate his dancers to excel. Michele Zonka reflected: "Every rule that you ever lived by, no matter what your culture is, he will throw that in your face. So you *never* get by, and that's what makes a good teacher" (interview, November 14, 2005). Similarly, Mehta echoed and expanded on Pandit Das's use of an individual's characteristics: "Chitresh-jī will use *anything* and *everything* to make you dance. . . . He will use your ethnicity; he will use your gender; he will use your age; he will use your body, your height . . . I'm telling you, ultimately, he'll use whatever he can get on you to make you dance better and stronger. Everything is his tool" (interview, April 6, 2003).

These comments suggest that all of those trained by Pandit Das, whether "Indian" or "non-Indian," heritage or affinity practitioners, were being othered in one way or another as they encountered issues of power, race, and gender in their study of kathak in its newer US environment. While in his creative work Pandit Das operated from the core principle directing him to "make everything one," seen most clearly in his development of kathak yoga, his style of community building was far more complex and regularly seemed to contradict this artistic philosophy. Certainly, working out ways to talk about dancers' individual similarities and differences helped Pandit Das articulate not only the company's multifaceted group identity but also his own positioning as a performer and teacher of kathak in the United States. Whether pitting students against one another or drawing them together, creating a learning environment that was demanding, joyous, distressing, inspiring, or some combination of these, Pandit Das worked to motivate his dancers to meet a higher standard of performance, ultimately with the goal of propelling the art and its practitioners forward.

7

Form and Freedom in Kathak Performance

November 7, 2002, San Francisco, California: It was the final rehearsal before Charlotte Moraga's first full-length solo concert. The concert was coming just months after the gaṇḍā bandan *ceremony that marked a shift in her relationship with Pandit Das from student and teacher to disciple and guru. To an extent, the imminent performance also would mark her transition from exclusively dancing as a member of the Chitresh Das Dance Company to additionally building a career as a solo artist.*

The tension in the practice room that evening was palpable, for up to that point practices had not gone as Moraga planned. In the few available rehearsals with the accompanying musicians from India, Pandit Das frustrated her attempts to set the concert program. If in her own practice she had worked out choreography or planned an order to the performance, she had not been able to go over this with sarodist Swapnamoy Banerjee and tabla player Kousic Sen. Instead, the "rehearsals" ran more like jam sessions between Pandit Das and these two musicians, who regularly performed with him.

The evening began with Moraga and the guest musicians all moving at a brisk pace, warming up their bodies and minds for the rehearsal ahead. Then Pandit Das joined the group, playing tabla and dancing. Because of his relationship with these musicians, because of his status in the group, because of his sheer strength and inventiveness as a dancer-musician, the musicians' attention naturally shifted to him. And despite Pandit Das's many supportive shouts to Moraga of "bahut acche!" *(an emphatic "very good!"), this supposed rehearsal for her solo concert was turning into another opportunity for the seasoned professionals to play with one another, with Moraga perhaps feeling that she was simply along for the ride.*

Eventually, Moraga became visibly upset. Though her frustrations were understandable, this tactic was quite purposeful on Pandit Das's part. In forcing her to let go of her earlier plans, and to be present and responsive to what was happening moment by moment in these sessions, Pandit Das was compelling Moraga to draw from, and ideally gain greater trust in, the embodied knowledge she had honed over years of practice. A trust in her own capacity to react instantaneously from this "reservoir" of accumulated knowledge would be crucial to the success of her upcoming performance, in which she would be expected to dance with some degree of upaj: *translated as spontaneity or improvisation (Campbell 2009, 121).*

Pandit Das's method of managing Moraga's first full-length solo preparation partially reveals the relative value he placed on different types of dance presentation, which included a regard for *upaj* as opposed to set choreography, solo over group dance, and "collaborative" projects rather than "fusion." In this chapter, I investigate each of these preferences, demonstrate how they supported or detracted from Pandit Das's vision of "traditional" kathak, and analyze the relationship of these types of kathak performance to the practical demands of the profession. To situate his artistic philosophy, I begin by discussing ways we may understand improvisation in this performance tradition. I then describe how dancers develop the capacity to perform in a spontaneous manner, examine musicians' roles in kathak, and discuss ways Pandit Das worked to resolve tensions between group choreography, spontaneity, and solo performance in his collaborative projects.

As the first dancers of their generation to perform full traditional solo concerts, Charlotte Moraga and Jaiwanti Das Pamnani, who had performed the previous year, set a precedent for up-and-coming dancers. During the year before their concerts, they each individually tied strings with Pandit Das in a ceremony formally marking them as *śiṣyas*. As discussed in previous chapters, various rituals marked their stages of commitment to the dance. The final stage is a *gaṇḍā bandan*, or string-tying ceremony, in which strings are tied around the wrists of guru and disciple to symbolize the bond between the two. In Pandit Das's own experience in India, a *gaṇḍā bandan* ceremony was undertaken when he was a child embarking on his study—he was just ten years old at the time of "tying strings" with his guru. Among Pandit Das's students, however, it was understood that, with few exceptions, the *gaṇḍā bandan* ceremony would not take place until one was ready both to make a lifetime commitment to the dance and to perform a full-length kathak solo. Rather than marking the beginning of study, in this context, the *gaṇḍā bandan* ritual was coupled with an adult dancer's first full solo performance—one which many describe as launching the beginning of a deeper level of study and understanding.

For students of Indian classical dances, the solo debut is often a major event, called an *arangetram* in bharatanatyam, *raṅgmañchpravesh* in odissi, and *raṅgapravesh* in other schools of kathak (Gorringe 2005, 101 fn. 4). Scholars suggest that it has taken on particular significance as a rite of passage for young women in diaspora communities, becoming an end in itself for some, who may then leave their dancing behind to focus on other goals such as school, family, or career (98; Greenstein and Bharadvaj 1998; Schwartz 2001, 87–93). In contrast to many dancers discussed in other studies, both Moraga and Pamnani were married and had children at the time of their first kathak solos. Both were seasoned performers who had danced in numerous productions as members of the Chitresh Das Dance Company; but, whether dancing as part of a group or as featured soloists, their repertoire until that point had consisted of choreographed material. In order to perform a solo as a *śiṣya* of Pandit Das, each needed to be able to improvise during the course of her performance. How does one learn the skills to do so? And what does improvisation mean in this context? The following discussion describes various forms of *upaj* found in kathak, examines how improvisation was taught by Pandit Das, and considers the valuation of *upaj* within this kathak community, affirming Rolf Groesbeck's contention that "the *meanings* of improvisation remain diverse and culturally constructed and grounded" (1999, 2).

Analyzing *Upaj*

Two primary aspects of improvisation in kathak can be roughly differentiated as choices involving movement (principally, but not exclusively limited to the upper body, and generally without sonic implications), and rhythm (movements that create percussive sound, mainly generated through footwork). Dancing in a spontaneous manner necessitates that the movement vocabulary of kathak is naturalized in dancers' bodies—often through years of rote drills and exercises—such that when they relax their dependence on choreographed hand, arm, and body motions and move "freely," those movements will still read as kathak. Rhythmically oriented improvisation also depends on repeated exercises and practices that help dancers develop an ability to work inventively within a specific rhythmic cycle. This skill, *layakārī*, allows dancers to improvise rhythmic phrases with footwork and to produce complex rhythmic formulae spontaneously.

While more recent academic work on improvisation, including Solis and Nettl (2009) and Nettl and Russell (1998), provides a growing number of ethnographic studies and perspectives on improvisational processes, I turn to an earlier essay by Bruno Nettl to frame this discussion. In considering various cultures' approaches to and concepts of musical composition and improvisation, Nettl observes that students generally first learn a model or models upon which to base improvisation (1974, 15).[1] One model involves what he calls "largely theoretical subject matter, consisting of verbal instructions and exercises" (16). A second model contains compositions that are memorized in entirety but would not, in themselves, typically constitute a proper performance. Models for these two bases of improvisation in kathak are discussed at length in this book. For example, chapter 5 describes fundamental exercises to learn *hastak*s and basic footwork patterns, and the sequence danced to the *bol*s "theī tā theī tā theī," which like others, is practiced by Pandit Das's students and utilized as a building block in other compositions, but it is not presented on its own in performance.

A third model Nettl discusses involves compositions that can be rendered in performance with or without improvisation. In kathak, students learn this type of model through choreographed versions of the various sections that comprise a kathak solo. *Ṭhāṭ*, for example, is a section of performance in which the dancer emphasizes subtle movements of the eyes, eyebrows, neck, hands, and breath, while "interspersing dramatic rhythmic flourishes which end quickly in crisp poses" (C. Das et al. 2001, 89). While less experienced students might perform *ṭhāṭ* exactly as they learned without diverting from the model, more advanced dancers will improvise within *ṭhāṭ* by drawing from the various building blocks of kathak performance in a way that—to a greater or lesser extent—is new each time (▶ compare videos 7.1 and 7.2, cue point 2:45–3:28).

Experienced dancers may bring the element of *upaj* both to nonnarrative, rhythmically oriented (*nṛitt*) portions and to sections of performance involving storytelling (*nṛitya* or *gat-bhāv*). For rhythmic compositions such as pithy *ṭukṛa*s and *toṛa*s, the way the composition is recited usually remains unchanged, but the manner in which the composition is danced will likely involve an element of spontaneity. In this instance, *upaj* refers to performing improvised variations of movement to a preexisting compositional (rhythmic) form. Additionally, *upaj* can refer to the spontaneous execution of a composition, drawn from one's repertoire in the midst of a performance. For example, over the course of their careers, kathak dancers learn several *tatkār ki bandish*es—compositions using the *bol*s of *tatkār* as described in chapter 1—and might spontaneously decide to perform one or more from their repertoire in the midst of a solo performance. *Upaj* also can be found in the spontaneous creation of rhythmic compositions, such as *tihāī*s. Most kathak dancers have a large repertoire of prepared *tihāī*s at their disposal. As with the examples above, solo dancers can be spontaneous in selecting a particular *tihāī* or in how they execute a *tihāī*. In *upaj*, one may even produce an entirely new *tihāī*, created on the spot in a moment of inspiration.

Inspiration, *feeling*, and *flow* are terms dancers have used to describe the experience of improvisation. As with most other forms of improvisation, what distinguishes *upaj* for kathak dancers is "the suddenness of creative impulse" (Nettl 1974, 3). Discussing Hindustani music, Bhaskar Chandavarkar writes: "Upaj can be translated as 'grown out of' or 'born out of.' *Upaj* cannot be taught. *Upaj* has to come into being on its own. It is the child of imagination and inspiration. Musicians in every culture experience these flashes of highly creative moments. Every musician would experience that curious feeling when music seems to flow entirely by itself, propelling itself effortlessly, leaving the musician in utter astonishment, almost as a bystander. It is during such moments that *upaj* in music takes place" (1987, 99).

Training to Improvise

If it cannot be taught, as Chandavarkar asserts, *upaj* certainly can be encouraged.[2] Moraga's development as a dancer illustrates this point. Early in her professional career she confided that working within the parameters of *tāl*, the specific rhythmic cycles of Hindustani music, had been one of the toughest hurdles in her training: "One of the most challenging things about kathak for me was not the *chakkar*s [swift turns], not the footwork, [but] just to be able to dance while listening to the *tāl* at the same time, and to be able to dance on *tāl*, to recognize parts of the *tāl*. [Formerly a professional jazz dancer,] I was used to dancing on the beat, to music, but not really noticing. [Kathak is] different because you have these *tihāī*s which are incredibly syncopated and difficult, so it was very different, and that was the most challenging thing" (interview, October 2, 2002). Three years after her first solo performance, with many more such performances under her belt, Moraga's attitude towards *upaj* was quite different, even effusive: "It just comes. It comes through you" (pers. comm., November 10, 2005).

Cultivating that effortless feeling, leading to "flashes of highly creative moments," in kathak requires, in part, solid grounding in the rhythmic framework through training with *ṭhekā*, the signature pattern of any *tāl* (Chandavarkar 1987, 99). *Ṭhekā* is recited or played cyclically, and in training with *ṭhekā* the dancer will perform other rhythmic compositions over this repeating pattern. Each beat of the *ṭhekā* has a specific weight and timbre, which helps dancers know where they are within the rhythmic cycle. Pandit Das reflects on how his guru utilized the playing of slow, unembellished *ṭhekā* to develop his disciples' rhythmic proficiency:

> My guru-jī never would allow any good tabla players to practice with us. He would allow only very lower-medium-range tabla players to play *just ṭhekā*—and at a slow speed. He would make us work around the *ṭhekā*, because if you

> work around the *ṭhekā*, your *layakārī* becomes very powerful. You become sharp in your mind; you become aware of the *ṭhekā*; you know how to move within the ringfence of the *ṭhekā*. *Ṭhekā* is a very important factor . . . first the dancer must listen to the *ṭhekā* and be able to dance on it, and then you can start improvising. You can become very sharp and can play and dance freely, [creating] spontaneous *tihāīs—upaj tihāīs*, not the fixed *tihāīs*. The *upaj tihāīs* begin to formulate in your psyche, not just in your mind, because it becomes your second nature. (C. Das interview, April 22, 2002)

More advanced drummers might become bored by long sessions of playing simple *ṭhekā* and might embellish the *ṭhekā* by filling in subdivisions of the beat or even playing the dancer's compositions along with them instead of playing the *ṭhekā*. At the "lower-medium" skill level Pandit Das discusses, however, tabla players can also benefit from long sessions of playing *ṭhekā*—focusing on their sound quality, tempo, or other aspects of their own playing. With only the skeletal pattern of the *ṭhekā* as a reference, dancers must attune themselves to the open spaces between beats and become more rhythmically precise. Pandit Das utilized his guru's technique in his own classes, particularly in his early years of teaching, as Gretchen Hayden describes: "In the early days he emphasized *tāl* with us and playing *ṭhekā*—us dancing on *ṭhekā*. Now there's the development that's been going on for some years of kathak yoga: reciting . . . singing and dancing. But at first it was more listening to the *ṭhekā*. He would play straight *ṭhekā* a lot, because he demanded that we would be able to do all our material on absolutely straight *ṭhekā*" (interview, January 18, 2003).

While Pandit Das continued to train his students to dance on basic *ṭhekā*, in subsequent years he also developed and encouraged other techniques to enhance the rhythmic awareness that would enable them to dance in an *upaj* manner, the most advanced of which was the practice of kathak yoga. Here, instead of relying on musicians for accompaniment, dancers mark the passage of the *tāl* themselves, by reciting the syllables of the *ṭhekā* and/or singing a corresponding melody called a *laharā* (see chapter 6). This process forces each dancer to develop an even keener awareness of the precise placement of dance compositions within the musical framework, as the dancer cannot avoid attending to these details while executing both.

Tihāīs and the "*Tihāī* Game"

Tihāīs are a particularly challenging area in which to develop spontaneity. Because of their rhythmic complexity, they often throw off the audience members' sense of the *tāl*, such that the performers' arrival on beat 1 (*sam*) may evoke a momentary feeling of surprise or wonder. And yet *tihāīs* are formulaic and rule bound; each involves the execution of the same rhythmic phrase (*palla*) three times, either without any gaps between the *pallas* (known as *bedam tihāīs*), or with gaps of equal duration between each phrase (called *damdār tihāīs*). To cause the last beat of the last *palla* to end on beat one of the concurrently moving rhythmic cycle would seem to take an incredible amount of forethought, if not a pencil and paper.[3] In fact, from the early years of training for Pandit Das's students, *tihāīs* were mastered not just through their repetition, but also at times by writing them out and analyzing the placement of each *palla* of the *tihāī* in relationship to the *tāl*.[4] A *tihāī* can be reinforced by reciting its *bols* while counting the *tāl* with the hands or playing *manjīra*, by reciting or dancing the *tihāī* along with an externally-produced *ṭhekā* as discussed above, and finally in this school of kathak, by dancing "with kathak yoga," producing the *ṭhekā* oneself through enunciating their syllables, often while singing a corresponding *laharā* (▶ see video 7.3).

An important portion of the *tihāī* repertoire for Pandit Das's senior dancers was a series of *tihāīs* called either the "*naṭavarī tihāīs*" or simply, "the sixteen *tihāīs*." Each of these *tihāīs* begins from a different *mātrā* (count) of *tīntāl*'s sixteen-count cycle: the "first-*mātrā tihāī*" from the first *mātrā* of the cycle, the "second-*mātrā tihāī*" from the second, and so forth.[5] This series develops facility in producing *tihāīs* of different lengths and in beginning *tihāīs* from different points within the rhythmic cycle. Considered a benchmark in a dancer's skill development, these *naṭavarī tihāīs* were practiced in almost every company dance class I observed.

Practicing the series, particularly with the kathak yoga component of enunciating the *ṭhekā* while singing a *laharā*, also served to build stamina, and more so because the typical ordering of the sequence allowed for little rest between each *tihāī*. Danced in direct ascending order, with each *tihāī* starting one beat later, would provide proportionately more and more rest between the *tihāīs* as they progressed. Instead, Pandit Das typically split the *tihāīs* into three groups: from the first through sixth *mātrās*, from the tenth to fifteenth *mātrās*, and from the seventh through ninth *mātrās*. His students alternated between the first two sets, dancing them in the following order: 1, 10, 2, 11, 3, 12, 4, 13, 5, 14, 6, 15, and then 7, 8 and 9.[6] In this staggered method, at the fast clip they were practiced in the dance company's classes, the entire series was completed in approximately five minutes, akin perhaps to a mile-long sprint.[7] Between the *tihāīs*, dancers would additionally perform *tatkār* (at the *solahguṇ* speed), other footwork, and/or turns to make the practice even more physically challenging.

We will consider the first three *tihāīs* danced in the *naṭavarī* sequence, beginning from beats one, ten, and two, in order to observe some of the characteristics and challenges of *tihāīs* of different lengths (▶ see video 6.5, cue point 0:08–1:00). Most *tihāīs* in this series are based on the *naṭavarī bols* "tiga dhā diga diga."[8] Writing in the Roman alphabet, members of the CDDC often shortened the *tihāīs*' key syllables, "tiga dhā diga diga," to "tddd" as seen in music examples 7.1, 7.2, and 7.3.[9] Beginning from beats 1, 10, and 2 in succession, the first-*mātrā tihāī* begins on beat 1 and ends on beat 1 (*sam*) of the next cycle of *tīntāl* (music example 7.1). With its completion, dancers have a gap of nine beats before beginning the tenth-*mātrā tihāī* (music example 7.2). The tenth-*mātrā tihāī* ends on the first beat, after which dancers launch directly into the second *mātrā tihāī* (music example 7.3).

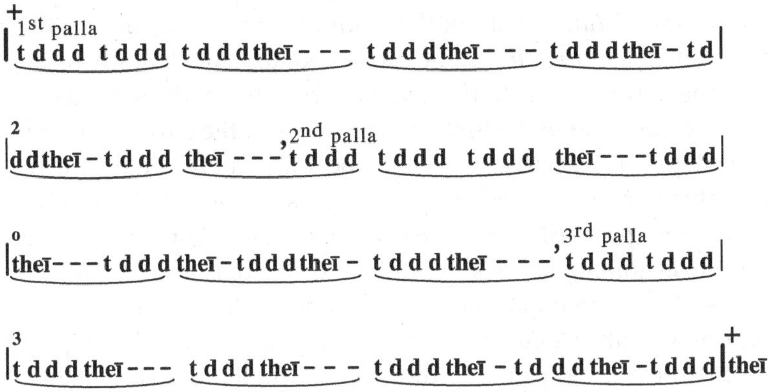

MUSIC EX. 7.1. First-*mātrā tihāī*

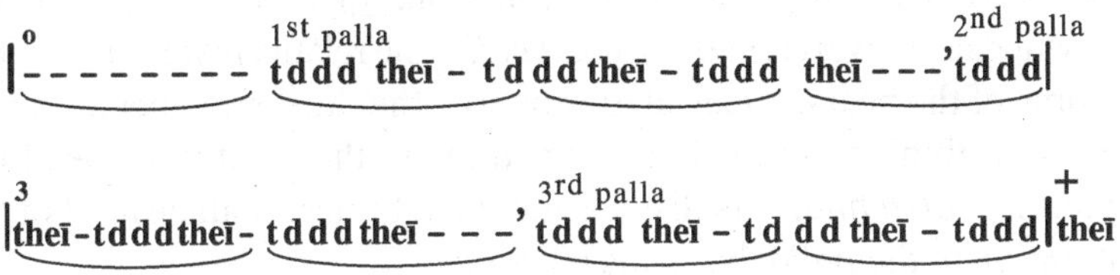

MUSIC EX. 7.2. Tenth-*mātrā tihāī*

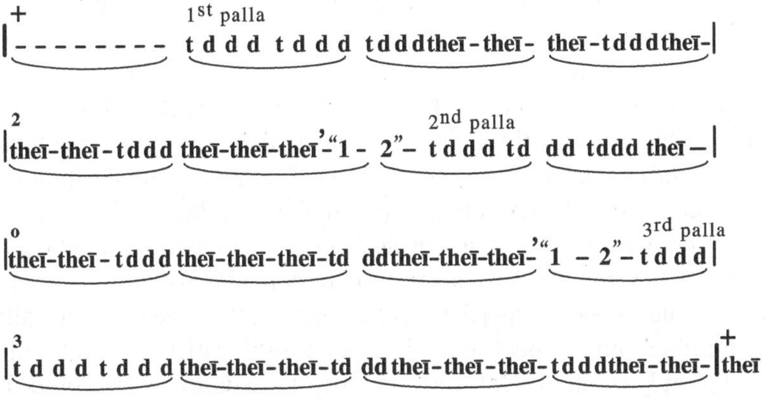

MUSIC EX. 7.3. Second-*mātrā tihāī*

The tenth-*mātrā tihāī*, the shortest and most straightforward of these three *tihāīs*, consists of the same phrase, "tiga dhā diga diga theī," repeated nine times, with each grouping of three separated by a half-beat gap. (The first- and second-*mātrā tihāīs* began with an expanded version of this phrase: "tiga dhā diga diga, tiga dhā diga diga, tiga dhā diga diga theī.") In practicing the tenth-*mātrā tihāī*, dancers will begin to recognize key rhythmic markers including the placement of each of its *pallas*, beginning on *mātrās* 10, 12½, and 15. The first-*mātrā tihāī* conforms to the *palla* placement standard for many "*sam* to *sam*" *tihāīs*, with *pallas* beginning on 1, 6½, and 12. In both the tenth- and first-*mātrā tihāīs*, the second *pallas* begin halfway through a *mātrā*, on the upbeat. In such *tihāīs*, the relationship of the second *palla* to the pulse is reverse that of the first and third *pallas*: the parts of the composition accented by their placement on the beat instead fall on the off-beat.

Of these three *tihāīs*, the second-*mātrā tihāī* is the most rhythmically complex. Its challenge primarily lies in the placement of its second *palla*, a quarter beat after the beginning of the seventh *mātrā*. There is a gap between each *palla* of this *tihāī* of three-quarters of a beat, and the first gap falls across two *mātrās*. To assist with beginning the second and third *pallas* at the proper time, dancers often fill these gaps by reciting "ek, do" (one, two), accompanied by unaccented right and left steps of the feet. Understanding the relationship of the *tihāī*'s bols to the beginnings of each *mātrā* is also important. In the first *palla*, *bols* that are naturally accented in recitation, "<u>ti</u>ga" and "thei," coincide with the downbeats; however, in the second *palla*, the relatively weak *bol* "<u>di</u>ga" lands on some of the beats. If executed properly, the third *palla* begins a half beat after the beginning of the eighth *mātrā*. As in the second *pallas* of the first- and tenth-*mātrā tihāīs*, its displacement continues a half beat off of the original iteration of the *palla*, but ends on *sam*.

As the brief discussion above indicates, this series is as rhythmically challenging as it is physically demanding. In their practice of the sixteen *tihāīs*, dancers strove for clarity in footwork and grace in upper-body movements, and they worked to maintain physical stamina and control of the voice while singing and reciting throughout. As students gained some mastery over this repertoire, they (either in class with Pandit Das or among themselves) began to work on their response time—on how quickly they could prepare for each *tihāī*. The "*tihāī* game" that evolved included having someone call out the number of any one of the sixteen *naṭavarī tihāīs* for a dancer to produce. At the beginning of a student's skill development, the number would be given several beats beforehand, providing time to consider which *tihāī* was required. As dancers became proficient at this game, the time between calling out the number and the beat itself decreased until, rather than a number, the caller simply shouted "Go!" or the name of the dancer who would then attempt the appropriate *tihāī* from the next beat (▶ see video 7.4).[10]

The purpose of this process was to develop a feeling for *tihāīs* that does not rely on an explicit thought process. Seibi Lee described this process: "The *tihāī* game gives you a starting point to becoming able to make a *tihāī* at any point in time. It's something of a halfway mark to being able to do full *upaj*. First, we practice the *naṭavarī tihāīs* so much so that they become almost second nature. So, then when we do the *tihāī* game, we take what we know really well and have to be able to just go from any point in time—to pull out the right one and bring it to *sam*. That's sort of part way [to dancing full *upaj*]" (interview, August 5, 2006).

Lee then distinguished between rhythmic *upaj* and spontaneity in movement: "At first, we dance [the *tihāīs*] exactly the same way we learn them in class, but then there's nothing to stop you from re-choreographing them—on the spot. That's sort of two-thirds of the way toward being fully spontaneous. . . . Ideally, then you develop a sense of the mathematics. When you get it in your body the amount of time each *palla* has to be from any point in order to get to *sam*, then I think you're getting close to being able to actually compose something on the spot. So, all this is a way of pushing you along" (interview, August 5, 2006).

These practices develop an ability to react instinctually, through kinesthetic knowledge and rhythmic facility, rather than through the analytic processes discussed above. As Dard Neuman notes, the rote repetition of preparatory exercises in Hindustani music training "emphasizes not just body-memory but body autonomy: a condition where the body acts as an independent 'mind' that explores on its own" (2012, 447 fn. 3). When I queried Pandit Das, he also reported that spontaneously producing *tihāīs* relied on noncognitive processing:

> Feeling. It depends on the mindset and environment. It's like karate or kung fu; you don't know what is coming and then have to react in the moment. *You can't think*. Sometimes I think, "I'm going to do this *tihāī*," but most of the time—and the more challenging—is to go with feeling. It's floating, floating, floating, and then you bring it in. Sometimes it comes and sometimes it misfires. It slips. That's the beauty of it. Life is like that. You can pray; you can do whatever, but it will come at a time that you least expect [snaps]. Love is like that too. (Interview, November 14, 2005)

Improvising Rhythmic Phrases

Another aspect of *upaj* involves improvising rhythmic phrases via footwork. Such phrases are most often produced during *savāl-javāb* or question-answer exchanges between dancer and tabla player or, less commonly, between dancer and melodic instrumentalist. If leading the *savāl-javāb*, the dancer must constantly produce new and interesting phrases for the instrumentalist to replicate (see video 7.5). Exercises for learning to improvise in this way were sometimes practiced in class with Pandit Das, but they took place more frequently during less formal practices. A group of dancers would usually stand in a circle practicing relatively quiet footwork (often *eṛī tatkār*) and reciting the *ṭhekā* while taking turns improvising footwork for the span of a cycle or some portion of a cycle of the *tāl*. As the exercise progressed, dancers observed one another's attempts, learning to judge what worked and what did not.

The proficient improviser might choose a novel footwork pattern, or work against the rhythmic feel already set up, perhaps by executing a triple-speed of footwork such as *chhegun̩* (three steps per beat) against the group's duple-feel *āṭhgun̩* or *solahgun̩ tatkār* (four or eight steps per beat).[11] Those less comfortable with the exercise might use the time between their own improvisational attempts to mentally work out their next phrase instead of following the progress of their dance-sisters. But more advanced dancers would pay attention to one another's phrases and might base their own improvised phrases on the themes the last dancer created. Taking a small phrase from the previous dancer's footwork and using it in a new way was considered ideal. The successful improviser would create a phrase that seemed to unfold naturally from the last, perhaps even ending with a *tihāī*. Better still, the *tihāī* also would make use of rhythmic phrases that had been explored over the course of the group's improvisation (cf. Lipiczky 1985, 159). In later years, due to the growing artistic relationship between Pandit Das and tap dancer Jason Samuels Smith, members of this kathak community also practiced what tap dancers call cutting contests. In this format, two dancers are pitted against one another, trading improvised phrases within a given number of beats until one is deemed the winner of the round.

In the footwork exercises described above, Pandit Das's dance students often utilized kathak yoga, accompanying themselves with basic melodic and rhythmic patterns of *laharā* and *ṭhekā*. Usually performed by accompanying musicians, *laharā* and *ṭhekā* are the staples of musical accompaniment, particularly in *nṛitt* (nonnarrative) sections of kathak performance. The function of the *laharā* is to keep time melodically while not taking attention away from the rhythmic complexities of dance and drumming (Massey 1999, 23). One might assume, given Pandit Das's relative emphasis on technical strength (*taiyārī*) and rhythmic complexity (*layakārī*), and from the description of his own training quoted above, that he preferred simple musical accompaniment in performance. However, as the next examples illustrate, Pandit Das instead looked for spontaneity in music accompaniment, challenging himself and the dancers he trained to be able to follow as well as lead.

"Matching" the Musicians

To further their capacity to perform in *upaj* style, Pandit Das utilized various techniques in helping his students learn to follow the musicians with whom they worked. For example, during advanced classes when musicians were present, Pandit Das sometimes asked the melodic instrumentalist to play *ālāp* (a nonmetric, improvisatory exploration of the melodic characteristics of a *rāg*) and instructed the dancers to improvise on the melodic contours. Because *ālāp* is rendered in free rhythm, dancers typically focused on movements of their upper bodies, as footwork may distract from the ambiance of this style of playing and inappropriately lead the dancer into a regular pulse. At other times, Pandit Das would ask the tabla player to play whatever he wanted and observed the dancers' attempts to follow. This practice taught his students to create footwork spontaneously based on the patterns they heard and, through trial and error, to identify which types of footwork may be appropriate for specific tabla patterns.

Pandit Das likewise instructed the musicians with whom he worked to match the movements of the dance, believing that dancer and musician should take turns leading and following. If done well, regardless of which artist is leading, this appears to the audience as simultaneous yet somehow synchronous improvisation. In Hindustani music, this practice, called *sāth saṅgat* (or *laṛant*), generally involves the tabla player following the melodic soloist, "imitat[ing] the rhythm of the soloist with a minimal time delay, occasionally even anticipating him" (Clayton 2000, 111). In practices with his students and in his own performances, Pandit Das would at times reverse this typical dynamic, instead following the tabla player or another musician. In their interactions, regardless of which artist was leading or following, he felt that "matching energies" was of paramount importance, particularly in the kathak solo.

Next, it was to the subject of "matching energies" that Pandit Das turned in the final rehearsal before Moraga's first full-length solo performance. As she became frustrated during this session, her final chance to practice with the accompanying musicians before a critical performance, Pandit Das chose to diffuse the situation with one of his many refrains: "musicians vs. dancers." I had been videotaping the rehearsal. Leaning closely into the video's frame, he announced, "The tabla players are faking! Video this! One thing that is happening with the tabla players is that they fake *while the* chakkars *[turns] are going on. I've been saying this for the last twenty-five years. . . . No, no, I am not trying to put down anybody," he said for the benefit of a visiting professional tabla player, "but it is very important to see what the body does! . . . So Charlotte, disciple, please."*

Reminding her of her relatively new status as his śiṣya, *Pandit Das indicated for Moraga to prepare to dance. Her* chakkars *(swift turns) were a place of joy and confidence, and she effortlessly executed a* tihāī *in* tīntāl *consisting of eighteen turns repeated three times (fifty-four total). Each turn on the left heel was punctuated by a slap of the right foot at the turn's completion. With each slap, a number was recited aloud to the rhythm "1–1– –2–2 ––3– 3––4 –4––" repeating the same number twice to highlight the turns' two-plus-three-beat rhythmic groupings overlaid atop a regular pulse. Each* palla *ended with "9–9" with no pause between the second "9" (the eighteenth turn) of one* palla *and the first turn of the next. When her demonstration was successfully completed, Pandit Das explained his outburst, exhorting the musicians to match the dancer's dynamism.*

Chakkars are most commonly performed in kathak by turning on the left heel. They are punctuated by the sound of the right foot slapping the floor before lifting into the next turn. Thus, while they require a great deal of energy from the dancer, they produce only one sound of the foot per turn. To "match energies," Pandit Das often emphasized the need for tabla players to "fill up" the time between each turn.

As Moraga retreated from centerstage, Pandit Das continued, "This is where most tabla players usually play this." He asked Kousic Sen to play a relatively simple version of what a tabla player might play to accompany chakkars *in this "1–1– –2–2 ––" rhythm. Sen then demonstrated similar accompaniment patterns of increasing rhythmic density ending with the* bols *"Dhā-tirakiṭatakaDhā-tirakiṭataka tirakiṭa" to create the "fill" Pandit Das was seeking for each set of turns (see music example 7.4).*[12] *Turning to sarod player Swapnamoy Banerjee, Pandit Das asked him to demonstrate the different levels of technical difficulty a stringed instrumentalist might choose. Utilizing instrumental* bols *including "dā" the sarod's downstroke, "rā" the upstroke, and the faster pairing "diri," Banerjee began by striking only one note for each turn the dancer would make, and then twice increased the density of notes (see music example 7.5).*[13] *Because the melodic instrumentalist's primary role is to maintain a constant melody* (laharā), *what changed in Banerjee's renditions was only the density of notes played (the number of times his pick struck the string) and not the number or placement of discrete pitches.*

Though these musicians did not utilize the same *bols* as the dancer, Pandit Das emphasized that their efforts should match. And particularly in a situation in which the dancer expends a great amount of energy—such as in this case performing fifty-four turns at a fast pace—he felt the musicians should work hard as well, next implying this was a relatively unique dynamic in the realm of kathak accompaniment.

|1 – 1 – – 2 – 2 – – 3 – etc.

|Dhā – Dhā – na Dhā – Dhā – na Dhā – etc.

|Dhā – – – Dhā ge ti ra kiṭa Dhā – – – Dhā ge ti ra ki ṭa Dhā – – – etc.

|Dhāghe teṭe Dhāge tira kiṭa Dhāgeteṭe Dhāge tirakiṭa Dhāgheteṭe etc.

|Dhā- - -ki ṭa taka Dhā- - -ki ṭa taka tira ki ṭa Dhā- - -ki ṭa ta ka Dhā- - - etc.

|Dhā -tira kiṭatakaDhā - tira kiṭataka tirakiṭaDhā -tira kiṭataka Dhā -tira etc.

MUSIC EX. 7.4. Kathak dancers' *chakkar* pattern with possible tabla accompaniment

|1 – 1 – – 2 – 2 – – 3 – etc.

|Dā – Dā – – Dā – Dā – – Dā – etc.

|Dā rā Dā rā dā Dā rā Dā rā dā Dā rā etc.

|Di ri di ri Di ri di ri di ri Di ri di ri Di ri di ri di ri Di ri di ri etc.

MUSIC EX. 7.5. Kathak dancers' *chakkar* pattern with possible instrumental accompaniment

At the finish of Banerjee's demonstration, Pandit Das asked the musicians, "So the question is: did you play like this before with any other kathak dancers?" One replied, smiling, "No comment." Pandit Das concluded the demonstration by stating: "We are all trying to work harder. We are all trying to understand one another: what is going on in tabla, what is sarod, what is kathak. This way, all working together, it brings the strength from tabla and sarod and the dancer all together. . . . We are trying to make a saṅgīt. Saṅgīt *means music, dance, and percussion all together.* Lau ban jai—*it becomes one."*

Several key attitudes emerge from this rehearsal: the importance of technical ability, the privileging of spontaneity, a striving for connectedness and mutual understanding leading to "oneness" in the course of performance (see chapter 6), and the notion that these values were not generally shared by all kathak dancers and their accompanying musicians. Pandit Das's emphasis on technical ability (*taiyārī*) applied not only to kathak dancers, but also to the musicians he employed; and those supporting Moraga's solo, although already accomplished performers, displayed signs of "trying to work harder" themselves by pushing to improve in speed and clarity. For example, these exhortations toward greater effort and technical excellence inspired Banerjee to wear light wrist weights while practicing *jhallā* on his sarod in imitation of Pandit Das's use of ankle weights and dumbbells while practicing dance.

In highlighting the skills of these professional kathak accompanists, Pandit Das was also, as he would say, "sending a message" to a musician observing the rehearsal. This guest tabla player was an emerging solo artist who also accompanied instrumentalists and vocalists—performances that held a higher position in the Hindustani music hierarchy.[14] While successful solo tabla players and melodic instrumentalists sometimes dissuade their students from playing with dance on musical grounds with warnings such as, "It will ruin your hand," kathak accompaniment is also seen as less prestigious. Musicians who work as kathak accompanists thus sometimes express frustration with their lower social status, their lack of recognition as artists, and with performing material that often is not sufficiently challenging.

"The Music Is Finished While You're Counting"

The repeating melodies called *laharā* (or *nagmā*) comprise the chief, but not the sole melodic facet of kathak performance. Kathak music also includes various kinds of songs that are most often used for sections of *nṛitya*: dance with a storytelling component. Genres taken from vocal music include *ṭhumrī*, *dādrā*, and *chaitī*; for *nṛitt*, or nonnarrative dance, the most common song genre is *tarānā* (cf. Bhate-Jathar 1990, 42). In addition to these and other song forms, kathak has seen the emergence of composers such as vocalist Pt. Atul Desai, who collaborated for many years with Smt. Kumudini Lakhia to compose melodies "through which Kathak's movement patterns could be highlighted" (R. Shah 2005, 147).

Regardless of the musical genre, musicians I interviewed generally felt their roles in kathak performance to be limiting. In discussing the performance of fixed compositions, Debasish Sarkar, an accomplished vocalist who accompanied top kathak and odissi dancers in India and abroad, described his most common experiences working with dance: "Most of the time I am just thinking: this line three times, this line two times. We have no flexibility, so I have to count: one, two, three, and then the next line" (Sarkar, C. Das, and anonymous interview, April 19, 2001). Another musician sitting in on the interview added, "the music is finished while you're counting."

While often couched in purely technical musical terms, reasons for the discouragement or disparagement of kathak accompaniment have as much to do with the historical associations of these roles. Today, the sitar, sarod, and other instruments commonly perform the task of melodic accompaniment in kathak; however, earlier, this was primarily the function of the sarangi, usually played by members of the Mirasi community (Daniel Neuman 1978).[15] Qureshi argues that the sarangi's very sound "conveys disrepute as part of a highly charged, ambivalent musical identity," that centers primarily upon its association with female courtesan performers (1997, 1). On folklore concerning the sarangi, Qureshi writes: "The story that dominates the sarangi happens at the side of the 'nautch girl,' in the hands of her teacher/accompanist/manager who supports her amorous song melody as well as her dazzling *kathak* footwork. Hence, the sarangi is inexorably linked to the licentious and immoral social space where a woman offers her art and, by implication, herself" (6).

If musicians' status had been negatively affected by their association with kathak, it makes sense that Pandit Das would lobby for greater respect for his accompanying musicians, in part as a way to advocate for respect of the dance itself. In a joint interview with two of his accompanists, Pandit Das responded to their frustrations: "I'm trying to force you to see that you're not ordinary musicians" (interview, April 19, 2001). Three aspects of Pandit Das's experience likely contributed to his attitude regarding the role of accompanying musicians: his general privileging of high technical standards, his nontraditional family background (particularly the influence of his mother, who pushed him to challenge societal prejudices), and his relative geographic distance from Indian social and artistic hierarchies. Even based in the United States, however, Pandit Das encountered prejudices regarding kathak accompaniment among the few elite Hindustani musicians in the San Francisco Bay Area. This led Pandit Das to encourage his accompanying musicians to take a prominent role in kathak performances early in his career, when many of Ali Akbar Khansahib's students accompanied him. Was pushing Khansahib's students a way for Pandit Das to prove something about kathak (and kathak accompaniment) to this towering musical master?

While Pandit Das taught at the Ali Akbar College of Music in the early 1970s, several music students played for dance classes and performances, particularly Peter van Gelder (sitar) and James Pomerantz (sitar). After

Pandit Das left the school, Pomerantz continued to accompany Pandit Das's concerts, stepping down from the role of primary melodic accompanist in 1981. At that time, Christopher Ris (sarod) took over and maintained that position until 2000. Ris recalled Pandit Das's often challenging emphasis on change and spontaneity: "He wanted everything to be exciting—everything to be unpredictable, spontaneous . . . He was always *changing* things; he saw it as good training for his students to always be quick [snaps his finger], to be able to adapt.[16] . . . What was amazing about Chitresh is, from the Indian music performances that I saw, the music was simply *laharā*. If there was a singer then the singer would sing a *ṭhumrī*, and the dancer would interpret the *ṭhumrī*; but by and large, instrumental music was simply there to keep the time" (interview, July 5, 2003). Ris described a fight that even "came to blows" with Pandit Das's brother, Ritesh Das who, having recently arrived in the United States from India, had found it presumptuous of Ris to take liberties with the *laharā*:

> When later we made peace, Babua [Ritesh Das] said, "I want to show you the way *laharā* should sound." And he played me something of Ramesh-jī [sarangi player Pt. Ramesh Mishra] playing *laharā*. He would change a note here, an ornament there, and occasionally he would go up to a high octave and hold a note to evoke some mood. And Babua said "*that's* how you should play."
>
> But Chitresh didn't want that. He wanted *music*. He wanted everyone to be alive and happening, to the extent that he said, "Chris, when you're playing, I want you to try and steal the spotlight from me. [laughing] *Just try!*" [He meant] be hot. And bring that quality to the music here. So, I would learn his *bols*, and sometimes his stories would just go. He would say "just play—follow me, but play." And so we would do, for example, the story of Draupadi and he would just improvise. I would improvise with him and the tabla would improvise with him, and we would just all be going for it. And sometimes it was great and sometimes it wasn't so great, but it was always exciting. (C. Ris interview, July 5, 2003)

Another musician with whom Pandit Das regularly worked in the first decade of the twenty-first century also mentioned accompanying the story of Draupadi's *bastraharaṇ* (Hindi: *vastraharaṇ*, disrobing): "There is such a difference . . . here we have freedom. In Draupadi, we know the story, but in the technical part—*Dādā*'s footwork—we will not know what he will do and will have to improvise accordingly" (Sarkar, C. Das, and anonymous interview, April 19, 2001). Responding to this comment, Pandit Das, who was also part of this interview, mentioned that the positioning of dancer and musicians in the modern proscenium context (in which the musicians typically are seated stage right) means that they have a side view of a dancer's facial expressions. Perhaps this difficulty in communicating with the musicians also encouraged him to follow them. Pandit Das described his experience in performance thus: "I don't know what they will do. They don't see my face, so I am floating on the rhythm. They play something and I will move. The rehearsal is one thing, but we don't memorize what feeling is going to come next." When Pandit Das made this point, one of his accompanists added, "We can never do the same thing in the next concert. Impossible." Pandit Das replied, "So it can be said that we are maintaining *saṅgīt* in the proper sense," providing the Sanskrit terms for the elements of *saṅgīt*, "*gītam* [song], *vātam* [instruments], and *nṛittam* [dance], all together." He concluded by stating, "I brought [these musicians] more into it. Because they got this freedom, they feel very high."

This type of "freedom" is only accessible to musicians with a solid training and high level of proficiency; as Pandit Das stated during my very first lesson with him, "real freedom comes from refined discipline with responsibility" (see chapter 1). This conviction was echoed by Pandit Das's senior students and disciples, including Charlotte Moraga: "Many young students may think that self-expression is freedom. But with a classical dance, self-expression does not come first. First you must acquire the language, the vocabulary with an emphasis in *taiyārī*" (Moraga 2003). For his accompanying musicians, the idea of freedom Pandit Das advocated was also in line with what he sometimes described as an "American" definition of freedom, meaning in part, freedom from social hierarchies and regulations (field notes, October 23, 1999). Within this context, *upaj* depends on the free-flowing exchange of melodic, rhythmic, and kinesthetic ideas facilitated by relative egalitarianism during performance. And for aspiring dancers, such spontaneity hinges on developing a thorough facility with kathak's movement vocabulary and rhythmic framework.

Mitigating Choreography

Despite his strong emphasis on *upaj*-style solo dancing, Pandit Das created several large choreographed works—a medium that typically privileges group dancing with tightly controlled choreography. During the years of my primary fieldwork, Pandit Das, the Chitresh Das Dance Company, or both performed a major new work every year: *Subali-Sugriwa*, 2000; *Sadhana*, 2001; *Pancha Jati*, 2002, and *East as Center*, 2003 (figure 7.1).[17] The emphasis of each of these works was either the storytelling aspect of the dance form or the rhythmic, as was the case in *Pancha Jati*.

Pancha Jati (2002) comprised six scenes, each based on specific South Indian rhythmic groupings, or *jātis*: three (*tiśra*), four (*chaturaśra*), five (*khaṇḍa*), seven (*miśra*), and nine (*sankīrṇa*).[18] The performance fused North and South Indian rhythmic theory; in its exploration of five South Indian rhythmic groupings, the work was structured within the North Indian rhythmic framework of *vilambit tīntāl* (slow cycles of sixteen beats). To the educated observer, the *tīntāl* cycle was made apparent in a variety of ways. Dancers at times recited the *jātis* while counting *tīntāl* with the hands, and Pandit Das (on tabla) played the *ṭhekā* of *tīntāl* throughout the piece. The melodic instrumentalists, however, played melodies suited to the movements of each section of the choreography rather than playing a *laharā*, or cyclic melody that would typically be utilized to reinforce the *tāl*.

In its introductory movement, dancers utilized all five *jātis* included in this work (groupings of three, four, five, seven, and nine), and focused on individual *jātis* in subsequent sections. To fit the five *jātis* into *tīntāl* during the first movement, a rest is included after each *jāti* phrase except for the last. This manner of grouping all five *jātis* can be recited and danced at varying densities relative to *vilambit* (slow) *tīntāl* (▶ see video 7.6 and music example 7.6).[19]

The middle sections of *Pancha Jati* were each devoted to the exploration of one or two specific *jātis*, and the final section brought all the *jātis* together again. Because of its use of South Indian rhythmic theory, Pandit Das employed Jim Santi Owen, a performer of both North and South Indian drumming traditions, to play South Indian percussion instruments including *thavil*, *kanjira*, and *morsing*. Pandit Das also encouraged the North Indian instrumentalists to play in a "South Indian style," for example, making use of a heavier and wider *gamak* (a vigorous shaking of the note, akin to vibrato) than is often used in Hindustani music. The melodic materials themselves further amplified the connection of North and South Indian classical traditions; the *rāg* used for much of the performance utilizes a pentatonic scale (SRGPD) common both in Hindustani music, where it is known as Bhupali, and in Karnatak music, where it is called Mohanam. Visually, the work was

Single:

+ 2 o 3

|Taki ṭa - takadimi| - ta kata ki ṭa - ta |ki ṭa takadimi - ta|ka ta ki ṭa takadimi|

Double:

+ 2

|Takiṭa - takadimi - takata ki ṭa - ta |kiṭa taka dimi - ta ka ta ki ṭa takadimi|

o 3

|Takiṭa - takadimi - taka ta ki ṭa - ta |kiṭataka dimi - ta ka ta ki ṭa takadimi|

MUSIC EX. 7.6. The five *jātis* within one cycle of *tīntāl* in single and double speeds more contemporary in presentation; instead of colorful, ornate costumes typically worn by kathak dancers, the dance company wore unadorned *śalvār qamīzes* of white satin. Rather than showing off individual dancers, these costumes highlighted the lighting design and the group as a whole—elements perceived to be more important within western modernist choreographic sensibilities (Venkataraman 1990; S. Wong 2006).

Other choreographic pieces staged between 2000 and 2003 relied on a strong storyline to hold together somewhat unconventional productions. *East as Center*, for example, depicted scenes from the Hindu epic the Rāmāyaṇa, and involved collaboration between dancers trained in kathak, South Indian kathakali, and Balinese dance.[20] Because each of these three dance forms utilizes specific vocabulary for depicting story and character as well as a tradition of enacting episodes from the Hindu epics, the dancers in this collaborative work each performed a specific role using distinct body carriage and characterization drawn from their own dance tradition.

Despite creating successful choreographed works, there remained in Pandit Das a philosophical discomfort with the medium of choreography itself. This unresolved tension between creating large-scale choreographed productions and feeling that improvised solo performances were more traditional and valuable led him to shift his attention back and forth between the two. In 2005, having returned from an extended winter trip to India, for example,

FIG. 7.1. *East As Center* at ODC Theater, San Francisco, May 28–June 7, 2003. Featuring (*left to right*): Ni Ketut Arini, Govindan Kutty, Chitresh Das.

Pandit Das shifted gears radically by temporarily disbanding his dance company, refraining from staging new choreographic works, and concentrating his energies on training his senior students as solo dancers. His decision as artistic director was not in line with the priorities of the dance company's executive director, whose energy was necessarily focused on securing grants. Despite Pandit Das's opposition to creating new choreography during that particular period, the business of American dance was based on producing "new works," as discussed by Pandit Das disciple Rina Mehta (then one of the organization's major fund-raisers):

> In the United States, dance is analogous with the performance of choreography. The concept of "new works" is very popular and grants, awards, and support [are] often provided by arts institutions to artists for the creation of new works. For an Indian classical artist, the concept of new works is less relevant. The traditional *kathaka* performs the traditional kathak solo again and again. However, while the framework may be the same, no one traditional kathak solo is like another because of the fact that improvisation is such an emphasis in the art form. In this sense, each traditional solo is a new work. (Mehta 2005)

The tendency for funders to support large-scale group choreography over individual solo performances also became the norm in India, where dance critic Leela Venkataraman notes "the ad-hocism of bureaucrats in the cultural establishment distributing the largesse of handsome grants for group ventures to all and sundry whose worth in this specialised field is yet to be proved. So we have a mushrooming crop of sub-standard efforts going by the name of 'dance ballets'" (1990, 29).

In 2002 Pandit Das described the relationship between the proscenium performance context and group choreography:

> The proscenium has revolutionized the Indian arts. Indian art is not meant for the proscenium, it is meant for very close [communication]. . . . If you want to promote this art worldwide, you have to go to the proscenium. And as soon as this art form goes to the proscenium, then you have to think about exits and entrances—choreography. . . . Prosceniums give an opportunity to do group thinking. . . . Choreography is not bad, but the idea [for] traditional Indian art form[s] is that you have to sing [and] dance for hours, alone. Because you come to this world alone, you go alone. First you have to establish that, and it takes time. (Interview, April 22, 2002)

Kathak's shift from smaller salon venues to larger proscenium stages resulted in diminished ability to communicate *nazākat*, the subtle movements of eyes, eyebrows, neck, wrists, and breath. Pt. Birju Maharaj also articulated this sentiment at a 1989 dance festival on choreography: "With dance transplanted from the warm mehfil and temple atmosphere on to the large impersonal proscenium stage, the subtleties of movement and abhinaya had lost their place in the total scheme, for no audience seated beyond the fourth row could see anything" (summarized by Venkataraman 1990, 29).

For this and other reasons discussed in this book, Pandit Das's primary emphasis as an artist and teacher was kathak's technical and rhythmic virtuosity, elements that carry across larger performance spaces. Some dance directors in India and abroad responded by emphasizing large-scale choreography, which also satisfied the tastes of audiences accustomed to the lavish song-and-dance numbers of the Bollywood film industry. In such performances, kathak ensembles emphasized "line" (in the balletic sense) and synchrony of movement not unlike that of a corps de ballet, as discussed by dance scholar Cynthia Jean Cohen Bull:

> Ballet choreography pays great attention to special precision. Shifting lines and clusters of dancers constitute major organizing principles of its composition, and formations of symmetrical bodies create visual harmony and hierarchy which frame and set off solo performers. The corps de ballet members strive to look as much alike as possible and to move in perfect unison; individuals must control inclinations to curve an arm less or lift a leg higher than the group ideal or they will ruin the overall visual design and motion. In contrast, the soloist may, indeed should, cultivate an ability to perform movement that looks stylistically unique. . . . Thus the soloist stands out by going beyond the basic pictorial unity of the ballet, playing at the edges of the strict boundaries to which the corps must adhere, and enhancing visual design with individual variation and rhythmic intricacy. (1997, 274)

Bull notes inherent differences in the aesthetic values and training required to produce the unison dancing of the corps de ballet and the distinctive movement qualities of a solo ballerina. This distinction is also found in kathak: in group choreography dancers must strive for synchronicity of movement in contrast to solo performances in which individual style is paramount. Despite the popularity of large group performances in India, Venkataraman suggests that choreographers can face difficulties recruiting willing dancers: "In the highly individualistic solo performance oriented dance scene, to expect capable dancers to subdue their individual status for a group need is not easy" (1990, 29).

Pandit Das adapted the large-scale production medium to align more closely with his values and to continue to challenge his dancers by emphasizing *upaj* within his productions. In *East as Center*, for example, although there was a narrative and musical framework, the performance outline was loose enough to allow the performers not only the expected spontaneity in *abhinaya* (facial expression and body language) but also in the footwork they utilized to depict their characters. Improvisation within a basic structure was particularly emphasized in *India Jazz Suites*, a collaboration between Pandit Das and tap dancer Jason Samuels Smith that premiered in 2005 and toured for several years. Whereas the dance forms represented in *East as Center* each had in common a tradition of portraying stories from the Hindu epics, tap and kathak share a rhythmic focus; without a strong storyline to adhere to, the performing artists had even more freedom to dance in *upaj* style (▶ see video 7.7 and figure 7.2).

Distinguishing collaborations such as these from "fusion" projects further fueled Pandit Das's rhetorical and creative processes. In collaboration, as he saw it, each dancer should perform in the style in which they were trained, interacting with other dancers who also should perform in a manner consistent with their dance training and tradition. The article "Don't Call It Fusion" quotes both Pandit Das and Jason Samuels Smith as emphasizing this fundamental aspect of their collaboration. "'There will be a lot of spontaneous rhythmic exploration,' Das says. 'But we will be dancing our own systems: him improvising in his tradition, and me in mine. And then we try to understand each other.' Smith adds, 'I think it's a powerful message, showing that people from two different backgrounds can communicate'" (Hunt 2005). The

FIG. 7.2. Chitresh Das and Jason Samuels Smith perform in *India Jazz Suites* world premiere at Cowell Theater, San Francisco, November 2005.

artistic connection between Pandit Das and Jason Samuels Smith served as the focal point for the 2013 documentary *Upaj: Improvise* (Uchiyama).

Creative projects have become common between kathak and other footwork-based dances, particularly tap and flamenco.[21] As Chakravorty notes, "the culture of globalization is resulting in many new experimental ventures in the dance world" (2000, 126). Pandit Das would differentiate projects like *India Jazz Suites,* which involved extensive collaboration between artists working in different traditions, from "fusion," which he perceived to be a superficial incorporating of other forms into one's dance for the purposes of a short-term project. Moving beyond the juxtaposition of similarity and difference is the project to create blended or hybrid forms—or, as contemporary dancemaker Parijat Desai describes, to "evolve new vocabularies via a serious and in-depth investigation into hybridizing technique and principle" (pers. comm., June 11, 2017). In this category, other artists including Chandralekha and Akram Khan have arguably worked to hybridize South Asian classical dances and other dance forms with similar depth and rigor as Pandit Das has worked within the kathak tradition (see Bharucha 1995; R. Mitra 2015).

Monica Dalidowicz describes the external motivations, among amateurs as well as professional performers in India, in developing what is called modern kathak:

> At the professional level, creation and innovation is a growing expectation, and artists are continually seeking new ways to use their art form, develop their own styles, and present contemporary issues. The emphasis on innovation in the professional world is echoed in the amateur practice of Kathak. During my fieldwork in Kolkata in 2004–5, I observed a prolific trend toward what was known as "modern Kathak." Modern Kathak had supplanted the traditional style on the proscenium stage; the traditional solo was replaced with elaborate group choreographies, innovative fusion pieces that combine Kathak with such other dance forms as flamenco, jazz, and even ballet, and endless other manifestations of Kathak that incorporate socially relevant themes far outside the traditional repertoire. (2010, 209)

Pandit Das expressed his feelings about such experiments in an interview two years before the Kolkata-based fieldwork that informed Dalidowicz's article:

> Nowadays people are doing fusion . . . people are trying different things. There's nothing wrong. With evolution, some things will change. When a river takes a new course, it will lose many chunks of land; big boulders will be displaced, salmon will change [their] course of migration . . . all these things will happen. [But] how much are you willing to experiment? . . . If you want to evolve as yourself, then you don't have room for fusion. I would suggest that the younger generation first establish yourself, then [experiment only] if you achieve in

> technique: speed and power, *khūbsūratī*, and . . . you have to portray masculine and feminine. (Interview, April 22, 2002)

While most kathak exponents similarly advocate "experimentation within traditional bounds," the parameters of those traditional bounds are often the subject of debate (P. Shah 1992, 79). Pandit Das experimented profoundly with the kathak tradition, yet he maintained a traditionalist stance in his rhetoric, valuing above all else solo performance that included *upaj*. With the stamp of success he eventually received in the West, his style—both innovative and tradition-oriented—gained an increasingly receptive audience in India in the first years of the twenty-first century.

8

Coming Full Circle

Saturday, June 12, 2003: As Thai Airways flight 313 descended on Kolkata's Dum Dum Airport, Pandit Das and I remarked on how rural the area looked in contrast to Bangkok, our stopover from California.[1] *It seemed as though the buildings below would be swallowed up at any moment by the dense greenery crowding in on all sides. Pandit Das took a moment to close his eyes, press his hands together and say a quiet prayer before returning to our conversation. "The first time I left this airport to come to America, I was so excited . . ."*

As we exited the airport's international building, we were hit with the intense heat and humidity of monsoon-season Bengal. At that time, Pandit Das usually traveled to India in winters, accompanied by several members of his dance company, for a full schedule of performances. This visit was to focus instead on teaching, and the only students accompanying him from the United States for the six-week trip were me and my dance-sister Rina Mehta, who had already arrived in Kolkata for the summer. Pandit Das and I scanned the gathering of "taxiwallas," each jostling for their next fare, when Rina appeared with a small group of young women I had never met—Pandit Das's Kolkata students. They greeted us with flowers and a welcome sign, and quickly led us through the crowds to the van that would take us to our lodgings. After we piled into the vehicle, Pandit Das introduced me to everyone with a smile, calling them, "my first real desī *students."*

In 2001, Pandit Das began teaching in Kolkata, and the following year he inaugurated the new school, naming it Chhandam Nritya Bharati in honor of his parents' institution, Nritya Bharati. This marked his official return to India as a teacher after thirty years abroad. Indrani Mallick, Kasturi Mishra, and Payel Basu comprised the core group of first students in Bengal since he left for the United States.

The van that took us from the airport to our rented flat in central Kolkata was also carrying another important passenger: an extra-large framed photo of Pandit Das's guru, Pandit Ram Narayan Mishra, requested by Pandit Das. There was no other time for his Kolkata students to bring him the image, because the very next day would be Guru Pūrṇimā, the annual full-moon holiday reserved for honoring one's teachers. Pandit Das told us this would be the first time he celebrated Guru Pūrṇimā in India since he left the country in 1970.

We had planned to celebrate Guru Pūrṇimā at the flat where Pandit Das's guru had lived, now occupied by his guru-brother Pt. Bachan Lal Mishra and family. That morning, however, it was decided that because Bachan-jī's students would be going there throughout the day to pay their respects and the space would be cramped already, it would be more appropriate to hold our own ceremony in our rented living quarters. Rina and I were suddenly, by default, the senior students, and we were anxious to carry ourselves properly during this important ceremony. As we prepared, we discussed what might be expected of us, our foremost question being whether we should touch Pandit Das's feet. Although the action is a common signal of respect to Indian elders, in the United States, Pandit Das would not allow us to touch his feet.[2] *However, this was a new situation in which it might be acceptable and indeed expected.*

We had little time to discuss the matter before Pandit Das called us into the room where the ceremony would take place. Fresh garlands adorned large framed pictures of his guru, Pandit Ram Narayan Mishra, and parents, Srimati Nilima Das and Nritya Acharya Prohlad Das. Dressed in white kurtā-pāyjāmā, *Pandit Das lit incense and deferentially circled it in front of the pictures of his guru, mother, and father. Setting down the incense, Pandit Das placed his hands together at his heart. After he intoned "Aum" and select Sanskrit verses, he began to sing the "Guru Vandanā," expressing reverence to gurus as vehicles for divine knowledge. With a small glance and flick of the hand, he motioned for us to join in: "Guru Brahma, Guru Vishnu, Guru Devo Maheshwara . . ."*[3]

Pandit Das touched his forehead to the base of each picture in turn. When he indicated that we might individually pay our respects, Rina, younger than me but senior in the dance, stepped forward. She followed the order Pandit Das had set, touching the base of each picture with her right hand and bowing slightly. Finally, she came to Pandit Das himself and touched his feet. He initially made a move to stop her, but quickly seemed to reconsider, and placed his hands atop her head in blessing. While she was offering her respects, the other students arrived and stood outside the open door. Seeing them watch us honor Pandit Das and his lineage, I became more conscious of the role we now occupied, as exemplars of tradition to his newer Indian students, and I was reminded of the long road Pandit Das had traveled from the time he first left India.

Returning to India with a "California *Gharānā*"

In the process of researching and writing this book, I came to understand more deeply the import and impact of Pandit Das's life trajectory on the style of kathak he developed. He was born at the tail end of the British Raj and was raised in independent India; as such, Pandit Das would argue, he was uniquely positioned to bridge multiple social and cultural worlds. Growing up in a home that doubled as the arts institution Nritya Bharati, he daily witnessed independence-era ways of training and promotion of traditional Indian arts that primarily involved middle-class members of society who were not hereditary practitioners of those forms. But through intense, one-on-one study with Pandit Ram Narayan Mishra, he was trained in the *guru-śiṣya paramparā*, or master-disciple tradition of artistic transmission. Furthermore, accompanying his guru to the *bāījī* quarters in Bowbazar as a young man, he was also able to observe the world of courtesan kathak training and performance, already in steep decline.

Pandit Das's relationship to his guru strongly impacted his own understanding of what it would mean to be a guru in a new cultural environment. As a young man in the heady days of 1970s California, he may have relished his role as guru to the "blondes and brunettes," but he also went through "tremendous struggles" to implement a culture of rigorous kathak training and artistic excellence in the United States. Pandit Das's early experiences of relative cultural isolation forced him, as he described, to deeply examine his own belief system in order to develop ways to translate or otherwise make his dance practices comprehensible to new students and audiences. He later reflected: "Because I was away, I could *see* India . . . [and] developing all these things while living outside has helped me to go back to India and teach a new way of looking, which is basically going deeper into the old school while adding new technique of my own" (interview, February 26, 2003).

My first trip accompanying Pandit Das to Kolkata, in 2003, took place during a period in which he was working to reconnect with Indian students and audiences; and in subsequent years, he traveled to India with increasing frequency.[4] He continued to teach in Kolkata and more notably in Mumbai, where his student Seema Mehta headed up Chhandam Nritya Bharati beginning in 2010. In India, students, journalists, and audiences enthusiastically received this style, this "new way of looking," particularly in the last ten years of his life, from 2004 to 2014 (interview, February 26, 2003; see also

Dalidowicz 2010). As he began to enjoy more widespread success in India than he felt he had experienced earlier in his career, Pandit Das's creative output blossomed, and he turned his attention to further articulating his philosophies of a life in dance, which included a greater emphasis on spirituality and charitable projects.

In addition to offering more concerts in India's major cities, Pandit Das began regularly teaching children of Kolkata sex workers a few years into the new millennium. He had become increasingly concerned for the girls he saw engaged in prostitution on the streets, and he spoke often of a wish to help get "at least one girl" out of the profession. During our 2003 summer trip, this interest manifested in preliminary involvement with two nongovernmental organizations that included teaching a kathak workshop to a small group of sex workers and speaking at a rally in Sonagachi, Kolkata's largest red-light district.

The following year, Pandit Das began a longer-term partnership with New Light, a public charitable trust working in the red-light district in Kolkata's Kalighat neighborhood that focused on educating the daughters of sex workers. Pandit Das began kathak classes for several girls in the New Light program and assigned his local students to teach them when he was abroad. Though these children had never previously studied kathak, the art form was arguably their birthright. As discussed earlier in this book, kathak was once the province of courtesans. Having lost public sanction for practicing the arts of music and dance during the latter decades of British colonization and into the independence era, courtesans were dispossessed of their social status, their audiences, and thus, their means of earning a livelihood; and most were left few options other than sex work. Although these girls were not necessarily the direct descendants of courtesans, their life conditions were shaped by these broader historical dynamics.

Pandit Das's kathak classes contributed to the girls' educations, designed to help broaden their perspectives and break the cycle of prostitution in their families. In teaching them dance, Pandit Das sought to help them experience an embodied connection to the divine through the practice of dance. He told them, "When you are feeling pain and sadness, light incense, do this prayer [singing and dancing three Sanskrit *śloka*s and *pranām*] and let your worries go" (translated by Antara Bharadwaj) (▶ see video 8.1, cue point 2:17). New Light founder Urmi Basu reports that being trained by someone of Pandit Das's stature gave them "a sense of self-esteem . . . and also a great deal of recognition" (video 8.1, cue point 4:50). And while, as Pandit Das expressed to the mothers of the "New Light girls," his intentions were not to train the girls as professional dancers, they did perform on several occasions including at Kolkata's famous Kalighat Kali Temple and at the Chhandam Nritya Bharati school shows, dancing alongside Pandit Das's other students (video 8.1, cue point: 6:56). Pandit Das also worked to expand access to kathak in the

United States; with tap dancer Jason Samuels Smith, he offered workshops to at-risk children in cities around the country, including in New Orleans, Los Angeles, and Chicago.

A focus on service to society became one in a set of formalized principles developed in 2007 and 2008 to consolidate and communicate his values. To articulate his philosophy for future dancers, Pandit Das turned to his senior students for input. A small group of dancers were asked to write about what they thought were the key tenets for learning kathak; from there, an even smaller group refined and honed these concepts in dialogue with Pandit Das. The Nine Principles, as they came to be known, were subsequently taught to students across the network of schools led by him and his disciples (figure 8.1). In describing the importance of the first principle, attitude and etiquette (*sadvyavahār aur tahazīb*), Pandit Das drew from his experience of training with his guru: "My Guruji was more concerned with how I walked into the dance class than with how I danced."[5] The next three principles, in order, focus on training in the technical aspects of kathak (*prashikshaṅ*), "practice with exertion" (*riyāz, mehnat ke sāth*), and deep study of "history, philosophy, music, mythology, and the rhythmical mathematics in the Indian classical system" (*sarvgyān*). With those skills and knowledge, a dancer is ready for the fifth principle, *upaj*, to improvise both on and off the dance floor. Pandit Das was insistent: "Improvisation in life is very important. One who can do that . . . [has] a flexible understanding of [the] human mind, human self, human world. Then you can be open" (in Lo 2007). From this basis, one's mission becomes the sixth principle, to "educate promote and preserve" the dance for future generations (*śikṣā, prachār aur surakṣā karnā*). This work involves "sacrifice and selfless service" (*tyāg* and *sevā*), listed as the seventh principle. Through this work, the dance might become a *sādhanā* or devotional practice (principle eight), ultimately taking place within and upholding the *guru-śiṣya paramparā* (principle nine).

The development of the Nine Principles serves as but one example of the dynamic relationship between Pandit Das and his students, which was collaborative yet clearly hierarchical, and central to his broader development of a characteristic style of kathak and of dance training. While Pandit Das maintained an emphasis on strong, powerful footwork throughout his career, as he and his disciples matured, their style of kathak in some ways became more fluid and subtle; at the same time, he delved deeply into the relationship of movement and music, particularly through his practice of kathak yoga. In his later years, Pandit Das continued to push himself and his students by increasingly working with complex rhythmic cycles involving half beats, such as 9½-, 10½-, and 12½-beat *tāls*, and by collaborating with dancers from other traditions, particularly tap and flamenco. He passionately proclaimed in *Upaj: Improvise*, a documentary about his years-long collaboration with

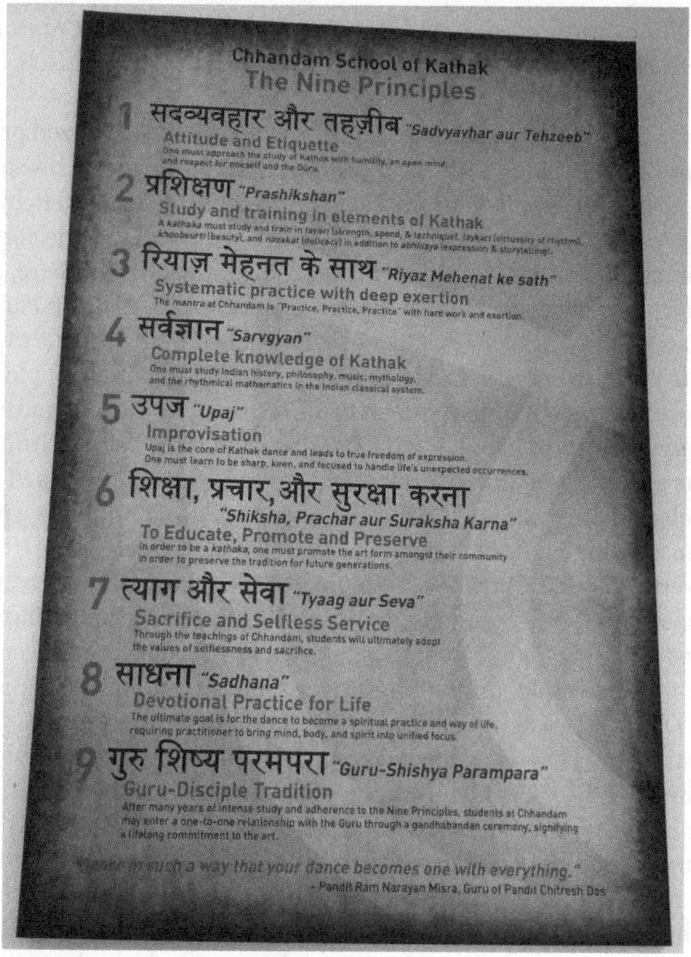

FIG. 8.1. The Nine Principles.

tap dancer Jason Samuels Smith: "You have to evolve with the audience and the time. You *have* to evolve, otherwise you'll be dead. You must understand your surroundings, your time, and your audience. You *must*. And the challenge is: how can *you* evolve with the time and with the audience, without giving up your integrity" (Pandit Das in Uchiyama 2013).

In his more experimental works, Pandit Das's preference for "collaboration" over "fusion" was present in productions such as *East as Center* (2001), and it found yet greater expression in the performances he created in the last ten years of his life, particularly the *India Jazz Suites* collaboration with tap dancer Jason Samuels Smith. *Yatra,* Pandit Das's final full performance, premiered in September 2014 with flamenco artist Antonio Hidalgo Paz and was intended to initiate a new collaboration. As a choreographer, in this period he revisited earlier works including *Pancha Jati*, which was presented in a dramatically revised version in 2014. While the concept, costumes, and lighting were similar to the 2002 production of the same title, the performance was almost completely rechoreographed with new, major technical and rhythmic challenges for the performing musicians and dancers. Both the 2002 and 2014 productions began with a section in which five rhythmic groupings (*jātis*) are included in one long phrase that fits into one cycle of *tīntāl* (see music example 7.6). While the 2002 version included single and double speeds of this phrase, the 2014 version also included triple and quadruple speeds of this phrase (▶ see video 8.2, cue points 4:14 and 4:59). And while the 2002 production showcased separate sections exploring the five *jātis* (3, 4, 5, and 7 and 9 combined), in 2014 Pandit Das began with the 4-beat *chaturaśra jāti* followed by the 5-beat *khaṇḍa jāti*.[6] The final three movements, however, explored *tāls* that added a half beat to each of the last three *jātis*: 5½, 7½, and 9½ (▶ see video 8.3).

In his *nritya* performances, Pandit Das delved into more difficult philosophical questions based in Hindu tradition. For example, in his version of dance-drama *Sita Haran* performed in 2010 by an all-female cast of CDDC members, Pandit Das chose to end with the killing of Bali (king of Kishkinda), intentionally ending at the moment of death in order to challenge the audience to question whether killing is ever acceptable. In *Shiva* (2014, 2016), the dancers played *aghorī*, or ascetic sadhus of the Shaivite tradition.[7] Set in cremation grounds, the piece depicts a guru, played by Seibi Lee, and his *śiṣyas*, who meditate and engage in esoteric practices (▶ see video 8.4 and figure 8.2). The guru character must deal with a *śiṣya* who suffers doubts along his spiritual path, a story that resonated with Pandit Das in his own relationship with some of his students.

Occasionally over the years Pandit Das and others would refer to his work as the "California *gharānā*" of kathak, using the term *gharānā* to indicate both the particular style of kathak he developed and the "lineage" or community of dancers who practice this style (see Chakravorty 2006, 127; Swapan 2015). As we know from the work of many scholars, *gharānā* is a mutable social concept (see Katz 2010; Kippen 1989; Daniel Neuman 1978, [1980] 1990; Silver and Burghardt 1976; Walker 2006, 2014). *Gharānā* identities are thought to have first been adopted by *k̲h̲āndānī* musicians—those within a direct lineage of Muslim musicians. Coming into full fruition in the twentieth century, the last one hundred years has seen the creation, development, and decline of many *gharānās*, beginning with solo vocal and instrumental *gharānās* and growing to include other instruments, including tabla, as well as kathak dance. As nonhereditary artists have become more prominent, lineage more often refers to ties of discipleship.

"The central structural feature of a gharana" Daniel Neuman notes, "is a 'core' lineage founded by an individual or sometimes two brothers" who can

FIG. 8.2. Image from *Shiva* at Z Space, San Francisco, October 27, 2013. Pictured (*left to right*): Labonee Mohanta, Rachna Nivas, Seibi Lee, Farah Yasmeen Shaikh.

be "distinguished from their own ancestors (who are also often known) by virtue of having made to Hindustani music a significant stylistic contribution which then comes to be regarded as the central distinctive feature" ([1980] 1990, 148). While the common determinants of a *gharānā* include a recognizable style and at least three generations of artists performing that style, these questions can be contentious. Neuman continues, "Controversy regarding what is and what is not a gharana, and who is and is not a member is still common and in many respects is political" (161). In examining changes to Pandit Das's ways of performing and teaching, this book is, in essence, tracing the birth of a new style kathak. Will this style be more widely considered a new kathak *gharānā*, a "California *gharānā*"? Because the concept of *gharānā* is a social as much as an artistic construct, the answer will depend largely on whether enough artists and influential members of the arts community recognize it as such. For that, only time will tell. One of the most important determinants in this process will be how many of Pandit Das's disciples and senior students, now teaching themselves, cultivate other disciples who claim his lineage and continue his philosophies, methods, and performance style.

As a teacher and guru, Pandit Das regularly gave his students a considerable amount of material, which seemed to grow exponentially toward the end of his life. In talking with dance-sisters in San Francisco, they would breathlessly tell me about the complexity of material they were learning, both with awe and overwhelm at the sheer amount of new material. When I attended the last annual kathak retreat Pandit Das led, in the summer of 2014, my experience confirmed their descriptions. He seemed to be driven to give us as much as possible; but the more material he shared, the more creativity he felt and the more there was to give. For years Pandit Das said, "If I can only dance like this at the age of seventy . . ." And on his seventieth birthday he indeed danced—at the Castro Theater in San Francisco with Jason Samuels Smith to accompany a screening of the documentary *Upaj: Improvise*, which detailed their collaboration, artistry, and related struggles and journeys.

Pandit Das's Passing

On the morning of January 4, 2015, Pandit Das experienced an acute aortic dissection, a tear in the lining of his aorta. He was rushed to the hospital, where medical personnel were unable to stabilize him for surgery and he passed away relatively quickly, less than two months after his seventieth birthday. He was survived by his wife, Celine Schein Das; by two young daughters: Shivaranjani, then three years old and born on India's Independence Day, and Saadhvi, born on the Fourth of July just a year and a half before his passing;[8] by his brother, Ritesh Das, who leads the Toronto Tabla Ensemble; and in spirit he is survived by countless kathak students, some "unofficial" disciples, and even fewer "official" disciples. Though for most of his life he resisted the term *guru*, calling himself a "modern-guru-in-training," by the end of his life, many called him Guru-jī regardless of whether or not they had officially tied strings with him in a *gaṇḍā bandan* ceremony. Seema Mehta, with whom he was planning to tie strings in the upcoming year, later reflected: "Just as he was always aspiring to be a Guru, in the truest sense of that word, so too I will always aspire to be his *śiṣya*—to be worthy of that position and that responsibility" (pers. comm., June 28, 2016).

Hundreds of people came to Marin County from as far away as India and Japan to mourn his passing. The funeral took place at the same funeral home and cemetery where Ustad Ali Akbar Khansahib was laid to rest, located just down the street from an early site of the Ali Akbar College of Music, where Pandit Das first taught kathak in California. After the public viewing and funeral, a smaller group gathered for a *pūjā*, led by a Hindu priest, and cremation of his body. As soon as the *pūjā* ended, "core" students and his longtime musical collaborator Jayanta Banerjee commenced in ringing bells, blowing conch shells, and singing the Sanskrit *ślokas* that were a regular part of our kathak practice, as we accompanied family members in processing his body to the cremation area. Unbidden and unplanned, one by one many chose to touch his feet, a final farewell and request for his blessings. We sang as his body was transferred into the crematory, and kept singing long after his brother pressed the button commencing his cremation, performing a modified version of the son or brother's duty to light the funeral pyre.

Pandit Das's death came unexpectedly, but his students were not unprepared. Rachna Nivas recalled: "As a guru, he talked about his death on a regular basis. . . . It became quite normalized. Four days before he passed he asked, 'What will you do tomorrow if I die today?' which wasn't unusual" (in Gilbert 2015). All his students heard him talk about his death and pose this and similar questions in the interest of preparing us. Nivas states, "What he was doing was constantly reminding us that this is not about receiving this energy from him. It's about invoking and generating that energy ourselves." Pandit Das spent the greater part of his life creating and molding the next generations of artists and arts activists, many who collectively and/or individually continue working to "educate, promote, and thus preserve" kathak in their specific communities.

Though not as commonplace as other practices and concepts from South Asia (such as yoga, meditation, and ideas such as "karma" and "enlightenment"), kathak is finding a place in contemporary multicultural America; Pandit Das and the Chitresh Das Dance Company did much to bring kathak broader recognition and acceptance. For example, in organizing and hosting two international festivals and symposia—*Kathak at the Crossroads* (2006) in San Francisco and *Traditions Engaged* (2010) held in San Francisco and Los Angeles—Pandit Das's organization succeeded both in positioning itself (if only temporarily) at the center of a continuing conversation about the nature of innovation and tradition within the broader Indian performing arts community, and in gaining mainstream media attention in the United States. September 28, 2006, the first day of *Kathak at the Crossroads*, was declared Kathak Day by the mayor of San Francisco (figure 8.3). Such recognition helped move kathak beyond the "ethnic" dance construct within which Pandit Das and his company worked for several decades. For his life's contributions, Pandit Das received a National Heritage Award in 2007.

While most support for kathak is still found in India, diasporic dancers have assertively joined the global conversation among kathak practitioners, scholars, and critics. Arunabha Deb writes of Pandit Das, "He was no less an ambassador for Kathak than Pandit Ravi Shankar was for the sitar" (2015). I argue, however, that his impact is more similar to that of Ustad Ali Akbar Khan, Pandit Das's role model and proclaimed *satguru* ("true guru," spiritual

FIG. 8.3. Chitresh Das with the Kathak Day proclamation by the mayor of San Francisco, September 28, 2006.

guru), who performed at the highest levels of excellence, but perhaps more importantly, deeply influenced generations of Americans through the relatively unassuming, ongoing work of teaching.

Retreating to Move Forward

In July 2015, the summer after Pandit Das's passing, *śiṣyas* and senior students gathered at a retreat center in Upstate New York to dance together, as he had wished, and to continue to process his loss and discuss how we might proceed as a community. Our retreat schedule took the same basic form as in previous years, beginning with rising at 6 a.m. for a 6:30 footwork session. As usual, our second dance session of each day involved *bol-paran*—compositions. But this year we focused on exercises and compositions that Pandit Das taught in the 1970s (see figure 5.5). Gretchen-dī led the class, and we learned exercises Pandit Das had taught years ago. We joked that he might respond to this session by asking, "Why are you going back to these *old* materials?" There was some excitement in practicing repertoire from Pandit Das's past teaching to which many, even some of the more senior dancers in the room, had not often been exposed. We decided, ultimately, that he would have wanted us to understand this embodied history so that we could be more informed dancers with a richer, fuller repertoire of movements. And practicing the exercises he taught in his early days in the United States helped us in trying to connect in a physical and emotional way with the depth of our own artistic heritage and move forward collectively.

Reflecting on how Pandit Das must have felt when his own guru passed, Jason Samuels Smith once remarked that "he probably kicked into another gear and felt like he had even more responsibility than he did before, and I understand that because after your masters leave, you know, you feel like it's up to you now" (in Uchiyama 2013). In their own ways, each of his senior students and *śiṣyas* similarly responded with great effort, focus, and commitment to their work. Over lunch during this retreat, we shared information and excitement about various recent projects. Charlotte Moraga enthusiastically told us about a concert by two members of the Chhandam Youth Dance Company, who had each performed an abbreviated kathak solo the previous weekend. Rachna Nivas was about to spend a month teaching in New York City, and she and Rina Mehta were collaborating with two esteemed tap dancers, Dormeshia Sumbry-Edwards and Michelle Dorrance, in a project called *SPEAK* (inspired by, but unique from the collaboration between Pandit Das and Jason Samuels Smith). Seibi Lee and I shared stories of working recently with kathak students in Los Angeles, and Seema Mehta told us about her upcoming solo performances in Mysore and Kolkata.

Along with this camaraderie, there were also heated discussions and even fierce disagreements about how to move forward. While we were confident that his closest, most invested and involved students and disciples would continue Pandit Das's work in various ways, would we have a collective identity? Would those separated by distances of states and countries—or those even in the same urban centers—continue to work together? Several dancers already led different organizations in different locales. Would there be a "Chhandam Global" or an otherwise labeled network of affiliated schools? As performing artists, would some continue to dance and create new works together? The biggest concerns and questions surrounded the future of the Chhandam

Chitresh Das Dance Company (CCDDC) in the Bay Area, where Pandit Das's presence was most consistent and where his energy and personality were most integrally a part of the fabric of everyday life. It was clear that no one person would be able to step into the multiple roles Pandit Das left vacant. Would a group of senior dancers jointly move the Chhandam school forward artistically? Would the Chitresh Das Dance Company continue, or would its members form new professional performance organizations?

In regularly discussing his own death, Pandit Das sometimes posited what would happen afterward: which dancers might align with which, and what projects they might undertake. Even as he anticipated that his disciples might splinter, he requested that we come together once a year in a retreat atmosphere to dance as a community. Each evening of the July 2015 retreat, we discussed these issues and more. We did not find concrete answers, but as the retreat came to an end, eleven of us sat on the floor in a circle, each representing various eras of Pandit Das's teaching and different sites of kathak transmission contributing to his legacy. We sang "Śri Krishno Chaitano" the song with which he often closed his performances (▶ see video 8.5). As we completed the song, many had tears in our eyes; we said a quiet *namaśkār* with palms pressed together at our hearts and sat for a long time in silence. I felt there was a comfort in continuing to sit silently with one another, and I imagined each of us was quietly supporting one another and sharing that fragile space of community before launching back into the various kinds of work we each felt compelled to do in our roles as lineage bearers, working to uphold Pandit Das's rich legacy. Finally, it was Gretchen-dī who broke the silence with a simple "We will try."

* * *

The passing of artists with strong vision and committed followers often brings about a period of intense change, and those trained by Pandit Das were catalyzed to move forward in various ways. As of 2019, the Chhandam School of Kathak continues, led by Artistic Directors Seibi Lee and Rachna Nivas. Other senior students and disciples have left the CCDDC to form their own schools or pursue their own performing careers, or both, including Farah Shaikh (Noorani Dance), Charlotte Moraga (Chitresh Das Institute), Antara Bhardwaj, and Labonee Mohanta, all based in the San Francisco Bay Area. Though not disbanded, the Chitresh Das Dance Company went on hiatus. In 2015, five artists trained by Pandit Das formed the Leela Dance Collective: Rina Mehta, Seibi Lee, Rachna Nivas, Sarah Morelli (author), and Shefali Jain (who had primarily studied with Gretchen Hayden). Without one person who could clearly fill Pandit Das's shoes and serve as artistic director of a dance company, this group felt the collective model served as a fruitful organizational structure to move the art forward, whereby we could support one another's growth as artists and create new works both individually and together.

My participation in this dance collective stemmed from feeling a greater responsibility to the art form following Pandit Das's passing. Pandit Das had occasionally told me that I would be a "different kind of ethnomusicologist"—someone established as both a scholar and a performer. Of course, many ethnomusicologists successfully develop careers involving varying degrees of performance, teaching, and scholarship. In saying this, I feel Pandit Das was encouraging me to take seriously my capacities as a performer and to continue to integrate those elements into my professional life. For many years, however, I privileged my scholarship and university-level teaching. Since Pandit Das's passing, I came to more fully embrace my role as a tradition bearer, which led to prioritizing my own continued training and helping develop the next generations of dancers. These changes also led to establishing a kathak school in Denver, the Sureela Academy (from *sur*, or tuning), to provide opportunities for University of Denver students to pursue more advanced kathak training postgraduation, and to serve others, particularly members of the South Asian American community, along the Denver Front Range. This teaching, along with participation in the Leela Dance Collective, helped me better understand the huge sacrifices and multiple responsibilities my guru-sisters took on as professional *kathakas*.

As I had heard Pandit Das tell a roomful of would-be students in Boston during my very first workshop with him, "Being a kathak dancer is not so easy!" His daily routine as a *kathaka* included spending each morning on the phone with various students and disciples from near and far, maintaining his own practice (including dance and running) in the early afternoons, and on most days, it included driving long distances to teach. In his later years, that full schedule was balanced with caring for two young children.

To be a *kathaka* in the ways Pandit Das expected required a great deal, including physical energy, mental acuity, interpersonal skills, and intrapersonal work. It necessitated ongoing study from external materials as well as internal reflection and self-examination in order to develop insights into the human condition needed for compelling performance. The process of becoming a kathak artist required one to absorb, retain, and maintain an ability to perform a tremendous amount of material, and also to make it one's own. It necessitated physical strength and agility, melodic and rhythmic understanding. Beyond the kathak elements of *taiyārī*, *layakārī*, *khūbsūratī*, and *nazākat*, it required a knowledge of history, philosophy, and religion to inform and inspire one's portrayal of different characters and emotions. And ultimately, it required enough ego to get up on stage but also an ability to let go of one's ego, to maintain an attitude of humility in order to channel fierce energies, and to remain a learner, even when your teacher is no longer living.

For those who joined the larger social-artistic network of a dance company or dance collective, being a *kathaka* required constant negotiations with a number of persons and personalities. It meant constantly being aware of and involved in multiple aspects of a particular production and the larger project of advancing the art form. It meant learning the various aspects of staging productions, from grant writing, marketing, and public relations, to costume, sound, and lighting design. Individually, unless one had other sources of financial support, it required doing the work necessary to pay one's bills while still reserving time and energy for training.

Being the type of *kathaka* Pandit Das modeled meant committing to teaching others and particularly to inspire and develop the next generations of *kathakas*. Doing so required an openness and willingness to go through the ups and downs of a student's journey. It necessitated cultivating an understanding of specific students' personalities and learning styles, and developing a sense for when to push a particular student and when to support, when to inspire, when to be forgiving, when to approach the student, and when to hold back and let the student come to you—and a willingness to be flexible in one's responses as situations required. Being a *kathaka* in the way that he envisioned for each of his *śiṣyas* and *śiṣyas*-in-training was transformational and all-encompassing.

As his *śiṣyas* negotiated large and small decisions and experiences without him in the months following his passing, many remarked to me, in various ways, that they were gaining a better understanding of how difficult it must have been for him to establish a kathak community so far from the place of his birth, and to maintain such a high standard over the course of so many years. In this, Pandit Das modeled a constancy in dedication to molding the next generations of *kathakas*. His students were the core of his legacy, as he expressed in an interview with a fourteen-year-old member of the Chhandam Youth Dance Company less than two months before his passing.[9] She asked him what he believed about the afterlife or reincarnation, to which he replied, "I believe that we came from somewhere—the energy comes from somewhere (and) it *has* to go somewhere. So, I don't know where it goes, because I don't know! But I know that in *this* life, . . . from the birth to death, our activities will show what we are. . . . after we leave our body then the legacy becomes our afterlife—*our* afterlife becomes our legacy . . . like you, *you* are my legacy" (Pai 2014).

Notes

Chapter 1. Encountering the Dance

1. See the appendix for definitions of *bol* and other basic terminology utilized in this book.

2. In this particular composition, the *bol*s are grouped rhythmically as "tā– theī– tattat theī– ā– theī– tattat theī–." See "Note on Musical Notation" before chapter 1.

3. Although referred to as "toe-flatting," the dancer actually places the ball of the foot (not the toe) on the floor behind the flat of the other foot. This pattern is repeated rhythmically: "flat ball flat ball," etc.

4. The rhythmic organization of this particular interaction is in the form of *savāl-javāb* (Hindi: "question-answer"). *Savāl-javāb* typically involves exchange between two performers, but in this case, it takes place between two characters enacted by the same dancer.

5. Pandit Das reported watching an Indian national television show on which Smt. Sitara Devi emphasized that artistic freedom could be obtained through *riyāz* with *mehnat*. The connection between "freedom" and "discipline" has been made by other Indian artists as well, including famed bharatanatyam dancer Smt. T. Balasaraswati, who stated, "It is freedom through discipline, not freedom from discipline" (quoted in Katrak 2001, 9–10).

6. *Saṅgīt* is defined in the Saṅgīt Ratnākar (ca. 1250) and elsewhere, as the confluence of instrumental, vocal, and dance performance. It is also the term used for a party held the night before a wedding in some South Asian communities.

7. The designation of "classical" is a fraught status constructed as part of a broader project to build India's postcolonial national identity. Dances previously reviled for being performed by those existing outside caste hierarchy and gender norms were formally embraced and "rehabilitated" in an effort to create national cultural traditions. Today, dances recognized as classical (*śāstrīya*) by the Sangeet Natak Akademi (India's National Academy for Music, Dance, and Drama), include kathak, bharatanatyam

(*bharatanāṭyam*), odissi (*oḍisī*), kuchipudi (*kuchīpuḍī*), mohiniattam (*mohinīaṭṭam*), kathakali (*kathakalī*), manipuri (*maṇipurī*), and most recently, sattriya (*satrīyā*). These forms are judged as classical on the basis of grounding in principles from the Nāṭya Śāstra, an approximately two-thousand-year-old treatise on the dramatic arts. It is important to note, however, that there has not been the continuity nor purity implied by official narratives around classical dance. Also, many female practitioners of newly "classical" traditions were systematically kept out of the revival process, which was dominated instead by upper-caste women and male gurus.

8. The creation of this format in solo kathak performance is credited to Smt. Maya Rao, Pt. Shambhu Maharaj's first nonhereditary female student at the Bharatiya Kala Kendra in New Delhi beginning in 1955 (Walker 2010, 293).

9. For example, in discussing the contributions of Pt. Birju Maharaj, doyen of the Lucknow *gharānā* (school) of kathak, Shyamanand Jalan, former vice chair of the Sangeet Natak Akademi noted, "He's not what his father was, or his grandfather was! He has changed all of kathak. Not only the presentation of kathak, but also the movements, also the sensibilities" (interview, July 31, 2003).

10. While *gharānās* may have developed in part to distinguish (Kalāvant) soloist performers from (Mirāsī) accompanists, through processes of change and adaptation, "most of the viable gharanas today were indeed founded by Mirasi accompanists" (Daniel Neuman 1978, 198; see also Walker 2014, 80–82).

11. In the mid-twentieth century, some writers also included Lahore as an important center for kathak (Walker 2014, 107, citing Bowers [1953] 1967).

12. *Tārikiṭa* footwork consists of an alternating four-step pattern in which a dancer strikes the floor with the sole of one foot and the heel of the other foot.

13. Whereas *tatkār*, described at the beginning of the chapter, is a pattern of eight steps, *nā dhin dhin nā* is a four-step pattern in which one foot is positioned behind the other. The ball of the back foot produces each "nā" step by quickly lifting and placing the ball of the foot back on the floor. The front foot brushes up and slightly away from its standing position to produce the first "dhin" and lands again for the second.

14. For example, Mekhala Natavar notes that in the great variety of footwork patterns she was taught by Jaipur *gharānā* kathak exponent Pt. Madan Maharaj, she learned one similar to the *tārikiṭa* technique utilized by Pandit Das as well as *tatkār* and *nā dhin dhin nā* patterns (personal communication, January 2, 2018).

15. Kay Kaufman Shelemay discusses three processes by which individuals become members of musical communities as descent, dissent, and affinity (2011). This book deals primarily with the categories of descent and affinity, though a loosely formed dissent group also existed, made up of former students of Pandit Das. See also Mark Slobin's discussion of affinity, which he differentiates from choice and belonging (1993, 55).

16. Pandit Das's then wife, Julia Maxwell, played a key role in establishing the Chhandam School of Kathak and the Chitresh Das Dance Company.

17. Gretchen Hayden and Joanna de Souza became formal disciples (*śiṣyas*) of Pandit Das in 1998.

18. As part of India's decolonization efforts, on January 1, 2001, the British spelling Calcutta was formally changed to Kolkata, more accurately reflecting its pronunciation by the city's majority Bengali- (*banglā*-) speaking inhabitants.

19. Various institutional changes took place just before and following Pandit Das's death on January 4, 2015. In 2014, the Sacramento branch of Chhandam closed because Pratibha Patel moved back to the San Francisco Bay Area. In 2015, Rina Mehta led the transition of the Los Angeles branch of Chhandam to an autonomous nonprofit, The Leela Institute for the Arts. In 2016, I began an affiliate school in Denver called Sureela, and two new institutions were opened in the Bay Area: the Chitresh Das Institute, with artistic direction by Charlotte Moraga; and Noorani Dance, led by Farah Shaikh. While some students of Pandit Das are still active in Kolkata, at the time of this writing Chhandam Nritya Bharati is now primarily located in Mumbai, where Seema Mehta maintains a thriving school.

20. The music for *Impressions of California Goldrush* was composed by George Ruckert and performed by Ruckert (sarod, fiddle, piano, keyboard and voice), Pranesh Khan (tabla), James Pomerantz (sitar), Brian Godden (guitar), and John Peterson (banjo).

21. See the appendix for a list of persons interviewed.

22. Kippen 2008 artfully discusses the particular challenges "of revealing a complex socio-musical being" in ethnographic writing focusing on North Indian gurus (134).

23. As examples of reflexive ethnography, see Babiracki (1997) 2008, Bakan 1999, Hagedorn 2001, Kisliuk 1998, and Shelemay 1991.

24. In Bhakti literature, the imagery of crossing the river or trying to reach the other side of the river suggests human longing to connect with the divine, such as in Bhakti saint Mirabai's poem, "Kadara [kidhar] piyā naiyā morī kaise lāge pār," ("Oh love, how will my boat arrive?"), used on occasion by Ali Akbar Khansahib as the textual basis for vocal composition.

25. Students of Pandit Das who were involved with the making of *Upaj: Improvise* (Uchiyama 2013) include Rina Mehta (executive producer), Antara Bhardwaj (producer), and Shipra Shukla.

26. The Chhandam Chitresh Das Dance Company did not publicly sell videos of Pandit Das or his dance company's performances, insisting that the video medium does not adequately convey the power and impact of live performance. Professionally recorded videos of Chhandam school shows were made available for purchase beginning in 2004, and then only to students and their parents. Several years after my primary fieldwork period, the community decided to make video clips available on YouTube, after thorough discussion of the ramifications of doing so. Most videos that accompany this book are excerpted from professional recordings.

27. Pandit Das's "official *śiṣyas*" include Gretchen Hayden, Joanna de Souza, Jaiwanti Das Pamnani, Charlotte Moraga, Pratibha Patel, and Seibi Lee. Before his death, he had also planned *gaṇḍā bandan* ceremonies to formalize his *guru-śiṣya* relationship with Rina Mehta, Rachna Nivas, and Seema Mehta. Other dance students and I consider ourselves his unofficial disciples.

28. Massage is often considered a student's duty to their teacher in India and elsewhere (e.g., Daniel Neuman ([1980] 1990, 46).

Chapter 2. Dancing History

1. The sarangi player on this recording was Pt. Ramesh Mishra. A recipient of the prestigious Sangeet Natak Akademi Award, Pt. Mishra was a childhood friend and longtime musical collaborator of Pandit Das. The terms used to describe each note are drawn from the Indian solfège system called *sargam*; see "Note on Musical Notation."

2. Kolkata-based video journalist Ajoy Roy recorded and edited most of the video employed during the performance.

3. The concept of *sādhanā* is explored more thoroughly in chapter 4.

4. Kathak also has been influenced by its development in communities outside South Asia in recent decades as well as by events throughout modern South Asian history largely outside the scope of this book, including British colonization, the independence movement, Partition, and the priorities of the independent countries of India, Pakistan, and Bangladesh.

5. There is enormous diversity in belief and practice among those who follow some form of Hinduism, which is more properly a geographical designation than a theological one (see, e.g., Flood 1996). The terms Hindu and India both derive from Greek and Persian alterations of the word Sindh, a river now better known as the Indus, which runs through Tibet, India, and Pakistan. Hindu adherents will often instead identify their practices with the term *sanātana dharma*, "eternal way" (P. Goldberg 2010, 3).

The Muslim world is too large and diverse for the designation Muslim to be adequate when examining the cultural elements informing kathak dance. Its "Muslim" aspects should more properly be considered geographically, as influences from Iran, Central Asia, and Afghanistan that were brought to the subcontinent through invasions beginning as early as the eighth century. These aesthetic elements of kathak were particularly cultivated in courts during the Mughal Era (1526–1857) and thereafter during British colonial rule.

6. This understanding of history, though problematized in some contemporary scholarship, particularly Walker 2014, is commonly repeated by most performers and many dance scholars. See also chapter 1. Regarding Muslim patronage, Chakravorty writes that "Muslim royalty did not change the basic aesthetic concepts associated with Hindu ritual practices of music and dance such as rasa, bhava and darshan (gaze), but secularized them and added technical complexity" (2008, 36–37).

7. As Walker describes, Smt. Maya Rao's contributions were particularly significant to establishing *ślokas* and *vandanās* in the kathak repertoire (2010, 294).

8. For example, as a young man Pandit Das's participation on school soccer, hockey, and cricket teams at times conflicted sharply with his responsibilities as a kathak disciple; "Once," he reminisced, "I was playing a football match instead of practising my dancing. My guru came to the field. He was so furious, he threw his walking stick at me. I had to abandon the match and go back with him" (Suraiya 1970, 19).

9. The placement of the image of a deity on the stage was an important shift in the presentation of India's dances, and in kathak, part of the explicit Hinduization of the dance form. For bharatanatyam, the practice "became the custom during the 1930s

. . . providing/restoring a semblance of a devotional setting" (Allen 1997, 79). Placing an idol on stage was vehemently criticized by hereditary dancer Smt. T. Balasaraswati, who according to Arudra, said "she would not show any disrespect to Nataraja's idol with her lifted foot pointing towards him in dance movements," (1986, 12, in Allen 1997, 79).

10. The Dramatic Performances Act of 1876 permitted colonial authorities to fine and/or jail citizens involved in presenting "dramatic performances which are scandalous, defamatory, seditious, obscene or otherwise prejudicial to the public interest" (in Bhatia 2004, 121). The June 15, 1984, interview with Pandit Das that is the source of this quotation appears to have been videotaped backstage before his performance at the 1984 Olympic Arts Festival in Los Angeles (C. Das 1984).

11. Ethnomusicological studies of courtesans in North India include Post (1987), Maciszewski (2001, 2006), Babiracki (2004), Qureshi (2006), and Walker (2010, 2014). See also Manuel (1989), Oldenburg (1990), and Rao (1990, 1996).

12. Oldenburg, for example, reveals that courtesans in Lucknow were subject to "heavy fines and penalties" as retribution for their support of the 1857 Indian rebellion against the British East India Company (1990, 260).

13. Anti-courtesan laws included the 1934 Bombay Devadasi Prostitution Act, the Madras Devadasi (Prevention of Dedication) Act of 1947, and its Andhra Pradesh amendment in 1956. The 1947 Madras Devadasi Act "was one of the first acts of the new Indian Parliament," suggesting these laws' symbolic value to newly independent India (Walker 2010, 290).

14. Anna Morcom documents the continued moral policing of lower class/caste women's performance; her 2009 article illuminates similarities in rhetoric between nineteenth- and early twentieth-century anti-nautch campaigns and those in early twenty-first-century Maharashtra that led to a ban in Mumbai on girls dancing in bars, leaving seventy-five thousand women jobless (125).

15. At the forefront of this shift in South India was Rukmini Devi Arundale, a Brahmin woman who was largely responsible for transforming the *devadāsī* dance form *sadir* into its present-day manifestation as bharatanatyam. The dance was renamed by Sanskritist V. Raghavan (Erdman 1987, 64), and today is one of India's most globally successful dance exports (see, e.g., O'Shea 2007).

16. Pandit Ram Narayan Mishra's students who became active as dancers or teachers include Ruby Bandyopadhyay, Sushmita Bannerjee, Maya Chaterjee, Chitresh Das, Chetna Jalan, Parimal Krishna, Arjun Mishra and Bachan Lal Mishra (neither directly related to Ram Narayan Mishra), and Kanon Sen. Some of these dancers took a second guru when Pandit Mishra died.

17. *Bhāv batāna* is described in greater detail in chapter 5.

18. One former student of Pandit Mishra in particular asked that I not reveal her identity, as she tearfully told me how she had worked to ensure that her children, who were in school and on track for "respectful" middle-class professions, would not learn about her family's history in the *koṭhās*.

19. This excerpt, and others below, are from one of two chapters authored by Pandit Das in a 32-page publication created by his then-wife, Julia Das (now Maxwell) (J. Das 1986a). Maxwell recalls: "For this part, I encouraged Chitresh to remember

things he saw, smelled, and heard. . . . My thinking was that it would draw the reader vicariously into the rich cultural context that had shaped Chitresh's discipleship and career" (2012, 120).

20. Of the three temples Pandit Das mentions here, the Shakti temple is more specifically a temple (*mandir*) to goddess Durga. This Durga Mandir and a Shiva Mandir are located on the opposite bank of the Ganga (or Hooghly) River from Kolkata's famous Dakshineswar Kali Temple. Only one *gaṇḍā bandan* ceremony was held elsewhere; Pandit Das's *gaṇḍā bandan* with Seibi Lee took place at her home in the San Francisco Bay Area on her fiftieth birthday, December 15, 2014.

Chapter 3. On the American Stage

1. Earlier court cases including *United States v. Balsara* (1910) and *A. Kumar Mazumdar* (1913) determined Indians eligible for citizenship because they were deemed to be Caucasian rather than Asian; as such, approximately one hundred Indians became naturalized US citizens between 1913 and the 1923 *Bhagat Singh Thind* decision (Rangaswamy 2000, 44). For Indians in the United States, various other laws impeded establishment of homes and communities, including a law barring the wives of Indian male laborers from accompanying them to the United States and antimiscegenation laws rendering it illegal for Indian men and "white" women to marry (P. Srinivasan 2012, 100; Leonard 1992).

2. First translated into English by Sir Charles Wilkins in 1785, there may be as many as 650 English-language versions of the Bhagavad Gita today (P. Goldberg 2010, 27).

3. Sensational media coverage continued during their stay in the United States. Journalists wrote about troupe members' struggles adapting and the tragedies they experienced. In particular, on January 3, 1881, Saheb gave birth to a baby who died just a few days later; and Ala Bundi died on February 2, 1881, due to typhomalarial fever (P. Srinivasan 2012, 50–51).

4. Though many writers reiterate St. Denis's claims that she gained initial inspiration for her works from an orientalist Egyptian poster or surmise that she gained further knowledge through library research (e.g., Desmond 1991, 38; Shelton 1981, 48), Priya Srinivasan argues that St. Denis's kinesthetic knowledge could only have come from directly witnessing and learning about Indian dance from actual Indian dancers and culture-bearers—including those performing on Coney Island in 1904 (2012, 71–73).

5. Notably, Graham later repudiated this training and asserted the modern dance she developed necessitated a break from tradition, including the "foreign" material practiced at the Denishawn School (Tomko 1999, 217; P. Srinivasan 2012, 105–7). Priya Srinivasan argues that "Graham discarded Denishawn's overt mimicry in favor of a more subtle, hidden appropriation," which "became the new face of orientalism, couched in the rhetoric of modernity" (2012, 107).

6. Madame Menaka (née Leila Roy) founded the Menaka Indian Ballet company in 1934; between 1935 and 1938 the company toured several cities in Europe as well as Southeast Asia and India (see D. Joshi 1989).

7. La Meri renamed the school the Ethnologic Dance Center when Ruth St. Denis moved to California in 1942 (P. Srinivasan 2012, 111–12; Shelton 1981, 254).

8. Ram Gopal notably studied both bharatanatyam and kathakali with Gurus Kunju Kurup and T. K. Chandu Panicker (kathakali) and Gurus "Madhuramba" and Meenakshi Sundaram Pillai, as well as Jaipur *gharāna* kathak from Guru Sohan Lal (Gopal and Dadachanji 1951, 81; Sai 2015). Early in his career, he also performed with La Meri in one of her tours of Asia (Burns 1998, 354).

9. Citing the La Meri Papers 1912–54 at the New York Public Library, Priya Srinivasan credits dance critic John Martin with coining the term *ethnic dance* in 1939 (2012, 108 and 193, fn. 11). The term was used soon thereafter by La Meri in her program notes.

10. The first LP of Hindustani music recorded outside South Asia, *Music of India: Morning and Evening Rāgas*, was recorded by Ali Akbar Khan and tabla player Pt. Chatur Lal while on a US tour in 1955 (Lavezzoli 2007, 59). Khansahib's and Ravi Shankar's massive influence on western understandings of Hindustani music is largely beyond the scope of this book (see e.g., Farrell 1997; Lavezzoli 2007; Reck 1985; Ruckert 1994; Shankar [1968] 2007 and 2001; Slawek 1991; Wade 1978; and Worth 1991).

11. The Beatles' best-known song utilizing Indian sonic materials is "Norwegian Wood." For discussions of western experiments with Indian musical materials from that era, see Cupchik forthcoming; Reck 1978 and 1985; Silver 1978; and Wade 1978.

12. As mentioned earlier, Balasaraswati first traveled to the United States in 1954, on a tour organized by the Asia Society (P. Srinivasan 2012, 188, fn. 26).

13. ASEA, later renamed the Center for World Music and Related Arts, relocated from San Francisco to San Diego in 1979.

14. A Unitarian church in Terra Linda served as the Ali Akbar College's first site in Marin County during the summer of 1969 and a few summers to follow. The college moved several times over the following years; other sites included two Girl Scout camp locations and a military academy (George Ruckert, pers. comm., July 10, 2015).

15. Throughout his life, Pandit Das would cite others who influenced him, often employing groupings of three. Depending on the period of his life and context, the names on his lists would differ somewhat. Near the end of his life, for example, he often cited his three primary influences as Swami Vivekananda, Japanese samurai (*rōnin*) Miyamoto Musashi, and Lord Krishna (Seema Mehta, pers. comm., July 5, 2015).

16. Pandit Das utilized the terms *kathaka*s and *kathak*s not to refer specifically to members of the "kathak" caste of hereditary performers (Walker 2006, 49), but to mean any kathak artists.

17. Given the meteoric rise to fame of Ravi Shankar, who among his many achievements, performed on the *Ed Sullivan Show*, this goal was not particularly far-fetched (Reck 1978, 9).

18. Following the 1984 premiere, Pandit Das performed *Twelve Minutes* several times, even as a discrete piece performed in the course of longer kathak solo performances (Joanna de Souza, pers. comm., August 18, 2015).

19. As mentioned in chapter 1, kathak dancers might instead begin with a formalized Muslim salutation called *salāmī* (Natavar 2000, 494).

20. This particular *tarānā* was introduced to Pandit Das by sitarist Peter van Gelder, one of Khansahib's first students to accompany Pandit Das.

21. "Madan Bhasma" was the only portion of *Twelve Minutes* to utilize prerecorded music, a choice likely made based on available resources rather than artistic preference.

22. Later quotations in this chapter are from this performance unless otherwise attributed.

23. Although many artists today believe Thakur Prasad to have been the guru of Wajid Ali Shah, Walker's research reveals inconsistencies in this history. As she notes, various authors cite either Thakur or his brother Durga Prasad as Wajid Ali Shah's guru, while in his own writings on kathak, Wajid Ali Shah mentions neither Thakur nor Durga Prasad (2014, 103, citing W. Shah [1877?] 1987).

24. This style of executing *chakkar*s with five sounds was not deliberately transmitted to his students, who tend, as is more common, to perform single-leg turns on a planted heel.

25. In tabla repertoire, the depiction of a train has been more common, and many tabla players make a connection between *relā* compositions and the *relgāṛī*.

26. Though she did not become as well-known, Baby Rani was a contemporary of Roshan Kumari-jī, the latter being most known for her performance in Satyajit Ray's *Jalsaghar* (1958).

27. In one account, Pandit Das described audience members requesting *The Train*; when he asked the audience whether he should dance with or without the tabla, a fellow artist who knew that the effect would not be as striking with the tabla player mischievously or maliciously shouted, "With tabla player!" (C. Das, pers. comm., July 26, 2003).

28. *Jāti* has varied meanings. In addition to its musical definition, these include "community or caste group" and "position fixed by birth," (sometimes implying a "good birth" or "high caste") as well as "kind, race; genus, species; nationality," and "family, lineage" (McGregor 1993, 367).

29. Pandit Das noted that "other North Indian musicians such as Ravi Shankar were borrowing from South India, and Uday Shankar was bringing in South Indian dancers" (interview, November 14, 2005). The use of *jātis* in kathak also has not been limited to Pandit Das. For example, Sushil Saxena comments that Pt. Sunder Prasad once demonstrated for him "how *tatkār* could be winsomely done as a kind of trelliswork upon the different *jātis*" (1991, 10).

30. Pandit Das taught his dancers to express *saṅkīrṇam* (9) most commonly as 2 + 3 + 4 ("taka takiṭa takadimi"). While the rhythmic mnemonics for groupings of three ("takiṭa") include a retroflex *ṭ* in the last syllable, Pandit Das's students (sometimes unfamiliar with retroflex consonants) tended to pronounce the phrase "takite."

31. I use a modified form of western staff notation to transcribe this performance for several reasons. While most kathak notation is prescriptive, acting as an outline of the rhythmic structure and *bol*s utilized by dancers, this transcription is descriptive, intended to convey the details of a performance for the purpose of analysis. Unlike most kathak compositions, *The Train* is not set within the context of a *tāl* framework, and because the performance was not recited, there is a less explicit relationship of footwork to corresponding *bols*. For some footwork patterns used, the corresponding *bol* patterns are obvious; for some portions of the performance, however, *bol*s may be

a somewhat artificial and arbitrary addition. For these reasons, I devised a system of notating types of footfall used solely for this transcription and analysis.

32. A note on transcription method: in certain portions of the video recording of this performance, I could not follow all the movements of Pandit Das's feet when the video played at normal speed. To more precisely create and verify this transcription, I alternated between watching the footage at 30 percent of the original speed (without sound), and listening to the sounds produced at their original speed.

33. I discuss this eight-step pattern, *tatkār*, in greater detail in chapter 4.

34. The *saṅkīrṇa-miśra* grouping was often used by Pandit Das in his own dancing and teaching; because 9 + 7 = 16, this pairing fits simply into the framework of sixteen-beat *tīntāl.*

35. Pandit Das also used the *jātis* as a structural device in large-scale choreographic works, discussed in chapter 7.

36. Monica Dalidowicz reports a similar directive, "to 'hear' the dance" in Pandit Das's disciple Seibi Lee's kathak classes in the Bay Area in the late 2000s (2015, 845).

Chapter 4. Teaching in a New Country

1. Kippen notes that the term *mashq* is also used occasionally among Lucknow *gharānā* tabla players to refer to *riyāz* (1988, 127). Just as both Sanskrit and Arabic-derived terms are used for the concept of practice, the Sanskrit words *guru* and *śiṣya* can be substituted with the Arabic-derived *ustad* and *śāgird*, terms more often used by Muslim musicians when referring to teacher and student.

2. Later quotations in this section are from *Sadhana* (2001) unless otherwise attributed.

3. Tabla master Ust. Ahmad Jan Thirakwa is also credited with using this technique to stay awake, and Daniel Neuman reports that he sat "where bugs and insects and scorpions used to bite . . . so he wouldn't feel sleepy" (Daniel Neuman [1980] 1990, 33, in Kippen 1988, 128).

4. Kippen's research finds that most musicians claim to partake in more daily *riyāz* than is supported by empirical evidence (1988, 128).

5. Because of immigration laws detailed in chapter 3, Pandit Das did not have many South Asian students during the first several years he taught in the United States. His first Indian American student was Amrit Mann, who moved to the United States in 1976. She began studying with Pandit Das in August 1978 and continued her training until her daughter was born in 1986. Amrit returned to her studies with Pandit Das in 2008 (pers. comm., August 16 and December 29, 2016).

6. Smt. Chetna Jalan (then Tewari) was in the United States as the daughter of a member of the Indian embassy in San Francisco. According to some who studied at the AACM at that time, she was picked up by an embassy car immediately following her teaching and did not spend much time getting to know the students outside of classes.

7. Urine therapy (uropathy) is a practice in which one ingests or absorbs urine using a variety of methods including drinking and massaging it into the skin. Its benefits were touted by former prime minister of India, Morarji Desai, who died in 1995 at the age of ninety-nine (Kroon [1993] 1996).

8. A different, more complete English translation of the couplet is included in Sethi's volume of Kabir poetry: "Master and God both stand / Face to face with me— / To whom should I pay my respects? / Hail to thee, my Master, / Who revealed the Lord to me!" ([1984] 1994, 649).

9. In his 2008 "Working with the Masters" essay, Kippen discusses several challenges for scholar-disciples, such as when loyalty to one's guru conflicts with one's interest in presenting musical material or a reading of history that might not be flattering to the guru's artistic family.

10. During my own years of navigating kathak student and scholar roles, my relationship with Pandit Das faltered for almost two years. At the time, as an untenured assistant professor with this book well underway, I was concerned about how the change would impact my career. Although it did not alter this book's narrative significantly, that period of time in which I was distanced from Pandit Das's charismatic orbit afforded me new perspectives on *guru-śiṣya* dynamics, reflected in this book. I was able to mend my relationship with Pandit Das several years before he passed away, and our teacher-student bond was arguably stronger for weathering the experience.

11. A number of "homegrown gurus" also became influential in the United States, including Sivaya Subramuniyaswami (born in 1927 as Robert Hansen), Swami Rudrananda (born in 1928 as Albert Rudolph), and Baba Ram Dass (born in 1931 as Richard Alpert), by mixing "Hindu sources with American metaphysical traditions, as well as American values such as individualism, egalitarianism, democracy, and a Protestant work ethic" (Gleig and Williamson 2013, 3).

12. Barker writes that the mass suicide at Jonestown reached a level of public awareness that at the time was "matched in the pollsters' experience only by the attack on Pearl Harbor and the explosion of the atom bomb" (1986, 330).

13. In India, too, the word *bābā* may be used sincerely or derisively to refer to *sādhus*, wandering mendicants who are "both respected and mistrusted" (Hausner 2007, 98).

14. While Moraga lists cultural differences as a factor, both non–South Asian dancers and dancers of South Asian descent reported similar responses from friends, family, and acquaintances.

15. The dance company usually wore standard kathak attire for performances; however, in *Impressions of the California Goldrush* (1990, discussed in chapter 1) they also experimented with nontraditional costume choices.

16. Stances are also referred to as *ṭhāṭ* in other schools (see, e.g., Maharaj 2002, 69 and 80). This use of the term privileges the positions held at/after *sam*, or beat one, during the performance section also called *ṭhāṭ*. Pandit Das instead distinguishes the two terms, using *ṭhāṭ* to describe the complete performance section in which dancers utilize *kharants* (stances).

17. Specific examples of the "scaffolding" of kathak skills at the Chhandam School, in particular building toward the practice of kathak yoga, are analyzed in detail by Monica Dalidowicz (2015).

18. *Tatkār* is generally produced while standing in place, but the footwork pattern can also be used when traveling to the left and right or forward and back.

19. The "brush" on the *bol* "tat" denotes a dual action of bringing the heel down and quickly lifting the foot, led by the toes, so that the foot is prepared to next slap the floor. Sometimes *eṛī tatkār* is performed with a more deliberate heel action rather than a brushing action.

20. The non-retroflex variant "*-gun*" can be substituted for *-guṇ*. Similarly, *diguṇ* is sometimes written and pronounced "*doguṇ*" or "*duguṇ*," and "*tiguṇ*" is interchangeable with *tīnguṇ*. Spellings in the text reflect the most common usage among Pandit Das's kathak community.

21. I generally translate *mātrā* as "beat" because most of the examples found in this book and its accompanying videos are in *vilambit* and *madhya layas*, slow and medium tempi at which the *mātrā* tends to be identical to the perceived pulse. As various scholars note, however, at much faster or slower tempi, the "beat" is not felt at the same rate as the passage of *mātrās*; because of this, Kippen instead uses the term "count" (2006, 96; see also Clayton 2000, 77).

22. This way of thinking about footwork in relation to the *tāl* applies particularly to slow and medium speeds of *tāl*: *vilambit* and *madhya layas*. For *drut laya* (fast tempo), it is easier to conceptualize the cycle as a whole. "Note on Musical Notation" provides basic information on the notation system employed in these music examples.

23. A similar style of arm movement is captured in Smt. Roshan Kumari's performance in Satyajit Ray's 1958 film, *Jalsaghar*. In the film, however, Kumari's arms are straighter, move along a more diagonal plane with the floor, and don't utilize a flipping of the hands that lends added movement and dimension to the California *chakkar*. Her feet also don't approximate the hovering technique of Pandit Das's style.

Chapter 5. Dancing Gender

1. Purnima Shah defines *abhinaya* as "the art of creative, imaginative, mimetic portrayal of the narrative theme through facial and bodily expressions," citing the etymology of the term, which implies "the translation of 'knowing' into 'telling'" (1998, 14 fn. 1).

2. Known more specifically as *bhāv-batānā*, this style of dance is associated with courtesan *ṭhumrī* singers and flourished in Benares (Vidyarthi 1959, 25, quoted in Walker 2014, 67). *Bhāv-batānā* was also considered a specialty of Pt. Shambhu Maharaj and his nephew, Pt. Birju Maharaj (see, e.g., Gottlieb 1988).

3. Addressing the divine as a lover is common in Bhakti literature and practice. The Bhakti religious movement can be traced to sixth-century South India; in the fourteenth and fifteenth centuries it spread through North India (see, e.g., Hawley 1988). The movement is characterized by a focus on individual communication with the divine in vernacular languages (once solely the privilege of priests chanting in Sanskrit). Devotees, regardless of their sex, may take on feminine gender identification in approaching the divine, such as in Gauḍīya Vaiṣṇavism, and may use the language and sensibilities of common relationships such as child and mother or lover and beloved (see, e.g., P. Shah 1998; Schweig 2002).

4. Here, Pandit Das meant "feminine ways of seduction"; other aspects of feminine power are explored later in this chapter (cf. Dalidowicz 2010).

5. A similar description of learning *abhinaya* from Guru Bandana Sen can be found in Chakravorty 2008, 107–8.

6. This is one of many efforts by South Asian dancers in the twentieth century to draw connections between contemporary practices and Sanskrit philosophies (see, e.g., Chakravorty 2006; Chatterjea 2004; Coorlawala 2004; O'Shea 1998; Walker 2010).

7. Soon after the kids' class got underway in Berkeley, Pandit Das began a second class for the mothers of those children with the help of CDDC members Noelle Barton and Michele Zonka, who was then also his longterm romantic partner.

8. When concentrating on footwork, hands instead tend to be clasped together in front of the chest. This is not a *hasṭak*, but a common position used in both practice and performance labeled the "rest position" in the Lucknow school (Lalli 2004, 27).

9. With the hands held in second *hastak* in front of the chest, the elbows were slightly lowered in comparison to the first *hastak* position, but were still held above the level of the hands. In some other styles of kathak, the elbows are held significantly lower.

10. In this particular exercise, the *bols* are grouped rhythmically as "theī–tātheī –tātheī– theī–theī– tat–tat–."

11. In his earlier teaching, Pandit Das somewhat dismissively characterized this second style as "spinning cobwebs" or "snacky dancing" (Barton interview, November 14, 2005).

12. Because his native language was Bengali, Pandit Das pronounced the Hindi word *sarpa* ("snake") with an *sh*. He generally encouraged his students in this and other matters of pronunciation to default to Hindi, reflected in the spelling *sarpa* for the remainder of this discussion.

13. "Sarpa Śīrṣa," a favorite of Pandit Das, was also performed with other melodies. In *Sadhana* (2001), Pandit Das sang it in *rāg* Bairagi while dancing (see video 5.4, cue point 1:25), and at a kathak intensive in the summer of 2014, he composed a melody for the song in *rāg* Basant.

14. Later quotations in this chapter are from this field recording unless otherwise attributed.

15. A dhoti is a lower-body wrap worn by men; for performance, it is usually white or off-white and made of light cotton. For more information on Guru Kelucharan Mohapatra, see Ileana Citaristi 2001.

16. This footwork pattern can be grouped into phrases of 3 + 3 + 2 syllables as shown in the main text; the footfalls are even, however, and can be written in rhythm across the span of two beats as "takiṭata kitadhina."

17. In 1975, Nimai Goswami was captain of the soccer team for the Mohun Bagan Athletic Club, one of the oldest soccer clubs in Asia (established in 1889).

18. Elsewhere in her dissertation, Mekhala Natavar argues that *lāsya*-style dancing became associated with the Lucknow *gharānā* and *tāṇḍava*-style dancing with the Jaipur *gharānā* because a number of women performed Lucknow-style kathak, whereas the Jaipur style was performed primarily by male dancers (1997, 66, fn. 48).

19. Of course, if other kathak dancers were taken into account in this discussion, these differences might be less pronounced. For example, contemporary male kathak

exponents including Pt. Rajendra Gangani of the Jaipur *gharānā* and brothers Ravi Shankar Mishra and Mata Prasad Mishra from the Benares *gharānā* all showcase vigorous styles of dancing. Nevertheless, a comparison between Pandits Maharaj and Das is striking. It is also interesting to note that the distinction inherent in their surnames—Maharaj ("king") and Das ("servant")—points to their different social positions within the hierarchy of this lineage-oriented dance form: Pt. Maharaj as a *gharānedār* dancer, or a direct descendent in a family with a distinctive artistic lineage, and Pandit Das without a clear line of descent.

20. Pandit Das often discussed his reverence for the power of the Mother (a category that included mother goddesses and human mothers). However, I never witnessed him attribute the entirety of his dance to connection with one particular deity; instead, he tended to discuss the specific attributes and energies of the divine manifestation he was invoking at a particular time, whether Lord Shiva, Krishna, Kali, or other.

21. Among his connections to Swami Vivekananda, Pandit Das held *gaṇḍā bandan* ceremonies (establishing formal guruship with his most serious disciples) on the bank of the Ganga (or Hooghly) River across from the Dakshineswar Kali Temple, where Vivekananda's guru, Sri Ramakrishna, spent much of his life.

22. Similarly, other "important historical figures such as Mahatma Gandhi, Jawaharlal Nehru, and Ananda Coomaraswamy all discovered India through leaving it" (Tarlo 1996, 299, fn. 10, cited in Dalidowicz 2010, 222, fn. 5).

23. As an example of this virtuosity, Pandit Das often played one *chhand* (rhythmic pattern/groove) on the tabla while improvising in a different one with his feet.

24. In 2013, for example, four male students studied kathak in Pandit Das's school of approximately four hundred.

25. Kathak dancer Vikram Iyengar describes another common stereotype in India, that boys play sports, and that only "effeminate" men pursue classical dance forms (2010, 229–30).

26. In her study of interpretations of *ardhanārīśvara* found in Indian iconography, hatha yoga theory, and Bhakti poetry, Ellen Goldberg notes that *ardhanārīśvara* may be translated as "lord who is half woman," indicating a gender hierarchy privileging the male half, denoted by the term *īśvara* (2002, 1).

Chapter 6. Dancing Unity, Articulating Difference

1. As Dalidowicz notes in her study of Pandit Das's cultural work, "Numerous scholars have detailed the historical development of a binary schema that opposes India and the west, spirituality and materialism, and that has provided the grounding for the ideas we see in Das's style (Chatterjee, P. 1993; Inden 1990)" (2010, 222 fn. 4).

2. In this practice, the *ṭhekā* serves as the sung text, and dancers in this community usually describe this process as "reciting the *ṭhekā* while singing the *laharā*."

3. When performing *tatkār* speeds with triple subdivisions of the beat (including *bārahguṇ* [12] included in music example 6.1), dancers usually also recite and/or sing the accompanying *ṭhekā* and *laharā* with triple rather than duple subdivisions.

4. This fifth-*mātrā tihāī* is one of the "sixteen *tihāīs*" discussed in chapter 7.

5. As seen in video 6.2, dancers sometimes perform the "1–2–" gap between each of the *tihāī*'s *pallas* with a double turn (completing two full rotations before bringing down the second foot) instead of two single turns.

6. Dalidowicz makes a similar argument in her 2015 article, asserting "the naming itself, 'kathak yoga' . . . signals an attempt to tap into ideas of ancient India's spiritual and ascetic practices and the Californian market of spiritual, holistic, and New Age practices" (849).

7. Because so many factors are involved in performing and in measuring the various aspects of kathak yoga (in contrast to the relatively straightforward practice of running on a treadmill, for example), the study was ultimately shelved.

8. Earlier, some kathak yoga presentations were included in smaller-scale student performances.

9. *Sargam* notation for the *laharā* in *rāg* Bairagi sung in video 6.4 can be found in music example 6.2. A version of the *laharā* Pandit Das sings in *rāg* Kalashri can be found in music example 6.1.

10. Clayton refers to this process as "divisive *laykārī*" (2000, 157).

11. Because Moraga was working in ten-beat *jhaptāl* instead of the more common sixteen-beat *tīntāl*, she employed a five-step footwork pattern rather than eight-step *tatkār*.

12. Chapter 7 discusses the kathak solo further.

13. See chapter 1 for a brief discussion of the terms *heritage* and *affinity*.

14. All five dance company members in figure 6.2, for example, began their study of kathak while in college: four started taking classes with Pandit Das while students at San Francisco State University or UC Berkeley, and the fifth dancer first studied kathak with Gretchen Hayden at Tufts University.

15. According to Julia Maxwell, Pandit Das first expressed the idea of a US "cultural bouquet" while they were meeting John Kridler of the Marin Foundation to review the CDDC's first grant (see Maxwell 2012, 111). Only once during my fieldwork was I present for discussion of this bouquet analogy: during a three-day intensive retreat in 2001, in which Pandit Das asked students to elaborate on its meaning. In the 1980s, the concept appears to have been in more frequent use.

16. Garlands hold symbolic importance in South Asian cultures; they often adorn Hindu deities, are exchanged in weddings, and are placed around the necks of the recipients of awards or various accolades. In California, this imagery was replicated in the poster for a concert celebrating Ali Akbar Khan's eightieth birthday: photos of several artists Khansahib supported in their US careers, and who performed in his honor for the occasion, were arranged around the poster's sides and bottom like a garland around a central image of Khansahib.

17. See chapters 3 and 7 for discussions of Pandit Das's use of *jātis*.

18. Theologian Richard Kyle describes the New Age as a nebulous and diffuse "cultural trend" drawing heavily on Indian and other Eastern religions as well as "Western occultism, . . . modern psychology, natural science, and even Christianity" (1995, 9, 75). Through the 2000s, New Age spirituality continued to be a noticeable cultural presence in the Bay Area and particularly Marin County. Several members of the CDDC, particularly those who grew up in the area, had a positive and accepting outlook

on beliefs and practices associated with the New Age; but, as with *hippie*, negative connotations associated with the term New Age led most in the kathak community to avoid its explicit use.

Chapter 7. Form and Freedom in Kathak Performance

1. While these categories are useful for organizing a discussion of types of *upaj* in kathak, more fundamentally, Nettl's article problematizes the binary categorizations of composition and improvisation and advocates for a more nuanced understanding of performances as lying along a spectrum from relatively more to relatively less fixedness. Additionally, he questions whether instead of considering relative degrees of improvisation, what differs between music cultures instead may be the concept of a musical "piece" itself, and the way it is to be appropriately rendered (1974, 9).

2. See, for example, Patricia Shehan Campbell's discussion of theories of learning to improvise from ethnomusicology, music pedagogy, and cognitive psychology (2009).

3. Various artists and scholars have worked out formulas for generating *tihāīs*, including this formula from George Ruckert for *bedam tihāīs* that begin and end on *sam*: $P = (nT+1) \div 3$. P stands for the number of beats in each *palla*, T is the number of beats in the *tāl*, and n is the number of cycles of the *tāl* (1994, 342–43).

4. While I have observed and taken part in formal and informal study situations with other kathak students during which *tihāīs* were written down and analyzed, I never witnessed Pandit Das's involvement in this type of learning.

5. The fifth-*mātrā tihāī* from this series is discussed in chapter 6.

6. The sequence was also sometimes practiced with a *tihāī* from the sixteenth *mātrā*, not included in the particular version discussed here. Another, more physically challenging version of the sequence included two versions of the sixth and seventh *mātrā tihāīs*, with all four performed in quick succession.

7. Following the sixteen *tihāīs*, dancers in the company's rehearsals usually moved immediately into a *paran*, a type of composition utilizing *bols* typical to the pakhawaj drum. Generally slower but longer, the *paran* required a different kind of endurance to complete the sequence.

8. *Naṭavarī bols* are pronounced and transliterated by some kathak dancers and authors as "tigdha dig dig." It is said that these bols originated in the sounds Lord Krishna's feet made dancing on the hood of the serpent-demon Kaliya as he rose victorious from the Yamuna River, a tale described in chapter 1.

9. Each consonant in "tddd" represents a phrase of equal length. Thus, "dhā" although only one syllable, fills the same amount of time as "tiga" or "diga." The "Note on Musical Notation" describes this style of notation.

10. A capacity to instantaneously produce *tihāīs* from any point in a *tāl* is one indicator of expertise in Hindustani music and kathak. See, for example, Lipiczky's description of a 1973 tabla solo by Pt. Sharda Sahai of the Benares *gharānā*: "While playing he challenged his audience to indicate at random when in the tala he should start a tihai. His repertory of formulas was so extensive and his command of them so proficient that no matter when he was signaled, he was able to play a tihai that ended on sam. Furthermore, each tihai was a natural outgrowth of the pattern he was working with at the moment the tihai began" (1985, 159).

11. See chapter 4 for a thorough discussion of different speeds and styles of *tatkār*.

12. For the sake of legibility, the rhythmic density of these in-text examples is half that typically performed and notated in music examples 7.4 and 7.5. In music examples 7.4 and 7.5, capitalization indicates where the musician's *bols* coincide with a slap of the dancer's foot.

13. These bols can also be transliterated as "ḍā," "ṛā," and "dir" or "ḍiṛ" (Miner 1993, 180–81).

14. While tabla players most often perform accompanying roles, their status may largely depend on the kind of performances they accompany, with kathak accompaniment generally being considered less prestigious than accompanying melodic instrumentalists and vocalists.

15. Pandit Das and the musicians with whom he worked never discussed caste/community with me or in my presence.

16. Ris shared a particularly vivid example of Pandit Das's tendency to change things at the last minute: "In the early days, Dada [Pandit Das] would often take wild chances in his performances. Once, while on tour in India in the early 1980s, Dada gave me a big surprise. We were beginning the story . . . of the abduction of Sita by Ravana—as part of a full concert at New Delhi's Kathak Kendra at the invitation of Birju Maharaj. This story had six characters, each with their own introductory theme and variations leading into the improvised dramatic sections. We had always practiced and performed this story in *tīntāl* but this time, after Dada announced the piece, he turned to the musicians and cued us for *rupak tāl*, the seven-beat rhythm cycle. On the spot, I had to recompose each of the themes and variations for the six characters and then follow his adaptation of the *bols* (rhythmic compositions) as he improvised to make them fit the seven-beat rhythmic cycle throughout the ten-minute piece" (pers. comm., August 11, 2013).

17. In addition to the 2002 version of *Pancha Jati*, Pandit Das also choreographed a substantially revised version later in his career (2014).

18. See chapter 3 for a more detailed discussion of the *jāti* rhythmic system.

19. In music example 7.6, the syllable beginning each iteration of the five *jātis* is capitalized.

20. Pandit Das and his dance company also collaborated with Balinese musicians and dancers of Gamelan Sekar Jaya for the 2000 production *Subali-Sugriwa*, which premiered in San Francisco and was staged at the Bali Arts Festival in Denpasar, Bali, later that year.

21. Some cross-cultural projects involving kathak and tap or flamenco have even come to be called Ka-tap and Kathamenco (Chakravorty 2006, 128). Other artists exploring connections between kathak and one or both of these dance forms have included Anjani Ambegaokar, Deepti Gupta, and Janaki Patrik, all based in North America (128). Pandit Das's disciples have also worked in collaboration with tap dancers, including Charlotte Moraga (performing with Dormeshia Sumbry-Edwards and Chloe Arnold in *India Jazz Progressions*, 2007), Seema Mehta (with Jason Samuels Smith in *Rhythm Rewritten*, which premiered 2015), and Rachna Nivas and Rina Mehta (with Dormeshia Sumbry-Edwards and Michelle Dorrance in *SPEAK*, 2016 and several subsequent performances). In September 2014, Pandit Das performed in

collaboration with flamenco dancer Antonio Hidalgo Paz (*Yatra*). See Miriam Phillips (1991; 2013) for more extensive discussion of the relationship between kathak and flamenco.

Chapter 8. Coming Full Circle

1. The official name of the airport in Kolkata is the Netaji Subash Chandra Bose International Airport. Dum Dum is the surrounding area of northwest Kolkata, so named because it was there that a British captain developed hollow-point bullets, or *dumdum*, in the 1890s.

2. See chapter 4 for more detailed discussion of touching feet and other forms of interaction between teachers and students.

3. The *vandanā*'s full text and translation: *gurū brahmā / gurū viṣṇu / guru devo maheśvara / gurur sākṣāt parabrahmā / tasmai śrī gurave namaha*. "The guru is (equal to) Brahma / the guru is (equal to) Vishnu / the guru is (equal to) Maheshwara (Shiva) / the guru alone is the Supreme Brahman / to the great Guru, I offer my respect." The text comes from the "Gurū Gīta," a section of the larger Hindu text, the *Skaṇḍa Purāṇa*, attributed to sage Vyasa.

4. I also briefly joined Pandit Das and CDDC members Jaiwanti Das Pamnani, Farah Shaikh, Jenny Baker, and Rachna Nivas during a trip to Kolkata in December 2000, when I was there as a music student of Ali Akbar Khansahib. A relatively new kathak student at the time, I attended a house concert where Pandit Das performed, and joined him and the company members for a few mealtime conversations.

5. This quote does not appear in the poster version of the Nine Principles seen in figure 8.1, but is included in a longer more detailed version of the document given to students at Pandit Das's and affiliated schools.

6. Within the *khaṇḍa* movement, he also overlaid concepts of the *pañcha bhūta* or five elements of creation: space (*ākāsh*), wind (*vāyu*), fire (*teja*), water (*apa*), and earth (*pṛithivī*).

7. *Shiva* was presented as a work in progress at Z Space, San Francisco, on October 26 and 27, 2013, and after Pandit Das's death, was performed in its entirety on February 27 and 28, 2016, at Zellerbach Hall in Berkeley.

8. I met with Pandit Das several times in the weeks following our last summer kathak retreat to review the video examples I had prepared to accompany this book. While we watched these clips, he imagined aloud how his daughters would perceive these videos in the future, make sense of them, and understand him a bit better through them and this project as a whole.

9. As a Catholic school student, this Chhandam Youth Dance Company member, Sruti Pai, had been charged with interviewing someone she saw as a model of spirituality. The recorded telephone interview was shared with Pandit Das's senior students and played at his funeral.

Appendix: Persons Interviewed by the Author

Ahluwalia, Cimeron. Personal interview, San Rafael, CA, 15 November 2004.
Anonymous. Personal interview, San Rafael, CA, 19 April 2001.
Anonymous. Personal interview, Kolkata, India, 3 August 2003.
Anonymous. Personal interview, San Rafael, CA, 2 November 2004.
Baker, Jenny. Personal interview, Berkeley, CA, 12 November 2004.
Bandyopadhyay, Ruby. Personal interview, Kolkata, India, 30 July 2003.
Bannerjee, Anindya. Personal interview, Kolkata, India, 6 August 2003.
Barton, Noelle. Personal interviews, San Rafael, CA, 14 June 2004 and 14 November 2005.
Birla, B. K. (Basant Kumar). Personal interview, Kolkata, India, 3 August 2003.
Biswas, Jaya. Personal interview, Kolkata, India, 5 August 2003.
Chakrabarty, Rajeev. Personal interview, Kolkata, India, 8 August 2003.
Chatterjee, Maya. Personal interview, Kolkata, India, 1 August 2003.
Das, Chitresh. Personal interviews, San Rafael, CA: 22 April 2002, 25 June 2002, 12 July 2002, 2 December 2002, 26 February 2003, 17 June 2004, 17 August 2005, 14 November 2005, and 11 May 2006. Kolkata, India: 20 July 2003, 25 July 2003, 31 July 2003, and 6 August 2003. Cambridge, MA: 14 April 2004.
Hayden, Gretchen. Personal interviews, Stow, MA: 18 January 2003, 31 March 2003, and 17 March 2004. Brookline, MA: 29 January 2004. E-mail, 13 May 2004.
Huq, Farhana. Personal interview, Somerville, MA, 11 January 2003.
Jalan, Chetna. Personal interview, Kolkata, India, 31 July 2003.
Jalan, Shyamanand. Personal interview, Kolkata, India, 31 July 2003.
King, Michele. Personal interview, Cambridge, MA, 19 October 2003.
Kutty, Govindan. Personal interview, San Mateo, CA, 23 May 2003.
Lee, Seibi. Personal interview, Richmond, CA, 18 November 2002. Telephone interviews, 6 October 2003, 4 January 2004, and 24 July 2004.
Maharaj, Prasanna. Personal interview, Ramakrishna Mission, Kolkata, India, 16 July 2003.

Mehta, Rina. Personal interviews, San Rafael, CA: 6 April 2003, 3 August 2003, and 18 June 2004. Telephone interviews: 28 February 2004 and 28 August 2004.
Meinl, Joanna. Personal interview, San Rafael, CA, 17 November 2004.
Misra, Bachan Lal. Personal interview, Kolkata, India, 30 July 2003.
Moraga, Charlotte. Personal interviews, San Francisco: 2 October 2002 and 19 December 2002. Telephone interview: 24 April 2004.
Nath, Anjali. Personal interview, Somerville, MA, 11 January 2003.
Pamnani, Jaiwanti Das. Personal interview, San Bruno, CA, 6 February 2006. Telephone interview, 8 September 2004.
Patel, Pratibha. Personal interview, San Bruno, CA, 17 June 2004.
Ris, Christopher. Personal interview, Fairfax, CA, 5 July 2003.
Ris, Marni Wieser. Personal interview, Fairfax, CA, 5 July 2003.
Roy, Abhijit. Personal interview, Kolkata, India, 4 July 2003.
Ruckert, George. Personal interview, Stow, MA, 18 January 2003.
Sarkar, Debasish, Chitresh Das, and anonymous. Personal interview, San Rafael, CA, 19 April 2001.
Sen, Hemen Chandra. Personal interview, Kolkata, India, 16 August 2003.
Sen, Kousic. Personal interview, San Rafael, CA, 19 April 2001.
Shaikh, Farah Noorani. Personal interview, San Francisco, CA, 12 December 2002.
Singh, Madhuri Devi. Personal interview, Kolkata, India, 3 August 2003.
Zonka, Michele. Personal interview, San Rafael, CA, 14 November 2005.

Glossary of Terms

All page numbers in parentheses refer to McGregor 1993.

abhinaya: "Acting" (48). In kathak, the portrayal of various characters through facial expression, body language, and gesture.

ālāp: Nonmetric, improvisatory exploration of the melodic characteristics of a *rāg*. *Ālāp* usually precedes other sections of a Hindustani performance.

āmad: "Coming, approach, arrival" (90). Slow compositions presented at or near the beginning of a kathak performance, utilizing the *bols* "tā theī tat."

āndolan: "Swinging" (76). In music, a slow oscillation of pitch akin to vibrato.

āṭhguṇ: "Eight-fold." See *guṇ*.

āṭh śabd: A style of *tatkār* footwork in which a slap of the whole foot is produced for each of the eight steps. See *tatkār*.

bāī-jī: A class of courtesan in North India.

bansuri [baṅsurī]: A keyless flute, typically made of bamboo.

barābar: "Equal," "even" (710). In relatively fast speeds of kathak footwork, *barābar* distinguishes duple subdivisions of the beat from *ḍeṛhī*, or triple subdivisions. See *ḍeṛhī*.

bārahguṇ: "Twelve-fold." See *guṇ*; *ḍeṛhī*.

bharatanatyam [bharatanāṭyam]: Originating in the South Indian state of Tamil Nadu as the dance form *sadir*, bharatanatyam is one of eight types of dance currently recognized as classical (*śāstrīya*) by the Sangeet Natak Akademi, the Indian government's national academy for the performing arts.

bhāv: "Emotion," also "expression, gesticulation" (765, 766). In kathak, the stylized portrayal of emotional states.

bhāv batāna: The performance of emotional states through facial expression, body language, and gesture. Associated with kathak's courtesan history, *bhāv batāna* is often performed while sitting and repeating one or more lines of song, interpreting the text's emotional tenor in various ways.

bol: "Utterance, word" (750). A term for the representative language indicating rhythmic pattern and often the manner of producing North Indian music and dance. Kathak makes use of *bols* derived from various drums (including tabla and pakhawaj) and some that are specific to the dance. In kathak there is not always a direct correspondence between *bols* and their technical delivery; *bol* patterns can thus be interpreted in a variety of ways.

chakkar: Turn, revolution. This term is used most often in kathak to refer to swift turns executed on the heel of one foot (usually the left).

chaubīsguṇ: "Twenty-four-fold." See *guṇ*.

chauguṇ: "Four-fold." See *guṇ*.

chhand: An accented, repeated pattern, groove.

chheguṇ: "Six-fold." See *guṇ*.

ḍeṛhī [or ḍeṛh]: "One and a half." The term is often used to describe fast speeds of footwork in triple subdivisions of the beat. Compare with *barābar*.

desī: "Indigenous" (512). People of a particular *deś* or region/country; colloquial: Indian or South Asian.

diguṇ [or doguṇ, duguṇ]: "Two-fold." See *guṇ*.

drut: "Speedy, swift" (516). In music and dance, *drut* refers to a fast tempo, between approximately 150 and 299 beats per minute. See *laya*.

eṛī: "Heel" (142). *Eṛī tatkār* is a style of *tatkār* in which the first and fifth steps are articulated by a slapping of the full foot on the floor, and the rest employ the heels. See *tatkār*.

gaṇḍā bandan: From *gaṇḍā*, a cord or colored threads, tied (*band*) by the guru around the wrist of the student, a ceremony formally marking the *guru-śiṣya* relationship.

gat bhāv: Performance of a story through dance movement and facial expression.

gharānā: From *ghar*, "house." *Gharānā* refers to the stylistic schools of Hindustani music and kathak dance, often named after the home city of its founder, such as the Jaipur and Lucknow *gharānās* of kathak.

ghuṅgharū: Dance bells, which in sets are tied around dancers' ankles.

guṇ: A "multiplicative suffix" (269). When appended to a number, *guṇ* corresponds to -fold, or times. For example, *tiguṇ* or *tīnguṇ* means "three-fold" or three times within a given beat or cycle. In kathak, *-guṇ* often refers to the number of times a footwork pattern is produced within one cycle of a given *tāl*.

hastak: Hand position, from *hasta*, "hand" (1066). In Pandit Das's school *hastaks* are usually labeled by numbers, "first *hastak*," "second *hastak*," etc.

Hindustani [hindustānī]: The classical music of North India, also performed in the broader region including Bangladesh, Pakistan, Nepal, and beyond.

jāti: "Birth" or "class"; a social "position fixed by birth" (367). In music and dance, *jāti* refers to a system of Karṇāṭak rhythmic groupings.

Karnatak [karṇāṭak]: The classical music of South India.

kathak: Originating in North India, kathak is one of eight types of dance currently recognized as classical (*śāstrīya*) by the Sangeet Natak Akademi.

kathakali (kathakalī): Originating in the southwestern state of Kerala, kathakali is one of eight types of dance currently recognized as classical (*śāstrīya*) by the Sangeet Natak Akademi.

kavitā: Poem.
kharant: Stance.
khūbsūratī: Beauty/handsomeness of face or form (243).
kramalaya: From *kram*, stepwise, regular process (220). The incremental increase in rhythmic density during a Hindustani music or dance performance. In kathak, *kramalaya* is often displayed using *tatkār* or, less commonly, other footwork patterns.
laharā: Also known as *nagmā*, a repeated melody usually of one *avartan* (cycle) of a given *tāl* in length, which provides rhythmic reference for kathak or tabla soloist.
laṛant: "Battle," a section of performance in which the tabla player and kathak soloist together engage in aggressive, dense improvisation, working to match or even anticipate one another's rhythmic phrases. Also known as *sāth saṅgat.*
lāsya: "Feminine" style dancing, characterized by soft, subtle and graceful movements.
lau: "Absorption of mind; deep meditation" (904).
laya [or lay]: Tempo. Most performances of Hindustani music or kathak are performed in any of three tempi: *vilambit* (slow), *madhya* (medium), and *drut* (fast).
layakārī: Rhythmic virtuosity. Facility in working inventively within rhythmic parameters.
madhya: "Middle; central" (788). In music and dance, *madhya* refers to a medium tempo, between approximately 75 and 149 beats per minute. See *laya*.
manipuri (maṇipurī): Originating in the northeastern state of Manipur, manipuri is one of eight types of dance currently recognized as classical (*śāstrīya*) by the Sangeet Natak Akademi.
manjīra: Handheld cymbals used to keep time in kathak practice and performance.
mātrā: Often glossed as "beat," "count," or "unit of time." *Mātrā* is used to define the number of metric pulses within a particular rhythmic cycle (*tīntāl* has 16 *mātrās*, *jhaptāl* has 10, etc.), and also indicates the expanse of time between two beats.
mehnat: "Labor, work," implying exertion or effort (833).
nagmā: See *laharā*.
naṭavarī bols: Dance mnemonics based on the syllables "tiga dhā diga diga," said to represent the sounds made by the feet of Lord Krishna (Naṭavar) as he danced on the hood of the serpent-demon Kaliya.
nāṭya: Drama.
nazākat: "Softness; delicacy; elegance," derived from Persian: *nāzuk* (541).
nṛitt [nṛtt]: "Pure dance," dance without narrative.
nṛitya [nṛtya]: Dance combining storytelling and rhythmic expression.
odissi [oḍisī]: Originating in the eastern state of Odisha, odissi is one of eight types of dance currently recognized as classical (*śāstrīya*) by the Sangeet Natak Akademi.
pallā: Each iteration of a rhythmic/melodic/danced phrase that is repeated three times to create a *tihāī*. Each *tihāī* has three *pallās*.
panje: A style of *tatkār* in which the heels remain fixed on the ground and the steps are articulated by tapping the toes and balls of the feet. See *tatkār*.
paramparā: Tradition.
pranām: A sanctification of the dance space performed before and after dancing.
rāg [or rāga]: A complex melodic concept utilized in Hindustani and Karṇāṭak music, as well as other South Asian music traditions. In Hindustani music, each *rāg*'s

characteristics may include the specific notes used, which notes are given greater or lesser importance, identifying melodic phrases, and particular ways of moving in ascent and descent, as well as other musical details and extra-musical associations.

riyāz: "Training, practice; toil" (864).

sādhanā: Spiritual practice; in the arts, practice done with regularity and devotion, and often in solitude.

sam: The moment of synchronicity in the Hindustani musical system usually expressed by a unison articulation by dancer and/or instrumentalists. Sometimes defined as "beat 1," *sam* should be differentiated slightly from the first *mātrā*. *Sam* occurs at the beginning of the first *mātrā*; the first *mātrā* comprises the time lapsed until the second *mātrā*, while *sam* is only the first moment of arrival. See *mātrā*.

saṅgīt: A term with several meanings and uses, *saṅgīt* is classically defined as performance combining instrumental, vocal, and dance elements. More commonly in Pandit Das's community this is conceived as the combination of melody, rhythm and movement.

sarangi [sāraṅgī]: A short-necked, box-shaped chordophone (stringed instrument). The sarangi is played with a bow and by pressing the fingernail or cuticle against the side of the main playing strings, which are made of gut. The instrument also has sympathetic strings (see *sarod*) and a goatskin head.

sarod: A twenty-five-string fretless lute instrument with a stretched goatskin head and steel fingerboard. The instrument has four main playing strings that are played with a pick (often made out of coconut shell) and by pressing the string against the fingerboard with the free edge of the fingernail. Some strings (*chikārī*) are used for rhythmic emphasis, and several others are considered "sympathetic" (*tarafdār*). Sympathetic strings are rarely plucked; instead each string, tuned to a specific note, will vibrate when the same note is played on the main strings.

sāth saṅgat: See *laṛant*.

savāl-javāb: A "question-answer" section of performances of Hindustani music and kathak dance. One performer will lead (often the instrumentalist or kathak dancer) by introducing a short phrase that is then imitated by the other primary performer (usually the tabla player). For kathak, the phrases focus on footwork. After trading a series of phrases, the performers then shift to phrases shorter by half of the previous. They may shorten the phrases again and again, usually ending with a *tihāī*.

śiṣya: "Pupil; disciple" (951).

sitar [sitār]: A stringed instrument with a long, hollow fretboard, movable frets, and a gourd that serves as a resonating chamber at its base. Like the sarod, the sitar has main playing strings, strings used for rhythmic emphasis and sympathetic strings (see *sarod*). The main strings are plucked with a wire plectrum (*mizrāb*) and can be individually pulled along a fret to create microtonal variations and glissandi, called *mīnḍ*.

solahguṇ: "Sixteen-fold." See *guṇ*.

svaramaṇḍāl: A zither often used to accompany Hindustani vocalists or kathak performances.

tabla [tablā]: The most popular drum in North Indian classical music today, the tabla consists of a set of two closed-bottomed drums, called the *bāyāṅ* (typically played by the left hand) and *dāyāṅ* (played by the right). Together, these drums create the complex catalog of sounds used in tabla solos, in accompanying Hindustani vocal and instrumental music and kathak dance, and in increasingly diverse genres of music around the world.

taiyārī: "Readiness." The physical agility and virtuosity of technique acquired through systematic practice.

tāl [or tāla]: "Clap." A rhythmic cycle of a given number of counts (*mātrās*) with a particular *ṭhekā*, or characteristic pattern of drum strokes. The *ṭhekā* of any *tāl* can be played or recited, with or without ornamentation, and minor stylistic variations may be found between schools.

tāṇḍava: Associated with the mythological dance of Shiva, this "masculine" style of dancing is characterized by sharp movements, strong footwork and robust movement (445).

tānpūrā: A long-necked, fretless stringed instrument (usually of 4–6 strings) used to generate a drone that is foundational to Hindustani music.

tatkār: The most basic footwork of kathak dance; a pattern of eight steps (right left right left, left right left right) vocalized as: "tā theī theī tat, ā theī theī tat." This pattern can be executed in various styles. See *āṭh śabd*; *eṛi*; *panje*.

t̠avā'if [or t̠avāyaf]: A class of North Indian courtesan.

ṭhā: From *ṭhaharnā*, "to stand still," "to pause" (411). In kathak, the term denotes the relatively slow (rhythmically sparse) execution of one set of footwork within one cycle of the *tāl*. See also *guṇ*.

ṭhāṭ [or ṭhāṭh]: The "stylized tuning of the mind and body" in which the dancer draws attention to subtle movements of the eyes, eyebrows, neck and wrists, often interspersed with sections of rapid footwork or turns (C. Das et al. 2001).

ṭhekā: See *tāl*.

tihāī: A thrice repeated musical or danced phrase generally ending on beat one (*sam*). Iterations of the phrase (*palla*) may be separated by a gap of any span of time, though the pause between first and second *pallas* must equal that between second and third *pallas*. *Tihāīs* are standard cadential formulae for Hindustani music and kathak.

tīnguṇ [or tiguṇ]: "Three-fold." See *guṇ*.

upaj: "Original idea; invention; fancy" (126). Spontaneity or improvisation in performance.

vilambit: "Delayed," "slow" (927). In music and dance, *vilambit* refers to a slow tempo, between approximately 25 and 74 beats per minute. See *laya*.

Bibliography

Abdullah, Ameena. n.d. "Mohammad Ali of Kathak." *Sun* (India), 27.

Abrahams, Ruth K. 2007. "Uday Shankar: The Early Years, 1900–1938." *Dance Chronicle* 30 (3): 363–426.

Ali Akbar College of Music. 2006. "History of the Music." Accessed November 15. http://www.aacm.org/history.html.

Allen, Matthew Harp. 1997. "Rewriting the Script for South Indian Dance." *TDR: The Drama Review* 41 (3): 63–100.

Arudra. 1986. "Thodaya Mangalam—2." *Sruti* 22-S: 11–12.

Babiracki, Carol M. (1997) 2008. "What's the Difference? Reflections on Gender and Research in Village India." In *Shadows in the Field: New Perspectives for Fieldwork in Ethnomusicology*, 2d ed., edited by Gregory Barz and Timothy J. Cooley, 167–82. New York: Oxford University Press.

——. 2004. "The Illusion of India's 'Public' Dancers." In *Women's Voices Across Musical Worlds*, edited by Jane A. Bernstein, 36–59. Boston: Northeastern University Press.

Bakan, Michael. 1999. *Music of Death and New Creation: Experiences in the World of Balinese Gamelan Beleganjur*. Chicago: University of Chicago Press.

Banerji, Projesh. (1942) 1947. *Dance of India*. Allahabad: Kitabistan.

Barker, Eileen. 1986. "Religious Movements: Cult and Anticult since Jonestown." *Annual Review of Sociology* 12: 329–46.

Barlow, Jon, and Lakshmi Subramanian. 2007. "Music and Society in North India: From the Mughals to the Mutiny." *Economic and Political Weekly* 42 (19): 1779–87.

Barz, Gregory, and Timothy J. Cooley, ed. (1997) 2008. *Shadows in the Field: New Perspectives for Fieldwork in Ethnomusicology*. 2d ed. New York: Oxford University Press.

Beckford, James A. 1985. *Cult Controversies: The Societal Response to the New Religious Movements*. London: Tavistock.

Bharucha, Rustom. 1995. *Chandralekha: Woman, Dance, Resistance.* New Delhi: HarperCollins.

Bhate-Jathar, Rohini. 1990. "The Concept of Creative Composition (Bandish) with Reference to Kathak." *Journal of the Indian Musicological Society* 21 (1–2): 41–43.

Bhatia, Nandi. 2004. *Acts of Authority/Acts of Resistance: Theater and Politics in Colonial and Postcolonial India.* Ann Arbor: University of Michigan Press.

Bhattacharya, Suryasarathi. 2018. "TM Krishna on #MeToo in Indian Classical Arts: Halo Around Artists Has Given Them Licence to Abuse." *Firstpost*, October 16, 2018. https://www.firstpost.com/india/tm-krishna-on-metoo-in-indian-classical-arts-halo-around-artists-has-given-them-licence-to-abuse-5367781.html.

Bhavani, Enakshi. 1965. *The Dance in India: The Origin and History, Foundations, the Art and Science of the Dance in India—Classical, Folk and Tribal.* Bombay: D. B. Taraporevala Sons.

Booth, Greg. 2005. "Pandits in the Movies: Contesting the Identity of Hindustani Classical Music and Musicians in the Hindi Popular Cinema." *Asian Music* 36 (1): 60–86.

Bowers, Faubion. (1953) 1967. *The Dance in India.* New York: AMS Press.

Browning, Barbara. 1995. *Samba: Resistance in Motion.* Bloomington: Indiana University Press.

Bull, Cynthia Jean Cohen. 1997. "Sense, Meaning, and Perception in Three Dance Cultures." In *Meaning in Motion: New Cultural Studies of Dance,* edited by Jane C. Desmond, 269–87. Durham, NC: Duke University Press.

Burns, Judy Farrar. 1998. "Meri, La." In *International Encyclopedia of Dance: A Project of Dance Perspectives Foundation, Inc.*, vol. 4, edited by Selma Jean Cohen, 354–55. New York: Oxford University Press.

Campbell, Patricia Shehan. 2009. "Learning to Improvise Music, Improvising to Learn Music." In *Musical Improvisation: Art, Education, and Society*, edited by Gabriel Solis and Bruno Nettl, 119–42. Urbana: University of Illinois Press.

Campi, Alicia J. 2005. *Closed Borders and Mass Deportations: The Lessons of the Barred Zone Act.* Immigration Policy Center. Accessed August 23, 2017. http://studylib.net/doc/8352297/the-barred-zone-act-of-february-4-1917.

Chakravorty, Pallabi. 1998. "Hegemony, Dance and Nation: The Construction of the Classical Dance in India." *South Asia* 21 (2): 107–20.

——. 2000. "Choreographing Modernity: Kathak Dance, Public Culture, and Women's Identity in India." PhD diss., Temple University.

——. 2000–2001. "From Interculturalism to Historicism: Reflections on Classical Indian Dance." *Dance Research Journal* 32 (2): 108–19.

——. 2004. "Dance, Pleasure and Indian Women as Multisensorial Subjects." *Visual Anthropology* 17 (1): 1–17.

——. 2006. "Dancing into Modernity: Multiple Narratives of India's Kathak Dance." *Dance Research Journal* 38 (1/2): 115–36.

——. 2008. *Bells of Change: Kathak Dance, Women and Modernity in India.* Calcutta: Seagull Books.

——, and Nilanjana Gupta, ed. 2010. *Dance Matters: Performing India*. New Delhi: Routledge.

Chandavarkar, Bhaskar. 1987. "Composition and Improvisation in Indian Music." In *Aspects of Indian Music*, edited by Sumati Mutatkar, 96–102. New Delhi: Sangeet Natak Akademi.

Chatterjea, Ananya. 2004. "In Search of a Secular in Contemporary Indian Dance: A Continuing Journey." *Dance Research Journal* 36 (2): 102–16.

Chatterjee, Partha. 1993. *The Nation and Its Fragments: Colonial and Postcolonial Histories*. Princeton, NJ: Princeton University Press.

Chatterjee, Sandra, and Cynthia Ling Lee. 2017. "'Our Love Was Not Enough': Queering Gender, Cultural Belonging, and Desire in Contemporary Abhinaya." In *Queer Dance: Meanings and Makings*, edited by Clare Croft, 45–65. New York: Oxford University Press.

Chattopadhyaya, Bimala Prosad. 1967. *A Primer of Music*. Burdwan: Burdwan Academy of Music.

Citaristi, Ileana. 2001. *The Making of a Guru: Kelucharan Mohapatra, His Life and Times*. Delhi: Manohar.

Clayton, Martin. 2000. *Time in Indian Music: Rhythm, Metre, and Form in North Indian Rāg Performance*. New York: Oxford University Press.

——. 2007. "Time, Gesture and Attention in a Khyal Performance." *Asian Music* 38 (2): 71–96.

Coorlawala, Uttara A. 1992. "Ruth St. Denis and India's Dance Renaissance." *Dance Chronicle* 15 (2): 123–52.

——. 2004. "The Sanskritized Body." *Dance Research Journal* 36 (2): 50–63.

Cowan, Jane K. 1990. *Dance and the Body Politic in Northern Greece*. Princeton, NJ: Princeton University Press.

Cowdery, James R. 1995. "The American Students of Balasaraswati." *UCLA Journal of Dance Ethnology* 19: 50–57.

Crooke, William C. 1896. *Tribes and Castes of the North-Western Provinces and Oudh*. 4 vols. Calcutta: Superintendent of Government Printing.

Cupchik, Jeffrey W. forthcoming. "George Harrison: South Asian Music, Subjectivity and Bricolage in the Era of Psychedelia." *Popular Music and Society*.

Dalidowicz, Monica. 2010. "Re-exporting 'Tradition': The Transcultural Practice of Kathak in Kolkata and the Creation of a New Female Body." In Chakravorty and Gupta, *Dance Matters*, 205–24.

——. 2012. "Learning Kathak: Crafting Bodies and Selves in the Guru-Shishya Parampara." PhD diss., Macquarie University.

——. 2015. "Crafting Fidelity: Pedagogical Creativity in Kathak Dance." *Journal of the Royal Anthropological Institute* 21: 838–54.

Danielson, Virginia. 1997. *The Voice of Egypt: Umm Kulthūm, Arabic Song, and Egyptian Society in the Twentieth Century*. Chicago: University of Chicago Press.

Das, Chitresh. 1984. Informal interview by anonymous. Videotaped backstage, Olympic Arts Festival in Los Angeles, June 15, 1984. CCDDC archive, San Rafael, CA.

——. 1985. Unpublished letter to Mr. Azad Bhawan, Indian Council for Cultural Relations. CCDDC archive, San Rafael, CA.

——. 1986a. "In Performance." In J. Das, *Chitresh*, 8–11.

——. 1986b. "Discipleship and the West." In J. Das, *Chitresh*, 26–32.

——. ca. 1988. Unpublished writing. CCDDC archive, San Rafael, CA.

——. 1999. *Toronto Tabla Ensemble in Concert: Special Guest, Kathak Dance Legend Chitresh Das* (live performance). Toronto: Harbourfront Centre, Du Maurier Theatre Centre, November 5. CCDDC archive, San Rafael, CA.

——. 2001. *Sadhana* (live performance). San Francisco: Cowell Theater, October 13. Accessed through unpublished video in author's private collection and CCDDC archive, San Rafael, CA.

Das, Chitresh, Gretchen Hayden Ruckert, Joanna Das, Michelle Zonka, Agnes Lee, and Sarah Morelli. 2001. *Kathak Handbook*. San Rafael, CA: Chhandam School of Kathak Dance.

Das, Julia. 1986a. *Chitresh: Calcutta to California*. San Anselmo, CA: Chitresh Das Dance Company.

——. 1986b. Unpublished letter to Michael Alexander, Alexander Artists Management. November 17, 1986.

Das, Prohlad. 1961. *Kathak Dance (Bol)*. Calcutta: Sri Amarendra Nath Paul.

Deb, Arunabha. 2015. "The Calcutta Mastaan." *Hindu: Business Line* (India), February 20, 2015. www.thehindubusinessline.com.

Desai, Ravija, Shruti Iyer, Vrushali Mundhe-Jawle, and Poonam Narkar. 2010. "What Is a Shishya?" Accessed August 25, 2010. https://kathaka.wordpress.com/2010/08/22/what-is-a-shishya/.

Desmond, Jane C. 1991. "Dancing Out Difference: Cultural Imperialism and Ruth St. Denis's 'Radha' of 1906." *Signs* 17 (1): 28–49.

——. 1993/1994. "Embodying Difference: Issues in Dance and Cultural Studies." *Cultural Critique* 26: 33–63.

Devi, Ragini. 1972. *Dance Dialects of India*. Delhi: Vikas Publications.

Devidayal, Namita. 2007. *The Music Room*. New York: St. Martin's Press.

Downing, Michael. 2001. *Shoes Outside the Door: Desire, Devotion, and Excess at San Francisco Zen Center*. Washington, DC: Counterpoint.

Eck, Diana L. 1993. *Encountering God: A Spiritual Journey from Bozeman to Banaras*. 2d ed. Boston: Beacon.

Eldershaw, Lynn P. 2007. "Collective Identity and the Postcharismatic Fate of Shambhala International." *Nova Religio* 10 (4): 72–102.

Erdman, Joan L. 1987. "Performance as Translation: Uday Shankar in the West." *Drama Review: TDR* 31 (1): 64–88.

——. 1991. "Inside Tradition: Scholar-Performers and Asian Arts." *Asian Theatre Journal* 8 (2): 111–17.

——. 1996. "Dance Discourses: Rethinking the History of 'Oriental Dance.'" In *Moving Words: Re-writing Dance*, edited by Gay Morris, 288–305. New York: Routledge.

Farnell, B. 1999. "Moving Bodies, Acting Selves." *Annual Review of Anthropology* 28: 341–73.

Farrell, Gerry. 1993. "The Early Days of the Gramophone Industry in India: Historical, Social and Musical Perspectives." *British Journal of Ethnomusicology* 2: 31–53.

———. 1997. *Indian Music and the West*. New York: Oxford University Press.

Feld, Steven. 1982. *Sound and Sentiment: Birds, Weeping, Poetics, and Song in Kaluli Expression*. Philadelphia: University of Pennsylvania Press.

Feuerstein, Georg. 1991. *Holy Madness: The Shock Tactics and Radical Teachings of Crazy-Wise Adepts, Holy Fools, and Rascal Gurus*. New York: Paragon House.

Flood, Gavin. 1996. *An Introduction to Hinduism*. Cambridge: Cambridge University Press.

Foster, Susan L. 2002. *Dances That Describe Themselves: The Improvised Choreography of Richard Bull*. Middletown, CT: Wesleyan University Press.

French, Harold W. 1974. *The Swan's Wide Waters: Ramakrishna and Western Culture*. Port Washington, NY: Kennikat.

Garlough, Christine L. 2013. *Desi Divas: Political Activism in South Asian American Cultural Performances*. Jackson: University Press of Mississippi.

Gere, David. ca. 1988. "Dance=MC^2." *Oakland Tribune*. CCDDC archive, San Rafael, CA.

Geurts, Catherine L. 2002. *Culture and the Senses: Bodily Ways of Knowing in an African Community*. Berkeley: University of California Press.

Ghosh, Anashua. 1981. "Taking Kathak Abroad: One of the Most Controversial Artistes Around Unwinds in an Informal Talk." *Telegraph* (India), September 22–28, 1981, 4–6.

Gilbert, Andrew. 2015. "Dance Card: The Passing of the Master of Kathak, Chitresh Das, Left His Mourning Followers Prepared to Carry On." *San Jose Mercury News*, January 26, 2015. www.mercurynews.com.

Gleig, Ann, and Lola Williamson, eds. 2013. *Homegrown Gurus: From Hinduism in America to American Hinduism*. Albany: State University of New York Press.

Goldberg, Ellen. 2002. *The Lord Who Is Half Woman: Ardhanārīśvara in Indian and Feminist Perspective*. Albany: State University of New York Press.

Goldberg, Philip. 2010. *American Veda: From Emerson and the Beatles to Yoga and Meditation—How Indian Spirituality Changed the West*. New York: Three Rivers.

Gopal, Ram, and Serozh Dadachanji. 1951. *Indian Dancing*. London: Phoenix House.

Gorringe, Magdalen. 2005. "*Arangetrams* and Manufacturing Identity: The Changing Role of a Bharata Natyam Dancer's Solo Debut in the Context of the Diaspora." In *Diasporas and Interculturalism in Asian Performing Arts: Translating Traditions*, edited by Hae-kyung Um, 91–103. London: RoutledgeCurzon.

Goswami, Satsvarūpa dāsa. 1981. *Only He Could Lead Them: San Francisco/India, 1967*. Vol. 3 of *Śrīla Prabhupāda-līlāmṛta: A Biography of His Divine Grace A. C. Bhaktivedanta Swami Prabhupāda*. Los Angeles: Bhaktivedanta Book Trust.

Gottlieb, Robert S., dir. 1988. *Circles-Cycles: Kathak Dance*. Berkeley: University of California Extension Media Center.

Greenstein, M. A., and Ramaa Bharadvaj. 1998. "Bharata Natyam: Translation, Spectacle and the Degeneration of Arangetram in Southern California Life." In *Proceedings, Society of Dance History Scholars, Twenty-First Annual Conference*, 127–34. Riverside: University of California, Society of Dance History Scholars.

Groesbeck, Rolf. 1999. "Cultural Constructions of Improvisation in Tāyampaka, a Genre of Temple Instrumental Music in Kerala, India." *Ethnomusicology* 43 (1): 1–30.

Guilbault, Jocelyne, and Roy Cape. 2014. *Roy Cape: A Life on the Calypso and Soca Bandstand*. Durham, NC: Duke University Press.

Hagedorn, Katherine J. 2001. *Divine Utterances: The Performance of Afro-Cuban Santería*. Washington, DC: Smithsonian Institution Press.

——. 2006. "Engendering Spiritual Power and Empowering Gendered Spirits: An Analysis of Batá Drumming in Afro-Cuban Santería." Paper presented at Center for the Study of World Religions colloquium, Harvard University, Cambridge, MA, April 19, 2006.

Hahn, Tomie. 2005. "Embodying Culture: the Transmission of Ṣhakuhachi Music." Paper presented for "Music of Asia" course taught by Nicholas Brooke, Bennington College, Bennington, VT, May 16, 2005.

——. 2007. *Sensational Knowledge: Embodying Culture through Japanese Dance*. Middletown, CT: Wesleyan University Press.

Hausner, Sondra L. 2007. *Wandering with Sadhus: Ascetics in the Hindu Himalayas*. Bloomington: Indiana University Press.

Hawley, John Stratton. 2004. "Global Hinduism in Gotham." In *Asian American Religions: The Making and Remaking of Borders and Boundaries*, edited by Tony Carnes and Fenggang Yang, 112–37. New York: New York University Press.

——, comp. 1988. *Songs of the Saints of India*. Translated by John S. Hawley and Mark Juergensmeyer. New York: Oxford University Press.

Hess, Gary R. 1969. "The 'Hindu' in America: Immigration and Naturalization Policies and India, 1917–1946." *Pacific Historical Review* 38 (1): 59–79.

Hunt, Mary Ellen. 2005. "Don't Call It Fusion." *Dance Magazine* 79 (11): 22.

Inden, Ronald. 1990. *Imagining India*. Oxford: Basil Blackwell.

Iyengar, Vikram. 2010. "The Lords of Dance: Changing Fortunes." In Chakravorty and Gupta, *Dance Matters*, 225–34.

Jairazbhoy, Nazir A. 1977. "The 'Objective' and Subjective View in Music Transcription." *Ethnomusicology* 21 (2): 263–73.

Joshi, Damayanti. 1989. *Madame Menaka*. New Delhi: Sangeet Natak Akademi.

Joshi, K. S. 1965. "On the Meaning of Yoga." *Philosophy of East and West* 15 (1): 53–64.

Karp, Ivan, and Martha B. Kendall. 1982. "Reflexivity in Fieldwork." In *Explaining Human Behavior: Consciousness, Human Action, and Social Structure*, edited by Paul Secord, 249–73. Beverly Hills, CA: Sage.

Katrak, Ketu. 2001. "Body Boundarylands: Locating South Asian Ethnicity in Performance and in Daily Life." *Amerasia Journal* 27 (1): 2–33.

Katz, Max G. 2010. "Hindustani Music History and the Politics of Theory." PhD diss., University of California, Santa Barbara.

——. 2012. "Institutional Communalism in North Indian Classical Music." *Ethnomusicology* 56 (2): 279–98.

Khokar, Mohan. 1979. *Traditions of Indian Classical Dance*. Delhi: Clarion Books.

Kinsley, David R. 1986. *Hindu Goddesses: Visions of the Divine Feminine in Hindu Religious Tradition*. Berkeley: University of California Press.

Kippen, James. 1988. *The Tabla of Lucknow: A Cultural Analysis of a Musical Tradition*. New York: Cambridge University Press.

——. 1989. "Changes in the Social Status of Tabla Players." *Journal of the Indian Musicological Society* 20 (1–2): 37–46.

——. 2006. *Gurudev's Drumming Legacy: Music, Theory and Nationalism in the Mṛdaṅg aur Tablā Vādanpaddhati of Gurudev Patwardhan*. Aldershot, UK: Ashgate.

——. 2008. "Working with Masters." In *Shadows in the Field: New Perspectives for Fieldwork in Ethnomusicology*, 2d ed., edited by Gregory F. Barz and Timothy J. Cooley, 125–40. New York: Oxford University Press.

Kisliuk, Michelle R. 1998. *Seize the Dance! BaAka Musical Life and the Ethnography of Performance*. New York: Oxford University Press.

Knight, Douglas M., Jr. 2010. *Balasaraswati: Her Art and Life*. Middletown, CT: Wesleyan University Press.

Kothari, Sunil. 1989. *Kathak: Indian Classical Dance Art*. New Delhi: Abhinav.

——. 2004. "Dance of the Masters." *Hindu*, November 21, 2004. https://www.thehindu.com/mag/2004/11/21/stories/2004112100460500.htm.

Kraut, Anthea. 2015. *Choreographing Copyright: Race, Gender, and Intellectual Property Rights in American Dance*. New York: Oxford University Press.

Kroon, Coen, van der. (1993) 1996. *The Golden Fountain: The Complete Guide to Urine Therapy*. Translated by Merilee Dranow. Mesa, AZ: Wishland.

Kyle, Richard G. 1995. *The New Age Movement in American Culture*. Lanham, MD: University Press of America.

Lalli, Gina. 2004. "A North Indian Classical Dance Form: Lucknow Kathak." *Visual Anthropology* 17 (1): 19–43.

"Largest Tour." 1933. *Time* 22 (18): 38.

Lavezzoli, Peter. 2007. *The Dawn of Indian Music in the West*. New York: Continuum.

Lee, Cynthia Ling. 2017. "Homeland as Beloved: Translating Viraha for (Post)Colonial Contexts." *Indian Theatre Journal* 1 (1): 39–53.

Leonard, Karen. 1992. *Making Ethnic Choices: California's Punjabi Mexican Americans*. Philadelphia: Temple University Press.

Lo, Louise, exec. prod. 2007. *Spark*. Season 5, episode 10, "Chitresh Das, Jackson, and Midori." KQED, San Francisco. 12 min. Accessed June 11, 2019. https://ww2.kqed.org/spark/pandit-chitresh-das/.

Lipiczky, Thom. 1985. "Tihai Formulas and the Fusion of 'Composition' and 'Improvisation' in North Indian Music." *Musical Quarterly* 71 (2): 157–71.

Maciszewski, Amelia. 1998. "Gendered Stories, Gendered Styles: Contemporary Hindusthani Music as Discourse, Attitudes, and Practice." PhD diss., University of Texas at Austin.

——. 2001. "Stories about Selves: Selected North Indian Women's Musical (Auto) biographies." *World of Music* 43 (1): 139–72.

——. 2006. "Tawa'if, Tourism, and Tales: The Problematics of Twenty-First-Century Musical Patronage for North India's Courtesans." In *The Courtesan's Arts: Cross-Cultural Perspectives*, edited by Martha Feldman and Bonnie Gordon, 332–51. New York: Oxford University Press.

Maharaj, Birju. 2002. *Aṅg Kāvya: Nomenclature for Hand Movements and Feet Positions in Kathak*. New Delhi: Har-Anand.

Mann, Gurinder Singh, Paul D. Numrich, and Raymond B. Williams. 2001. *Buddhists, Hindus, and Sikhs in America*. New York: Oxford University Press.

Manuel, Peter. 1989. *Ṭhumrī in Historical and Stylistic Perspectives*. Delhi: Motilal Banarasidass.

Massey, Reginald. 1999. *India's Kathak Dance: Past, Present, Future*. New Delhi: Abhinav Publications.

Maxwell, Julia. 2012. *Lifting the Jewel from Its Filigree*. Denver, CO: Outskirts.

McGregor, R. S., ed. 1993. *The Oxford Hindi–English Dictionary*. New York: Oxford University Press.

Meduri, Avanthi. 1988. "Bharatha Natyam—What Are You?" *Asian Theatre Journal* 5 (1): 1–22.

——. 1996. "Nation, Woman, Representation: The Sutured History of the Devadasi and Her Dance." PhD diss., New York University.

Mehta, Rina. 2005. Unpublished document. May 2005. Personal collection.

Miner, Allyn. 1993. *Sitar and Sarod in the 18th and 19th Centuries*. Wilhelmshaven, Germany: Florian Noetzel.

Mishra, Upendra, prod. 2014. *Chai with Manju: Chitresh Das*. Hosted by Manju Sheth. Waltham, MA: INE Multimedia, November 3, 2014. Accessed August 2, 2015. https://www.youtube.com/watch?v=crYhyGOAZYE.

Mitra, Jayasri. 2004. "Dancing in California." *Statesman* (India), February 24, 2004, 6.

Mitra, Royona. 2015. *Akram Khan: New World Choreographies*. London: Palgrave Macmillan.

Molekhi, Pankaj. 2010. "Yogic Twirls: Kathak Exponent Introduces the New Form of Dance." *Economic Times*, August 8, 2010. http://economictimes.indiatimes.com.

Moore, Dick. 1979. "A Hurricane-Force Explosion of Artistry." *Marin Independent-Journal*, July 30, 1979.

Moraga, Charlotte. 2003. "Innovation in Kathak." Unpublished document, November 2003. Personal collection.

Morcom, Anna. 2009. "Indian Popular Culture and Its 'Others': Bollywood Dance and Anti-nautch in Twenty First Century Global India." In *Popular Culture in a Globalised India*, edited by K. Moti Gokulsing and Wimal Dissanayake, 125–38. London: Routledge.

Morelli, Sarah. 2010. "Intergenerational Adaptation in North Indian Kathak Dance." *Anthropological Notebooks* 16 (3): 77–91.

———. 2016. "'A Superior Race of Strong Women': North Indian Classical Dance in the San Francisco Bay Area." In *The Music of Multicultural America: Performance, Identity, and Community in the United States*, edited by Kip Lornell and Anne Rasmussen, 340–67. Jackson: University Press of Mississippi.

Morris, Holly, dir. 2001. *Adventure Divas*. Season 1, episodes 3 and 4, "India: Holy Cow." Aired October 26, 2001, and November 2, 2001, on PBS. Seattle: Adventure Divas.

———. 2006. *Adventure Divas: Searching the Globe for Women Who Are Changing the World*. New York: Villard.

Muller, Carol, and Sathima Bea Benjamin. 2011. *Musical Echoes: South African Women Thinking in Jazz*. Durham, NC: Duke University Press.

Narayan, Shovana. 1998. *Rhythmic Echoes and Reflections: Kathak*. New Delhi: Roli Books.

Natavar, Mekhala. 1997. "New Dances, New Dancers, New Audiences: Shifting Rhythms in the Evolution of India's Kathak Dance." PhD diss., University of Wisconsin–Madison.

———. 2000. "Music and Dance: Northern Area." In *South Asia: The Indian Subcontinent*, vol. 5 of *The Garland Encyclopedia of World Music*, edited by Alison Arnold, 492–506. New York: Garland.

Nathan, Archana. 2018. "#MeToo: In World of Carnatic Music and Bharatanatyam, Women Say Harassment Is an Open Secret." *Scroll.in*, October 15, 2018. https://scroll.in/.

Nettl, Bruno. 1974. "Thoughts on Improvisation: A Comparative Approach." *Musical Quarterly* 60 (1): 1–19.

Nettl, Bruno, and Melinda Russell, ed. 1998. *In the Course of Performance: Studies in the World of Musical Improvisation*. Chicago: University of Chicago Press.

Neuman, Daniel. 1978. "*Gharanas*: The Rise of Musical 'Houses' in Delhi and Neighboring Cities." In *Eight Urban Musical Cultures*, edited by Bruno Nettl, 186–222. Urbana: University of Illinois Press.

———. (1980) 1990. *The Life of Music in North India: The Organization of an Artistic Tradition*. Chicago: University of Chicago Press.

———. 1984. "The Ecology of Indian Music in North America." *Bansuri* 1: 9–15.

Neuman, Dard. 2012. "Pedagogy, Practice, and Embodied Creativity in Hindustani Music." *Ethnomusicology* 56 (3): 426–49.

Nimjee, Ameera. 2018. "Playing Dance and Dancing Music: The Work of Intimacy in Kathak." In *Dance Matters Too: Markets, Memories, Identities*, edited by Pallabi Chakravorty and Nilanjana Gupta, 176–89. New Delhi: Routledge.

Nketia, J. H. Kwabena. 1963. *Drumming in Akan Communities of Ghana*. Edinburgh: Published on behalf of the University of Ghana by T. Nelson.

Nuttall, Denise I. 1998. "Embodying Culture: Gurus, Disciples and Tabla Players." PhD diss., University of British Columbia.

——. 2007. "A Pathway to Knowledge: Embodiment, Experience and Dreaming as a Basis for Understanding the Other." In *Extraordinary Anthropology: Transformations in the Field*, edited by Jean-Guy Goulet and Bruce G. Miller, 323–51. Lincoln: University of Nebraska Press.

Oldenburg, Veena Talwar. 1990. "Lifestyle as Resistance: The Case of the Courtesans of Lucknow." *Feminist Studies* 16 (2): 259–87.

O'Shea, Janet. 1998. "'Traditional' Indian Dance and the Making of Interpretive Communities." *Asian Theatre Journal* 15 (1): 45–63.

——. 2007. *At Home in the World: Bharata Natyam on the Global Stage*. Middletown, CT: Wesleyan University Press.

Pai, Sruti. 2014. Interview with Chitresh Das. Telephone interview, November 10, 2014. Personal collection.

Panchali. 1977. "Chitresh Das—A Volatile Kathak-Dancer." *Cine Advance*, February 16, 1977.

Pandit, Bansi. 1992. *The Hindu Mind: Fundamentals of Hindu Religion and Philosophy for All Ages*. Glen Ellyn, IL: B & V Enterprises.

Pawar, Yogesh. 2014. "Why's Pt Chitresh Das Dancing at 70?" *DNA* (Mumbai), April 19, 2014. http://www.dnaindia.com/lifestyle/report-why-s-pt-chitresh-das-dancing-at-70-1979920.

Phillips, Miriam. 1991. "Both Sides of the Veil: A Comparative Analysis of Kathak and Flamenco Dance." MA thesis, UCLA.

——. 2013. "Becoming the Floor/Breaking the Floor: Experiencing the Kathak-Flamenco Connection." *Ethnomusicology* 57 (3): 396–427.

Post, Jennifer. 1987. "Professional Women in Indian Music: The Death of the Courtesan Tradition." In *Women and Music in Cross-Cultural Perspective*, edited by Ellen Koskoff, 97–110. New York: Greenwood.

Pradhan, Aneesh. 2008. "*Sangat*: The Role of *Tabla* Accompaniment to Hindustani Music and Dance." *Journal of the Indian Musicological Society* 39: 103–14.

Prickett, Stacey. 2012. "Defying Britain's Tick-Box Culture: Kathak in Dialogue with Hip-Hop." *Dance Research* 30 (2): 169–85.

Princep, James. 1832. "Census of Population of the City of Benaras." *Asiatic Researches* 17: 470–98.

Purkayastha, Bandana. 2005. *Negotiating Ethnicity: Second-Generation South Asian Americans Traverse a Transnational World*. New Brunswick, NJ: Rutgers University Press.

Qureshi, Regula Burckhardt. 1991. "Whose Music? Sources and Contexts in Indic Musicology." In *Comparative Musicology and Anthropology of Music*, edited by Bruno Nettl and Phillip V. Bohlman, 152–68. Chicago: University of Chicago Press.

——. 1997. "The Indian Sarangi: Sound of Affect, Site of Contest." *Yearbook for Traditional Music* 29: 1–38.

——. 2000. "Confronting the Social: Mode of Production and the Sublime for (Indian) Art Music." *Ethnomusicology* 44 (1): 15–38.

——. 2006. "Female Agency and Patrilineal Constraints: Situating Courtesans in Twentieth-Century India." In *The Courtesan's Arts: Cross-Cultural Perspectives*, edited by Martha Feldman and Bonnie Gordon, 312–31. New York: Oxford University Press.

Rahaim, Matthew. 2012. *Musicking Bodies: Gesture and Voice in Hindustani Music*. Middletown, CT: Wesleyan University Press.

Ramberg, Lucinda. 2014. *Given to the Goddess: South Indian Devadasis and the Sexuality of Religion*. Durham, NC: Duke University Press.

Rangaswamy, Padma. 2000. *Namasté America: Indian Immigrants in an American Metropolis*. University Park: Pennsylvania State University Press.

Rao, Vidya. 1990. "'Thumri' as Feminine Voice." *Economic and Political Weekly* 25 (17): WS31–WS39.

——. 1996. "Thumri and Thumri Singers: Changes in Style and Life-Style." In *Cultural Reorientation in Modern India*, edited by Indu Bangla Jaidev, 278–315. Simla: Indian Institute of Advanced Study.

Ray, Satyajit, dir. (1958) 2011. *Jalsaghar* (*The Music Room*). Irvington, NY: Criterion Collection. 95 min.

Reck, David. 1978. "The Neon Electric Saraswati: Being Reflections on the Influences of Indian Music on the Contemporary Music Scene in America." *Contributions to Asian Studies* 12: 3–19.

——. 1985. "Beatles Orientalis: Influences from Asia in a Popular Song Tradition." *Asian Music* 16 (1): 83–149.

Reed, Susan A. 1998. "The Politics and Poetics of Dance." *Annual Review of Anthropology* 27: 503–32.

Rice, Timothy. 1987. "Toward the Remodeling of Ethnomusicology." *Ethnomusicology* 31 (3): 469–88.

Rinehart, Robert E., and Synthia Sydnor, eds. 2003. *To the Extreme: Alternative Sports, Inside and Out*. Albany: State University of New York Press.

Robbins, Thomas. 1978. Review of *All God's Children: The Cult Experience—Salvation or Slavery?*, by Carroll Stoner and Jo Anne Parke. *Sociological Analysis* 39 (2): 180–81.

Robinson Locke Collection, 1680–1976 [bulk 1870–1920]. *Robinson Locke Scrapbook Covering the Life and Career of Augustin Daly*. Billy Rose Theatre Division, New York Public Library of the Performing Arts, New York City.

Roy, Parama. 1998. *Indian Traffic: Identities in Question in Colonial and Postcolonial India*. Berkeley: University of California Press.

Roy, Sandip. 2006. "Umrao Jaan, the Story Untold." *Telegraph* (Kolkata), October 29, 2006. https://www.telegraphindia.com/1061029/asp/look/story_6914758.asp#.

——. 2007. "Kathak in California." *Times of India*, April 29, 2007. http://timesofindia.indiatimes.com/articleshow/1974187.cms.

Ruckert, George. 1991. *Introduction to the Classical Music of North India*. Book 1 of *The Classical Music of North India: The Music of the Baba Allauddin Gharana as Taught by Ali Akbar Khan at the Ali Akbar College of Music*, general editor Ali Akbar Khan. [Staunton, VA] : East Bay Books.

——. 1994. "The Music of Ali Akbar Khan: An Analysis of His Musical Style through the Examination of His Composition in Three Selected Ragas." PhD diss., University of California, Berkeley.

——. 2004. *Music in North India: Experiencing Music, Expressing Culture*. New York: Oxford University Press.

Ruskin, Jesse D., and Timothy Rice. 2012. "The Individual in Musical Ethnography." *Ethnomusicology* 56 (2): 299–327.

Sai, Veejay. 2015. "A Visual Tribute to Ram Gopal, India's Forgotten Dance Superstar." *Scroll.in*, January 23, 2015. https://scroll.in.

Sarker, Sanghamitra, prod. N.d. *Anwesha*. Calcutta: Integrated TV.

Sax, William S. 2002. *Dancing the Self: Personhood and Performance in the Pāṇḍav Līlā of Garhwal*. New York: Oxford University Press.

Saxena, Sushil K. 1991. *Swinging Syllables: Aesthetics of Kaṭhak Dance*. New Delhi: Sangeet Natak Akademi.

Schechner, Richard. 1985. *Between Theater and Anthropology*. Philadelphia: University of Pennsylvania Press.

Schippers, Huib. 2007. "The Guru Recontextualized? Perspectives on Learning North Indian Classical Music in Shifting Environments for Professional Training." *Asian Music* 38 (1): 123–38.

Schofield, Katherine Butler. 2010. "Reviving the Golden Age Again: 'Classicization,' Hindustani Music, and the Mughals." *Ethnomusicology* 54 (3): 484–517.

Schwartz, Susan L. 2001. *Rasa: Performing the Divine in India*. New York: Columbia University Press.

Schweig, Graham M. 2002. "Humility and Passion: A Caitanyite Vaishnava Ethics of Devotion." *Journal of Religious Ethics* 30 (3): 421–44.

Self-Realization Fellowship. 2017. "Locations." Accessed July 3, 2017. https://members.yogananda-srf.org/CenterSearch/SearchMap.aspx.

Sethi, V. K. (1984) 1994. *Kabir: The Weaver of God's Name*. Punjab: Radha Soami Satsang Beas.

Shah, Purnima. 1992. "Innovation in Contemporary Kathak." MA thesis, UCLA.

——. 1998. "Transcending Gender in the Performance of Kathak." *Dance Research Journal* 30 (2): 2–17.

——. 2008. "Negotiating Gender in Contemporary Kathak Dance Choreography." *Sāmīpya: Adhyayana Ane Saṃśodhananuṃ Traimāsika* 25 (1–2): 1–9.

Shah, Reena. 2005. *Movement in Stills: The Dance and Life of Kumudini Lakhia*. Ahmedabad: Mapin.

Shah, Wajid Ali. (1877?) 1987. *Bani*. Translated into Hindi by Roshan Taqi and Krishna Mohan Saxena. Lucknow: Sangeet Natak Academi.

Shankar, Ravi. (1968) 2007. *My Music, My Life*. San Rafael, CA: Mandala.

——. 2001. *Raga Mala: The Autobiography of Ravi Shankar*. New York: Welcome Rain.

Shelemay, Kay Kaufman. 1991. *A Song of Longing: An Ethiopian Journey*. Urbana: University of Illinois Press.

——. 2001. *Soundscapes: Exploring Music in a Changing World*. New York: W. W. Norton.

——. 2011. "Musical Communities: Rethinking the Collective in Music." *Journal of the American Musicological Society* 64 (2): 349–90.

Shelton, Suzanne. 1981. *Divine Dancer: A Biography of Ruth St. Denis*. New York: Doubleday.

Sikand, Nandini. 2016. *Languid Bodies, Grounded Stances: The Curving Pathway of Neoclassical Odissi Dance*. New York: Berghahn Books.

Silver, Brian. 1978. "Henry Cowell and Alan Hovhaness: Responses to the Music of India." *Contributions to Asian Studies* 12: 54–81.

——, and R. Arnold Burghardt. 1976. "On Becoming an Ustad: Six Life Sketches in the Evolution of a Gharānā." *Asian Music* 7 (2): 27–58.

Singha, Rina, and Reginald Massey. 1967. *Indian Dances: Their History and Growth*. New York: George Braziller.

Slawek, Stephen. 1991. "Ravi Shankar as Mediator between a Traditional Music and Modernity." In *Ethnomusicology and Modern Music History*, edited by Stephen Blum, Philip V. Bohlman, and Daniel M. Neuman, 161–80. Urbana: University of Illinois Press.

——. 1996. "Engrossed Minds, Embodied Moods and Liberated Spirits in Two Musical Traditions of India." *Bansuri* 13: 31–41.

——. 2000. "The Classical Master-Disciple Tradition." In *South Asia: The Indian Subcontinent*, vol. 5 of *The Garland Encyclopedia of World Music*, edited by Alison Arnold, 457–67. New York: Garland.

Slobin, Mark. 1993. *Subcultural Sounds: Micromusics of the West*. Hanover, NH: Wesleyan University Press.

Smith, Cecil M. 1950. *Musical Comedy in America*. New York: Theatre Arts Books.

Solis, Gabriel, and Bruno Nettl, ed. 2009. *Musical Improvisation: Art, Education, and Society*. Urbana: University of Illinois Press.

Soneji, Davesh. 2012. *Unfinished Gestures:* Devadāsīs, *Memory, and Modernity in South India*. Chicago: University of Chicago Press.

Spielvogel, Laura. 2004. Review of *Sport, Dance and Embodied Identities*, edited by Dyck, Noel and Eduardo P. Archetti. *Journal of the Royal Anthropological Institute* 10 (4): 943–44.

Srinivasan, Amrit. 1985. "Reform and Revival: The Devadasi and Her Dance." *Economic and Political Weekly* 20 (44): 1869–76.

Srinivasan, Priya. 2012. *Sweating Saris: Indian Dance as Transnational Labor*. Philadelphia: Temple University Press.

St. Denis, Ruth. 1939. *Ruth St. Denis, An Unfinished Life: An Autobiography*. London: G. G. Harrap.

Strauss, Sarah. 1997. "Re-Orienting Yoga: Transnational Flows from an Indian Center." PhD diss., University of Pennsylvania.

——. 2005. *Positioning Yoga: Balancing Acts across Cultures*. Oxford: Berg.

Sundar, Pushpa. 1995. *Patrons and Philistines: Arts and the State in British India, 1773–1947*. Delhi: Oxford University Press.

Suraiya, Jug. 1970. "Chitresh Das, Kathak Dancer: A Dedicated, Talented Artiste Talks to Jug Suraiya." *JS* (Calcutta), October 3, 1970, 18–19.

Swapan, Ashfaque. 1996. "Kathak Maestro Celebrates 25 Years." *India West*, October 4, 1996, B1, B16.

——. 2015. "Poetry in Motion: An Affectionate Ode to Chitresh Das." *India West*, January 6, 2015. http://www.indiawest.com.

Tang, Patricia. 2005. "Negotiating Performance in Senegalese Popular Music: Sound, Image, and the Ethnomusicologist as Exoticized 'Other.'" *Journal of Popular Music Studies* 17 (3): 275–300.

——. 2007. *Masters of the Sabar: Wolof Griot Percussionists of Senegal*. Philadelphia: Temple University Press.

Tarlo, Emma. 1996. *Clothing Matters: Dress and Identity in India*. Chicago: University of Chicago Press.

Thobani, Sitara. 2017. *Indian Classical Dance and the Making of Postcolonial National Identities: Dancing on Empire's Stage*. London: Routledge.

Tircuit, Heuwell. 1978. "The West Is Becoming the East for Indian Culture." *San Francisco Chronicle*, September 3, 1978.

Tomko, Linda. 1999. *Dancing Class: Gender, Ethnicity, and Social Divides in American Dance, 1980–1920*. Bloomington: Indiana University Press.

Tucker, Marilyn. 1986. "A Dancer's Vision of Ancient Tales." *San Francisco Chronicle*, July 14, 1986, 53.

——. 1990. "A Tame Indian's Take on the Golden West—Chitresh Das." *San Francisco Chronicle*, September 9, 1990, 48.

Uchiyama, Hoku, dir. 2013. *Upaj: Improvise*. San Francisco: Hindipendent Films.

Urban, Hugh B. 2005. "Osho, From Sex Guru to Guru of the Rich: The Spiritual Logic of Late Capitalism." In *Gurus in America*, edited by Thomas A. Forsthoefel and Cynthia Ann Humes, 169–92. Albany: State University of New York Press.

Van Ness, Peter H. 1999. "Yoga as Spiritual but Not Religious: A Pragmatic Perspective." *American Journal of Theology and Philosophy* 20 (1): 15–30.

Veal, Michael E. 2000. *Fela: The Life and Times of an African Musical Icon*. Philadelphia: Temple University Press.

Venkataraman, Leela. 1990. "Choreography for Group Dance: Problems and Challenges." *Sruti* 66: 27–31.

Versluis, Arthur. 1993. *American Transcendentalism and Asian Religions*. New York: Oxford University Press.

Vidyarthi, Govind. 1959. "Melody through the Centuries: A Chapter from Ma'danul Moosiqi Written in 1856 by Hakim Hohammad Karam Imam, a Courtier of Wajid Ali Shah of Lucknow." *Sangeet Natak Akademi Bulletin* 11–12: 13–26, 33.

Viswanathan, T., and Matthew Harp Allen. 2004. *Music in South India: the Karṇāṭak Tradition and Beyond*. New York: Oxford University Press.

Vosen, Elyse Carter. 2001. "Seventh-Fire Children: Gender, Embodiment, and Musical Performances of Decolonization by Anishinaabe Youth." PhD diss., University of Pennsylvania.

Wade, Bonnie. 1978. "Indian Classical Music in North America: Cultural Give and Take." *Contributions to Asian Studies* 12: 29–39.

Walker, Margaret. 2004. "*Kathak* Dance: A Critical History." PhD diss., University of Toronto.

——. 2006. "Ancient Tradition as Ongoing Creation: The Kathavacaks of Uttar Pradesh." *Canadian Journal for Traditional Music* 33: 48–63.

——. 2010. "Courtesans and Choreographers: The (Re)Placement of Women in the History of *Kathak* Dance." In Chakravorty and Gupta, *Dance Matters*, 279–300.

——. 2014. *India's* Kathak *Dance in Historical Perspective*. Surrey, UK: Ashgate.

Wallis, Roy. 1988. "Paradoxes of Freedom and Regulation: The Case of New Religious Movements in Britain and America." *Sociological Analysis* 48 (4): 355–71.

Welsh, Anne M. 1994. "Classic Kathak Dance Transcends Culturalism: Art Matters, Not Artists' Skin Color." *San Diego Union-Tribune*, April 21, 1994, 24.

Williams, Sean, and Lillis Ó Laoire. 2011. *Bright Star of the West: Joe Heaney, Irish Song Man*. New York: Oxford University Press.

Winnig, Clifford Jason. 1999. "The Ali Akbar College of Music: Changing Identities Within and Without." MA thesis, University of Texas at Austin.

Witzleben, J. Lawrence. 1997. "Whose Ethnomusicology? Western Ethnomusicology and the Study of Asian Music." *Ethnomusicology* 41 (2): 220–42.

——. 2010. "Performing in the Shadows: Learning and Making Music as Ethnomusicological Practice and Theory." *Yearbook for Traditional Music* 42: 135–66.

Wong, Deborah. 2000. "The Asian American Body in Performance." In *Music and the Racial Imagination*, edited by Ronald Radano and Philip Bohlman, 57–94. Chicago: University of Chicago Press.

Wong, San San. 2006. Oral presentation, Association of Performing Arts Presenters conference, New York City, January 20, 2006.

Worth, Howard, prod. 1991. *Raga*. New York: Mystic Fire Video.

Zonka, Michele. 1993. "The Flowering of Chhandam." *India Currents*, June, C42.

——. n.d. "Sadhana." Chhandam Chitresh Das Dance Company. Accessed November 12, 2004. http://www.kathak.org.

Index

Note: Page numbers set in *italics* indicate pictures or photographs; the letter "t" indicates a table or diagram. Honorifics such as "Pandit" (Pt.), "Shrimati" (Smt.), and "Ustad" (Ust.) are treated as transparent and are ignored in the alphabetization of personal names containing them.

SARAH MORELLI is an associate professor of ethnomusicology at the University of Denver and a performing kathak artist.

MUSIC IN AMERICAN LIFE

Only a Miner: Studies in Recorded Coal-Mining Songs *Archie Green*
Great Day Coming: Folk Music and the American Left *R. Serge Denisoff*
John Philip Sousa: A Descriptive Catalog of His Works *Paul E. Bierley*
The Hell-Bound Train: A Cowboy Songbook *Glenn Ohrlin*
Oh, Didn't He Ramble: The Life Story of Lee Collins, as Told to Mary Collins *Edited by Frank J. Gillis and John W. Miner*
American Labor Songs of the Nineteenth Century *Philip S. Foner*
Stars of Country Music: Uncle Dave Macon to Johnny Rodriguez *Edited by Bill C. Malone and Judith McCulloh*
Git Along, Little Dogies: Songs and Songmakers of the American West *John I. White*
A Texas-Mexican *Cancionero*: Folksongs of the Lower Border *Américo Paredes*
San Antonio Rose: The Life and Music of Bob Wills *Charles R. Townsend*
Early Downhome Blues: A Musical and Cultural Analysis *Jeff Todd Titon*
An Ives Celebration: Papers and Panels of the Charles Ives Centennial Festival-Conference *Edited by H. Wiley Hitchcock and Vivian Perlis*
Sinful Tunes and Spirituals: Black Folk Music to the Civil War *Dena J. Epstein*
Joe Scott, the Woodsman-Songmaker *Edward D. Ives*
Jimmie Rodgers: The Life and Times of America's Blue Yodeler *Nolan Porterfield*
Early American Music Engraving and Printing: A History of Music Publishing in America from 1787 to 1825, with Commentary on Earlier and Later Practices *Richard J. Wolfe*
Sing a Sad Song: The Life of Hank Williams *Roger M. Williams*
Long Steel Rail: The Railroad in American Folksong *Norm Cohen*
Resources of American Music History: A Directory of Source Materials from Colonial Times to World War II *D. W. Krummel, Jean Geil, Doris J. Dyen, and Deane L. Root*
Tenement Songs: The Popular Music of the Jewish Immigrants *Mark Slobin*
Ozark Folksongs *Vance Randolph; edited and abridged by Norm Cohen*
Oscar Sonneck and American Music *Edited by William Lichtenwanger*
Bluegrass Breakdown: The Making of the Old Southern Sound *Robert Cantwell*
Bluegrass: A History *Neil V. Rosenberg*
Music at the White House: A History of the American Spirit *Elise K. Kirk*
Red River Blues: The Blues Tradition in the Southeast *Bruce Bastin*
Good Friends and Bad Enemies: Robert Winslow Gordon and the Study of American Folksong *Debora Kodish*
Fiddlin' Georgia Crazy: Fiddlin' John Carson, His Real World, and the World of His Songs *Gene Wiggins*
America's Music: From the Pilgrims to the Present (rev. 3d ed.) *Gilbert Chase*
Secular Music in Colonial Annapolis: The Tuesday Club, 1745–56 *John Barry Talley*
Bibliographical Handbook of American Music *D. W. Krummel*
Goin' to Kansas City *Nathan W. Pearson Jr.*

"Susanna," "Jeanie," and "The Old Folks at Home": The Songs of Stephen C. Foster from His Time to Ours (2d ed.) *William W. Austin*
Songprints: The Musical Experience of Five Shoshone Women *Judith Vander*
"Happy in the Service of the Lord": Afro-American Gospel Quartets in Memphis *Kip Lornell*
Paul Hindemith in the United States *Luther Noss*
"My Song Is My Weapon": People's Songs, American Communism, and the Politics of Culture, 1930–50 *Robbie Lieberman*
Chosen Voices: The Story of the American Cantorate *Mark Slobin*
Theodore Thomas: America's Conductor and Builder of Orchestras, 1835–1905 *Ezra Schabas*
"The Whorehouse Bells Were Ringing" and Other Songs Cowboys Sing *Collected and Edited by Guy Logsdon*
Crazeology: The Autobiography of a Chicago Jazzman *Bud Freeman, as Told to Robert Wolf*
Discoursing Sweet Music: Brass Bands and Community Life in Turn-of-the-Century Pennsylvania *Kenneth Kreitner*
Mormonism and Music: A History *Michael Hicks*
Voices of the Jazz Age: Profiles of Eight Vintage Jazzmen *Chip Deffaa*
Pickin' on Peachtree: A History of Country Music in Atlanta, Georgia *Wayne W. Daniel*
Bitter Music: Collected Journals, Essays, Introductions, and Librettos *Harry Partch; edited by Thomas McGeary*
Ethnic Music on Records: A Discography of Ethnic Recordings Produced in the United States, 1893 to 1942 *Richard K. Spottswood*
Downhome Blues Lyrics: An Anthology from the Post–World War II Era *Jeff Todd Titon*
Ellington: The Early Years *Mark Tucker*
Chicago Soul *Robert Pruter*
That Half-Barbaric Twang: The Banjo in American Popular Culture *Karen Linn*
Hot Man: The Life of Art Hodes *Art Hodes and Chadwick Hansen*
The Erotic Muse: American Bawdy Songs (2d ed.) *Ed Cray*
Barrio Rhythm: Mexican American Music in Los Angeles *Steven Loza*
The Creation of Jazz: Music, Race, and Culture in Urban America *Burton W. Peretti*
Charles Martin Loeffler: A Life Apart in Music *Ellen Knight*
Club Date Musicians: Playing the New York Party Circuit *Bruce A. MacLeod*
Opera on the Road: Traveling Opera Troupes in the United States, 1825–60 *Katherine K. Preston*
The Stonemans: An Appalachian Family and the Music That Shaped Their Lives *Ivan M. Tribe*
Transforming Tradition: Folk Music Revivals Examined *Edited by Neil V. Rosenberg*
The Crooked Stovepipe: Athapaskan Fiddle Music and Square Dancing in Northeast Alaska and Northwest Canada *Craig Mishler*

Traveling the High Way Home: Ralph Stanley and the World of Traditional Bluegrass Music *John Wright*
Carl Ruggles: Composer, Painter, and Storyteller *Marilyn Ziffrin*
Never without a Song: The Years and Songs of Jennie Devlin, 1865–1952 *Katharine D. Newman*
The Hank Snow Story *Hank Snow, with Jack Ownbey and Bob Burris*
Milton Brown and the Founding of Western Swing *Cary Ginell, with special assistance from Roy Lee Brown*
Santiago de Murcia's "Códice Saldívar No. 4": A Treasury of Secular Guitar Music from Baroque Mexico *Craig H. Russell*
The Sound of the Dove: Singing in Appalachian Primitive Baptist Churches *Beverly Bush Patterson*
Heartland Excursions: Ethnomusicological Reflections on Schools of Music *Bruno Nettl*
Doowop: The Chicago Scene *Robert Pruter*
Blue Rhythms: Six Lives in Rhythm and Blues *Chip Deffaa*
Shoshone Ghost Dance Religion: Poetry Songs and Great Basin Context *Judith Vander*
Go Cat Go! Rockabilly Music and Its Makers *Craig Morrison*
'Twas Only an Irishman's Dream: The Image of Ireland and the Irish in American Popular Song Lyrics, 1800–1920 *William H. A. Williams*
Democracy at the Opera: Music, Theater, and Culture in New York City, 1815–60 *Karen Ahlquist*
Fred Waring and the Pennsylvanians *Virginia Waring*
Woody, Cisco, and Me: Seamen Three in the Merchant Marine *Jim Longhi*
Behind the Burnt Cork Mask: Early Blackface Minstrelsy and Antebellum American Popular Culture *William J. Mahar*
Going to Cincinnati: A History of the Blues in the Queen City *Steven C. Tracy*
Pistol Packin' Mama: Aunt Molly Jackson and the Politics of Folksong *Shelly Romalis*
Sixties Rock: Garage, Psychedelic, and Other Satisfactions *Michael Hicks*
The Late Great Johnny Ace and the Transition from R&B to Rock 'n' Roll *James M. Salem*
Tito Puente and the Making of Latin Music *Steven Loza*
Juilliard: A History *Andrea Olmstead*
Understanding Charles Seeger, Pioneer in American Musicology *Edited by Bell Yung and Helen Rees*
Mountains of Music: West Virginia Traditional Music from *Goldenseal* *Edited by John Lilly*
Alice Tully: An Intimate Portrait *Albert Fuller*
A Blues Life *Henry Townsend, as told to Bill Greensmith*
Long Steel Rail: The Railroad in American Folksong (2d ed.) *Norm Cohen*
The Golden Age of Gospel *Text by Horace Clarence Boyer; photography by Lloyd Yearwood*
Aaron Copland: The Life and Work of an Uncommon Man *Howard Pollack*
Louis Moreau Gottschalk *S. Frederick Starr*

Race, Rock, and Elvis *Michael T. Bertrand*
Theremin: Ether Music and Espionage *Albert Glinsky*
Poetry and Violence: The Ballad Tradition of Mexico's Costa Chica *John H. McDowell*
The Bill Monroe Reader *Edited by Tom Ewing*
Music in Lubavitcher Life *Ellen Koskoff*
Zarzuela: Spanish Operetta, American Stage *Janet L. Sturman*
Bluegrass Odyssey: A Documentary in Pictures and Words, 1966–86 *Carl Fleischhauer and Neil V. Rosenberg*
That Old-Time Rock & Roll: A Chronicle of an Era, 1954–63 *Richard Aquila*
Labor's Troubadour *Joe Glazer*
American Opera *Elise K. Kirk*
Don't Get above Your Raisin': Country Music and the Southern Working Class *Bill C. Malone*
John Alden Carpenter: A Chicago Composer *Howard Pollack*
Heartbeat of the People: Music and Dance of the Northern Pow-wow *Tara Browner*
My Lord, What a Morning: An Autobiography *Marian Anderson*
Marian Anderson: A Singer's Journey *Allan Keiler*
Charles Ives Remembered: An Oral History *Vivian Perlis*
Henry Cowell, Bohemian *Michael Hicks*
Rap Music and Street Consciousness *Cheryl L. Keyes*
Louis Prima *Garry Boulard*
Marian McPartland's Jazz World: All in Good Time *Marian McPartland*
Robert Johnson: Lost and Found *Barry Lee Pearson and Bill McCulloch*
Bound for America: Three British Composers *Nicholas Temperley*
Lost Sounds: Blacks and the Birth of the Recording Industry, 1890–1919 *Tim Brooks*
Burn, Baby! BURN! The Autobiography of Magnificent Montague *Magnificent Montague with Bob Baker*
Way Up North in Dixie: A Black Family's Claim to the Confederate Anthem *Howard L. Sacks and Judith Rose Sacks*
The Bluegrass Reader *Edited by Thomas Goldsmith*
Colin McPhee: Composer in Two Worlds *Carol J. Oja*
Robert Johnson, Mythmaking, and Contemporary American Culture *Patricia R. Schroeder*
Composing a World: Lou Harrison, Musical Wayfarer *Leta E. Miller and Fredric Lieberman*
Fritz Reiner, Maestro and Martinet *Kenneth Morgan*
That Toddlin' Town: Chicago's White Dance Bands and Orchestras, 1900–1950 *Charles A. Sengstock Jr.*
Dewey and Elvis: The Life and Times of a Rock 'n' Roll Deejay *Louis Cantor*
Come Hither to Go Yonder: Playing Bluegrass with Bill Monroe *Bob Black*
Chicago Blues: Portraits and Stories *David Whiteis*
The Incredible Band of John Philip Sousa *Paul E. Bierley*

"Maximum Clarity" and Other Writings on Music *Ben Johnston, edited by Bob Gilmore*
Staging Tradition: John Lair and Sarah Gertrude Knott *Michael Ann Williams*
Homegrown Music: Discovering Bluegrass *Stephanie P. Ledgin*
Tales of a Theatrical Guru *Danny Newman*
The Music of Bill Monroe *Neil V. Rosenberg and Charles K. Wolfe*
Pressing On: The Roni Stoneman Story *Roni Stoneman, as told to Ellen Wright*
Together Let Us Sweetly Live *Jonathan C. David, with photographs by Richard Holloway*
Live Fast, Love Hard: The Faron Young Story *Diane Diekman*
Air Castle of the South: WSM Radio and the Making of Music City *Craig P. Havighurst*
Traveling Home: Sacred Harp Singing and American Pluralism *Kiri Miller*
Where Did Our Love Go? The Rise and Fall of the Motown Sound *Nelson George*
Lonesome Cowgirls and Honky-Tonk Angels: The Women of Barn Dance Radio *Kristine M. McCusker*
California Polyphony: Ethnic Voices, Musical Crossroads *Mina Yang*
The Never-Ending Revival: Rounder Records and the Folk Alliance *Michael F. Scully*
Sing It Pretty: A Memoir *Bess Lomax Hawes*
Working Girl Blues: The Life and Music of Hazel Dickens *Hazel Dickens and Bill C. Malone*
Charles Ives Reconsidered *Gayle Sherwood Magee*
The Hayloft Gang: The Story of the National Barn Dance *Edited by Chad Berry*
Country Music Humorists and Comedians *Loyal Jones*
Record Makers and Breakers: Voices of the Independent Rock 'n' Roll Pioneers *John Broven*
Music of the First Nations: Tradition and Innovation in Native North America *Edited by Tara Browner*
Cafe Society: The Wrong Place for the Right People *Barney Josephson, with Terry Trilling-Josephson*
George Gershwin: An Intimate Portrait *Walter Rimler*
Life Flows On in Endless Song: Folk Songs and American History *Robert V. Wells*
I Feel a Song Coming On: The Life of Jimmy McHugh *Alyn Shipton*
King of the Queen City: The Story of King Records *Jon Hartley Fox*
Long Lost Blues: Popular Blues in America, 1850–1920 *Peter C. Muir*
Hard Luck Blues: Roots Music Photographs from the Great Depression *Rich Remsberg*
Restless Giant: The Life and Times of Jean Aberbach and Hill and Range Songs *Bar Biszick-Lockwood*
Champagne Charlie and Pretty Jemima: Variety Theater in the Nineteenth Century *Gillian M. Rodger*
Sacred Steel: Inside an African American Steel Guitar Tradition *Robert L. Stone*
Gone to the Country: The New Lost City Ramblers and the Folk Music Revival *Ray Allen*

The Makers of the Sacred Harp *David Warren Steel with Richard H. Hulan*
Woody Guthrie, American Radical *Will Kaufman*
George Szell: A Life of Music *Michael Charry*
Bean Blossom: The Brown County Jamboree and Bill Monroe's Bluegrass Festivals *Thomas A. Adler*
Crowe on the Banjo: The Music Life of J. D. Crowe *Marty Godbey*
Twentieth Century Drifter: The Life of Marty Robbins *Diane Diekman*
Henry Mancini: Reinventing Film Music *John Caps*
The Beautiful Music All Around Us: Field Recordings and the American Experience *Stephen Wade*
Then Sings My Soul: The Culture of Southern Gospel Music *Douglas Harrison*
The Accordion in the Americas: Klezmer, Polka, Tango, Zydeco, and More! *Edited by Helena Simonett*
Bluegrass Bluesman: A Memoir *Josh Graves, edited by Fred Bartenstein*
One Woman in a Hundred: Edna Phillips and the Philadelphia Orchestra *Mary Sue Welsh*
The Great Orchestrator: Arthur Judson and American Arts Management *James M. Doering*
Charles Ives in the Mirror: American Histories of an Iconic Composer *David C. Paul*
Southern Soul-Blues *David Whiteis*
Sweet Air: Modernism, Regionalism, and American Popular Song *Edward P. Comentale*
Pretty Good for a Girl: Women in Bluegrass *Murphy Hicks Henry*
Sweet Dreams: The World of Patsy Cline *Warren R. Hofstra*
William Sidney Mount and the Creolization of American Culture *Christopher J. Smith*
Bird: The Life and Music of Charlie Parker *Chuck Haddix*
Making the March King: John Philip Sousa's Washington Years, 1854–1893 *Patrick Warfield*
In It for the Long Run *Jim Rooney*
Pioneers of the Blues Revival *Steve Cushing*
Roots of the Revival: American and British Folk Music in the 1950s *Ronald D. Cohen and Rachel Clare Donaldson*
Blues All Day Long: The Jimmy Rogers Story *Wayne Everett Goins*
Yankee Twang: Country and Western Music in New England *Clifford R. Murphy*
The Music of the Stanley Brothers *Gary B. Reid*
Hawaiian Music in Motion: Mariners, Missionaries, and Minstrels *James Revell Carr*
Sounds of the New Deal: The Federal Music Project in the West *Peter Gough*
The Mormon Tabernacle Choir: A Biography *Michael Hicks*
The Man That Got Away: The Life and Songs of Harold Arlen *Walter Rimler*
A City Called Heaven: Chicago and the Birth of Gospel Music *Robert M. Marovich*
Blues Unlimited: Essential Interviews from the Original Blues Magazine *Edited by Bill Greensmith, Mike Rowe, and Mark Camarigg*

Hoedowns, Reels, and Frolics: Roots and Branches of Southern Appalachian Dance *Phil Jamison*
Fannie Bloomfield-Zeisler: The Life and Times of a Piano Virtuoso *Beth Abelson Macleod*
Cybersonic Arts: Adventures in American New Music *Gordon Mumma, edited with commentary by Michelle Fillion*
The Magic of Beverly Sills *Nancy Guy*
Waiting for Buddy Guy *Alan Harper*
Harry T. Burleigh: From the Spiritual to the Harlem Renaissance *Jean E. Snyder*
Music in the Age of Anxiety: American Music in the Fifties *James Wierzbicki*
Jazzing: New York City's Unseen Scene *Thomas H. Greenland*
A Cole Porter Companion *Edited by Don M. Randel, Matthew Shaftel, and Susan Forscher Weiss*
Foggy Mountain Troubadour: The Life and Music of Curly Seckler *Penny Parsons*
Blue Rhythm Fantasy: Big Band Jazz Arranging in the Swing Era *John Wriggle*
Bill Clifton: America's Bluegrass Ambassador to the World *Bill C. Malone*
Chinatown Opera Theater in North America *Nancy Yunhwa Rao*
The Elocutionists: Women, Music, and the Spoken Word *Marian Wilson Kimber*
May Irwin: Singing, Shouting, and the Shadow of Minstrelsy *Sharon Ammen*
Peggy Seeger: A Life of Music, Love, and Politics *Jean R. Freedman*
Charles Ives's *Concord*: Essays after a Sonata *Kyle Gann*
Don't Give Your Heart to a Rambler: My Life with Jimmy Martin, the King of Bluegrass *Barbara Martin Stephens*
Libby Larsen: Composing an American Life *Denise Von Glahn*
George Szell's Reign: Behind the Scenes with the Cleveland Orchestra *Marcia Hansen Kraus*
Just One of the Boys: Female-to-Male Cross-Dressing on the American Variety Stage *Gillian M. Rodger*
Spirituals and the Birth of a Black Entertainment Industry *Sandra Jean Graham*
Right to the Juke Joint: A Personal History of American Music *Patrick B. Mullen*
Bluegrass Generation: A Memoir *Neil V. Rosenberg*
Pioneers of the Blues Revival, Expanded Second Edition *Steve Cushing*
Banjo Roots and Branches *Edited by Robert Winans*
Bill Monroe: The Life and Music of the Blue Grass Man *Tom Ewing*
Dixie Dewdrop: The Uncle Dave Macon Story *Michael D. Doubler*
Los Romeros: Royal Family of the Spanish Guitar *Walter Aaron Clark*
Transforming Women's Education: Liberal Arts and Music in Female Seminaries *Jewel A. Smith*
Rethinking American Music *Edited by Tara Browner and Thomas L. Riis*
Leonard Bernstein and the Language of Jazz *Katherine Baber*
Dancing Revolution: Bodies, Space, and Sound in American Cultural History *Christopher J. Smith*
Peggy Glanville-Hicks: Composer and Critic *Suzanne Robinson*
Mormons, Musical Theater, and Belonging in America *Jake Johnson*

Blues Legacy: Tradition and Innovation in Chicago *David Whiteis*
Blues Before Sunrise 2: Interviews from the Chicago Scene *Steve Cushing*
The Cashaway Psalmody: Transatlantic Religion and Music in Colonial Carolina *Stephen A. Marini*
Earl Scruggs and Foggy Mountain Breakdown: The Making of an American Classic *Thomas Goldsmith*
A Guru's Journey: Pandit Chitresh Das and Indian Classical Dance in Diaspora *Sarah Morelli*

The University of Illinois Press
is a founding member of the
Association of University Presses.

Composed in 10/13 Georgia
with Gill Sans Std display
by Lisa Connery
at the University of Illinois Press
Cover designed by Becca Alexander
Cover illustration: Promotional image for *Masters of Tradition* performances with Swapan Chaudhuri, April 2001, in California. Photo by Marty Sohl.

University of Illinois Press
1325 South Oak Street
Champaign, IL 61820-6903
www.press.uillinois.edu